MW00851005

PRAISE FOR MAGIC OF TH

"In this deep, wise, and beautifully v
explore the complex interweaving of our personal imag...
with community, society, and environment...Fio and Jane's introductions to each point in the pentacle offer honest and courageous insights on how to acknowledge and mitigate the effects of colonialism, racism, and gender bias in our spiritual practices. With the additional contributions of ten respected witches from the Reclaiming Witchcraft tradition, I found this book to be a powerful and practical introduction into one of the core principles of the Reclaiming tradition, and a helpful and integral guide for any of us who wish to deepen our own spiritual and magical practice."

—**WENDY RULE**, internationally acclaimed singer, songwriter, and witch

"This beautiful offering...provokes the reader to truly reflect on their practice, to deconstruct it and analyze how one might, if brave enough, emerge from the sense of vulnerability and discomfort which this work will undoubtedly evoke, into a place of beauty and strength.... Fio Gede Parma and Jane Meredith draw together their own wisdom, and the wisdom of powerful, inspiring teachers, elders, and great thinkers to present yet another visceral and transformative journey which you are invited to undertake."

—**MHARA STARLING**, author of *Welsh Witchcraft* and *Welsh Fairies*

"Jane Meredith and Fio Gede Parma present an in-depth examination of the somewhat lesser known of these two magical tools, offering its transformative potency to practitioners everywhere. Learn how the Pearl Pentacle can help to heal psychic and emotional wounds, transforming them into something beautiful. The authors share their personal experiences working with and teaching this tool, as well as the perspectives of several other teachers and practitioners, providing a more rounded view of this nuanced subject. Filled with essays, interviews, rituals and more, *Magic of the Pearl Pentacle* offers the world a powerful tool of healing, harmony, grace, and community."

—**STORM FAERYWOLF**, author of *The Satyr's Kiss*

"A beautiful exploration of the human experience that calls us to walk a path of magic that fosters personal growth, community harmony, and divine relationship....An invaluable resource for anyone seeking to deepen both their understanding of self and their connection to the world. Drawing from the rich traditions of Reclaiming and Feri, this book challenges us to engage with our own stories, to confront the complexities of our relationships, and to embrace the beauty that emerges from vulnerability and connection. Each chapter serves as a portal, inviting readers to reflect on their own experiences and to actively participate in the magic of community."
—JHENAH TELYNDRU, author of *The Ninefold Way of Avalon*

"Jane Meredith and Fio Gede Parma explore the multifaceted magic of Love, Law, Wisdom, Liberty, and Knowledge and offer it to us as a spell to awaken beautiful, beloved community. Along with their own insights, they gather an array of voices of witches who have lived this work and speak to us with real, honest, loving truth. This book is both an invitation to connect to the gifts of the Pearl Pentacle and a vessel holding the living history of Reclaiming."
—ANTHONY RELLA, author of *Slow Magic*

"An impressive and influential book. The sheer knowledge and experience that comes from the ten wonderful teachers that have contributed to the book as well speaks of the power within the pages. This is a book of self-discovery and one of transformation, the journey may not be easy, but it will be life changing if you are prepared to put the work in. You won't be alone, as the words within these pages provide you with guidance as you traverse your inner and outer worlds. You might not agree with everything, you may challenge some of it, most of it should resonate with you, but that's the point—it will provoke you to take action."
—RACHEL PATTERSON, witch, high priestess, podcast host, and bestselling author

MAGIC OF THE

PEARL
PENTACLE

©Luke Brohman

©Christopher James Bate

JANE MEREDITH is an Australian writer and ritualist. Her books include *Magic of the Iron Pentacle, Elements of Magic, Falling Through the Tree of Life, Rituals of Celebration, Journey to the Dark Goddess,* and *Aspecting the Goddess.* Jane is passionate about myths and magic, co-created ritual, trees, rivers, and dark chocolate. The Kabbalistic Tree of Life is one of her special loves. She teaches internationally and is a teacher within the Reclaiming tradition. Visit her at JaneMeredith.com.

FIO GEDE PARMA is a Balinese-Australian non-binary witch, magical mentor, and international teacher. Fio is a cofounder of the Coven of the Wildwood and a midwife of the Wildwood tradition. They have been initiated into four traditions of the Craft and serve and celebrate as priestex and lover with many spirits and gods. Fio's books include *Elements of Magic, The Witch Belongs to the World,* and *Magic of the Iron Pentacle.* Visit them at FioGedeParma.com.

MAGIC OF THE

PEARL
PENTACLE

RECLAIMING LOVE, LAW, WISDOM, LIBERTY & KNOWLEDGE

JANE MEREDITH • FIO GEDE PARMA

Foreword by Phoenix LeFae

LLEWELLYN
WOODBURY, MINNESOTA

FIRST EDITION
First Printing, 2025

Cover design by Kevin R. Brown
Illustrations by Llewellyn Art Department

Llewellyn Publications is a registered trademark of Llewellyn Worldwide Ltd.

Library of Congress Cataloging-In-Publication Data
Names: Meredith, Jane, author. | Parma, Gede, author. | LeFae,
  Phoenix, writer of foreword.
Title: Magic of the pearl pentacle : reclaiming love, law, wisdom, liberty
  & knowledge / Jane Meredith, Fio Gede Parma ; foreword by Phoenix LeFae.
Description: First edition. | Woodbury, Minnesota : Llewellyn, [2025] |
  Includes bibliographical references. | Summary: "Through its five
  attributes of Love, Law, Wisdom, Liberty, and Knowledge, the Pearl
  Pentacle shows you how to engage intimately with your community and
  develop a deep and dynamic connection with yourself and others through
  numerous hands-on activities. Featuring contributions by ten authors and
  teachers, *Magic of the Pearl Pentacle* is written from the Reclaiming
  Witchcraft perspective"—Provided by publisher.
Identifiers: LCCN 2024049297 (print) | LCCN 2024049298 (ebook) | ISBN
  9780738777306 (paperback) | ISBN 9780738777436 (ebook)
Subjects: LCSH: Magic. | Witchcraft. | Self-actualization
  (Psychology)—Miscellanea.
Classification: LCC BF1611 .M475 2025 (print) | LCC BF1611 (ebook) | DDC
  133.4/3—dc23/eng/20241231
LC record available at https://lccn.loc.gov/2024049297
LC ebook record available at https://lccn.loc.gov/2024049298

Llewellyn Publications
A Division of Llewellyn Worldwide Ltd.
2143 Wooddale Drive
Woodbury, MN 55125-2989

www.llewellyn.com

Printed in the United States of America

We dedicate this book to Copper Persephone (1962–2020), Rose May Dance (1948–2021), and Todd K. Herriot (1970–2023).

These three teachers of ours, beloveds and lovers of many, continue to inspire us with their fierce love and joyful wisdom.

Colleen, Jana d'Madrid, John Brazaitis, Kala, Lizann, Luanne, River, Wildflower, and others named and unnamed—all Reclaiming witches and priestexes who danced with the pearlescence of the skies, seas, and their own hearts.

Beloved and Mighty Dead of Reclaiming

ACKNOWLEDGMENT OF COUNTRY

We conjured the spell of this book at the cliffs facing the east, the great Pacific Ocean, where the moon rises and shines on the shimmering blue of the pearlescent sea.

We have dreamed, written, edited, and called together these words across time and place, and enjoined with many lifetimes—other people's lifetimes. Our contemplations and explorations into the Pearl Pentacle points of Love, Law, Wisdom, Liberty, and Knowledge have been supported and challenged by our understandings of and connections with First Nations people and relationship with land.

We acknowledge the sacred lands—many of them stolen, invaded, occupied by empires and colonizers—in which the contributions were written or recorded by willing and skillful Reclaiming witches and priestexes. We acknowledge the elders of these places and all Indigenous and First Nations peoples past, present, and emerging.

The sacred lands that we have woven this book within include:

- » Gadigal and Bidjigal country—close to the site of the British invasion of so-called Australia
- » Darug and Gundungurra country—Katoomba, in the Blue Mountains
- » The ancient lands of the Iceni and their Queen Boudica—named London by the Romans
- » Glastonbury, Avalon, Somerset
- » Throughout the lands of the ancient Gallic tribes, now called France
- » Wurundjeri country, Naarm, so-called Melbourne
- » Yuggera, Jagera, and Turrbal country, in the lands of the great River Maiwar (so-called Brisbane River)

PEARL PENTACLE ACKNOWLEDGMENT

We acknowledge the lineage and history of the Pearl Pentacle as arising from the Iron Pentacle taught and cherished by Victor and Cora Anderson of the Feri tradition.

We acknowledge the early teachers of what would become Reclaiming—Starhawk, Diane Baker, Kevyn Lutton, Lauren Liebling, Macha Nightmare, Rose May Dance, Cybele, Pandora O'Mallory, and others—and their work with Iron and Pearl Pentacles.

We wish to acknowledge our original Reclaiming teachers of the Pearl Pentacle: Ravyn Stanfield, World Tree Lyceum (Raven Edgewalker and Chelidon), Dawn Isidora, and SusanneRae.

We acknowledge all of our co-conspirators, beloveds, those who have taught and learned alongside us in myriad online and in-person core classes and events singing with the currents of Pearl.

We acknowledge Fio's teachers, mentors, and provocateurs in Feri who passed them the magics of Pearl Pentacle, and . . .

We honor and deeply respect the Pearl Pentacle itself, which continues to emanate Love—Law—Wisdom—Liberty—Knowledge.

For all those who seek this magic.

Moonlight swirls across the sea in ripples and tides, a magical script in silver, rewritten every second. We stand on the cliffs, entranced, called home to the beauty and mystery of this world. Pearlescent and shimmering, moonlight on water, a call to the deep and the bright.

We look up to the stars our world is born from, we breathe the sea air deep into our bodies, we remember life came from the ocean and the stars, and we call to the Pearl Pentacle.

We remember Love. We open the crowns of our heads to the starlight, to the great stream of existence, and feel it moving through us like a great wave. Love. Love. Love is the law.

We open to the land and the directions, and our very cells and atoms call through us, reminding us of their entire histories; we feel their laws deep and unfolding within us. The law of the ocean waves before us, the law of the moon's relationship with the ocean and the earth, the law of gravity holding our bodies to the rock. Law. Holding the law as sacred, we lean into wisdom.

The deep ocean below the waves shimmers darkly beyond our vision. The depths. Some of us seek wisdom, some are blessed by wisdom, and some of us are torn apart by it. The ritual unfolds itself, and we call and speak into each point of the Pearl Pentacle, feeling ourselves held within it. This is a wisdom passed to us, a wisdom we inherit, a wisdom we participate in that opens the gate to liberty.

The waves crash on the rocks and we sing to them of moonlight, of pearl, of freedom from and freedom to. Liberation, liberté, liberty. Freed from the old and into the new, the liberty to step forth, to dare, to seek, to create. We arc on the crest of a wave from liberty to knowledge.

Here we have performed sacred rituals. Here we have wept, here loved. Here we join hands, make offerings of rose petals and song and prayer; here we taste the fruit, juice on our lips mixed with sea spray. The moon overhead, the rock beneath, the sea making love with both, and we fragile humans daring initiation, daring to taste knowledge and be transformed by it.

Love. Law. Wisdom. Liberty. Knowledge.

The magic of the Pearl Pentacle awaits…

CONTENTS

FOREWORD

What does a girl from Northern California have in common with two amazing witches who live in Australia? The short answer is the Reclaiming tradition of witchcraft, and I (the girl from Cali) couldn't be happier about that fact.

My relationship with the Reclaiming tradition of witchcraft started when I walked into my first public ritual in the mid 1990s. I was totally new to witchcraft, in my teens, and painfully shy. But another witchy friend encouraged me to go to this ritual with her, and my life was forever changed. Suddenly all the things I had been reading about and learning about had an experiential context. Magic was alive, and for the first time in my brief witchcraft explorations, I was having a palpable experience of it.

I attended public rituals for almost two decades, happy for that to be my only foray into being with a larger community. But, in 2009, I decided I needed more from community. I wanted to be with other witches; I wanted to deepen my practice, and I knew that could only happen with the support of other experienced witches. This led me to sign up for my first round of Elements of Magic, which is one of the core classes in the Reclaiming tradition.

Later that same year I took the Iron Pentacle class. I was terrified of the magic of the Iron Pentacle. Just reading the words of the energy points—Sex, Pride, Self, Power, Passion—brought up all kinds of uncomfortable feelings in me. I worried that it would be hard, emotional, and triggering. In actuality, it was revelatory, eye-opening, and healing.

After Iron Pentacle, I was ready to take on the power of the Pearl Pentacle. Going into the Pearl Pentacle weekend intensive class, the names of the energy centers—Love, Law, Wisdom, Liberty, Knowledge—felt like old friends. And since Iron wasn't so bad, I figured Pearl would be a magical walk in the park for me. Boy, was I wrong.

You see, a pearl is formed due to irritation. The soft body of the oyster gets a grain of sand stuck in its shell. This is annoying and painful. And like your tongue touching a sore tooth over and over again, the soft body of the oyster touches that irritant over and over again. Each time it adds a coating of nacre to that spot until it becomes smooth, shiny, and beautiful.

The Iron and Pearl Pentacles helped me explore the finer points of running energy through my body. These tools helped me touch those sore spots in my spirit and find a way to make them beautiful gems. Our human bodies are pretty miraculous things. Even with all of the trials and health issues a body can have, the sequence of events that makes each life possible is nothing short of miraculous. Beyond the sinew, bone, and neurons, we also hold the capacity to move energy through these fleshy vehicles of spirit. How awesome is that?

The idea of energy moving through, in, and around the body isn't a new concept; it's quite ancient. How energy moves through the body has been studied, discussed, and taught in cultures all over the planet. This modern interpretation that we call the Pearl Pentacle may be a newer tool, but it holds deep power. Pearl Pentacle offers the body as an energetic pentacle, with the points of that star holding the power of Love, Law, Wisdom, Liberty, and Knowledge.

The work of the Pearl Pentacle was really challenging for me. Doing the magic of the Pearl Pentacle had me face the places where I was too hard on myself. The energy of it had me looking at my own brightness and the places where I had the ability to shine. Pearl Pentacle showed me that it was time for me to step into the community and allow myself to be seen.

It's been thirty years since that first public ritual and fifteen years since first walking into the Elements of Magic class. Now I have been blessed to share Reclaiming magic with hundreds of people all over the world. And of all the five Reclaiming core classes, I have taught Pearl Pentacle the most often.

Reading this book brought me back to the magic of that first weekend intensive Pearl Pentacle class that I took so many years ago. The mysteries that are shared here come from many voices with many years of experience, and they reveal the soothing yet challenging magic of stepping into the brightness of Pearl Pentacle magic. While working the exercises offered in these pages, I could once again feel the shifts I felt in my heart and spirit when this tool was first shared with me. Ultimately, witchcraft is not an armchair sport. It requires us to get up and do things. The magic shared in this book gives you the opportunity to get up and do that magic too.

I would encourage anyone who reads these words to contemplate them, meditate on them, dig into their mysteries, and then, most importantly, do the exercises that are shared here. Really make space for this work in your practice. Feel the power of the Pearl Pentacle move through your body. Explore the power of each of these energy points. Feel it, do it, be it.

The things that create irritation hold the potential for glorious beauty. Voilà—magic! The pearl would never form if the oyster just *thought* about the irritation. The oyster has to literally touch it, feel it, connect with it, and transform it.

When life has taught you to hide your light under a bushel, when you are a believer in the tall poppy syndrome, when you have been told to be quiet and not allow yourself to be seen, the Pearl Pentacle is a gateway to releasing those shackles of lies. The power of this tool helps us to shine more brightly and step into who we truly are in order to better serve community. And beyond our personal development as witches, the Pearl Pentacle gives us a powerful tool for taking this magic into our everyday. It is more than a weekend workshop or WitchCamp or even a book. It is life-changing magic.

Fio and Jane Meredith are two witches that I am honored to know. I have had the pleasure of working with, learning from, and collaborating with both of them. I have an overwhelming feeling of gratitude for the work that they have done on this book and their other books, *Elements of Magic* and *Magic of the Iron Pentacle*, because it has allowed so many people to connect with the web of Reclaiming magic. They are both prolific writers, skilled facilitators, and deeply magical beings.

Jane Meredith has a smile that could launch a thousand ships. Her witchcraft runs in a deep current that is palpable when you are near her. She is thoughtful with her magic, and she has a deep understanding of the flow of energy. Jane Meredith knows when to push, when to speak, and when to keep silent. These are skills that are an innate part of her flesh and blood.

Fio is a lithe and sensuous being. They help facilitate a sense of belonging and wonder even when doing mundane things! Being in their presence, you know that they have seen into the depth of mystery, and they hold an understanding of magic that most humans never will. Fio seems to shapeshift and call up magic from the depths of their soul.

For both of them, witchcraft is more than what they do; it is who they are.

This book is a gift to the Reclaiming community and the wider world of witchcraft. It is a gift to our elders and the lineage of this magic.

PHOENIX LEFAE
January 2024

INTRODUCTION

The Pearl Pentacle is a magical map, a mystery teaching, a portal to discovering more about being alive and being human than we might think possible. Through its five attributes of Love, Law, Wisdom, Liberty, and Knowledge the Pearl Pentacle invites intimate engagement in community. It provides a vision and ethos for human relationships and our connections with each other. The Pearl Pentacle calls us forth through the desires of love, our longings for the truth of law, our surrender into wisdom, the lived necessity of liberty, and the mysteries of knowledge.

Pearl Pentacle arises out of the primal and ecstatic magic of witches and mystics who desire deep and dynamic connection through the lifeforce with self and other. A pentacle is the ancient and sacred symbol of a geometrically perfect five-pointed star, sometimes held within a circle. A pearl is the manifestation of lustrous beauty born first of irritation or wounding from within a mollusk such as an oyster. Through a gradual process that takes many moons, perhaps years, pearls are formed.

We sometimes speak of *pearls of wisdom* and of *not casting pearls before swine*. In Chinese cultures dragons may be depicted holding pearls in their claws, and this is said to have originated with an old folktale of a young boy who discovers a pearl, only to be transformed into a dragon because he must protect this pearl from greedy men. Pearls are enigmatic, oceanic, gorgeous, and valuable to us. We seek the pearl, we reach out toward it, filled with longing. Together, a pentacle and a pearl form the Pearl Pentacle. Here is a powerful portal of magical inquiry and an opening to explore the mystery of being alive in deeper ways.

We write this book from our perspective as Reclaiming witches, priestexes, teachers, and students as well as in collaboration with each other's lineages, voices, experiences, and passions. Within these pages are also ten original essays authored by ten experienced Reclaiming teachers who know and love the work of the Pearl Pentacle, each writing on topics they have a specialization within.

Reclaiming has always been an open-source tradition in that our classes, rituals, and WitchCamps—magical residential intensives of three to seven days—are open to all people, whether or not they identify as being part of or belonging to Reclaiming. Many efforts are made, and still work is being done, to improve accessibility for marginalized peoples, whether that marginalization be through economic status, age, color, gender, sexuality, or physical ability. At Reclaiming gatherings and classes, skills are taught to support and empower all those who show up to learn—and this book, as well as our previous books, offers the same. Maybe you open this book interested in or coming from a background of personal development, political activism, radical ecology, psychology, witchcraft, Traditional Wicca, Goddess tradition, or a broad paganism. Regardless of your current or previous magical affiliations, regardless of your prior knowledge and experience, the shimmering of the Pearl Pentacle invites you to explore its great themes of Love, Law, Wisdom, Liberty, and Knowledge—to take them into your heart, learn with them and through them, and step through their gateways into vibrant community, ritual, and magic.

Since writing *Magic of the Iron Pentacle* (Llewellyn, 2016), this Pearl Pentacle book has lingered as a thread of possibility between us, inviting us further into the mystery. And here we are writing these words as a kiss to the moon, the sea, and the stars in our blood. This book is an offering and an invitation to all the people and communities who might take up this work.

HISTORY OF THE PEARL PENTACLE

The Pearl Pentacle comes to us from the Feri tradition, which many of those writing in this book are initiates of. Feri—which is sometimes spelled Faery, Faerie, or Fairy—is a dynamic form of American traditional witchcraft that emerged in the US between the 1940s and 1960s. The original Grandmasters of Feri, Victor and Cora Anderson, are in many ways indivisible from Feri, so people often write Anderson Feri to distinguish this particular form of witchcraft from others. Key elements of Feri include a deep and profound sexual or sensual mysticism that pervades our magic and enjoins us to God Herself, whom we also name the Star Goddess. From this rapturous and intimate connection cultivated over the years—and surrendered into within a moment—Feri practices include soul alignment, rites of unbinding and cleansing with water, breath, sound, and chant, as well as all manner of sorceries, rituals, and trance work. Feri witchcraft acknowledges and works with several important precepts including the Black Heart of Innocence, the Iron Pentacle, a warrior ethos, and, in most branches, the Pearl Pentacle.

Pearl Pentacle is taught as one of five core classes in the Reclaiming tradition: Elements of Magic, Iron Pentacle, Pearl Pentacle, Rites of Passage, and the Community class. Reclaiming began as an experiment in fusing feminist ethos and processes with witchcraft ritual and magical skills. Through this braiding, the early Reclaiming witches felt it was necessary to bring their feminist witchcraft into nonviolent direct action and acts of civil disobedience. Not only this, but the feminist concept that *the personal is political* and the consciousness-raising groups of these influences and roots nourish our tradition to this day. More than forty years on, Reclaiming has evolved to become a vital and international network of pagans, witches, spirit workers, artists, activists, and scientists who participate in ecstatic and life-affirming ritual, the work of justice, and magical transformation.

Reclaiming and Feri traditions are sometimes viewed as cousins or siblings. It is from Feri that the Iron and Pearl Pentacles come. Within Reclaiming—via the work of many covens, core classes, and Witch-Camps—the Iron and Pearl Pentacles have become entire landscapes of work and mystery. In Reclaiming, the order the points are journeyed through may be "around the circle" or "through the star." The running of the pentacle's magical current from point to point through the pentagram of the body—head, foot, hand, hand, foot, back to head—derives from the work of Gabriel Carrillo (1948–2007) and his BloodRose school of Feri witchcraft. Some early Reclaiming witches studied with Gabriel in the BloodRose school in the 1980s and thus

LOVE

WISDOM

KNOWLEDGE

LAW

LIBERTY

Figure 1: In Reclaiming, the Pearl Pentacle's current begins at the love point and then continues to law, wisdom, liberty, and knowledge.

the influence was brought into the tradition. Victor Anderson often cautioned people to not become reliant or locked into certain parts of the body being anchors for certain pentacle points as this might cloud the magic. In the spirit of paradox, we offer the provocation that we are able to hold the points as themselves and also experience them through the living human animal form. As well, we might consider that just as the magical current of the Pearl Pentacle can move through us, we can move through it.

POINTS OF THE PEARL PENTACLE

The Pearl Pentacle is said to emanate from the Iron Pentacle. The five points of Pearl arise from Iron's five points. Another way to look at this could be that these points are actually each other viewed or experienced from different angles. While in Anderson Feri lineages Iron is almost always passed from the teacher to the student before Pearl, in Reclaiming people may come to these bodies of work at different times.

The points of the Iron Pentacle in the original order given by Victor Anderson and going around the circle clockwise, as we look at it on the page, are Sex, Self, Passion, Pride, and Power. The points of the Pearl Pentacle in the original order around the circle are Love, Wisdom, Knowledge, Law, and Power. In this teaching both pentacles possess power points. T. Thorn Coyle—a mystic who was a key teacher in early Reclaiming days—learned directly from the Andersons and was passed the name Liberty for what is sometimes still called Power in the Pearl Pentacle. In this book we honor and acknowledge the sequence of these points as originally offered by Victor and Cora Anderson around the circle and have chosen to structure our book as the magical current is run through the landscape of body.

In the Reclaiming tradition we often consciously direct the currents of the pentacles from head to right foot, up to the left hand, through the heart and across to the right hand, then down to the left foot before returning to the head. One somatic mnemonic device used to figure out this flow is to imagine that the Goddess or a Great One is standing in front of you and drawing an invoking pentagram on you that begins at the top point and then sweeps down to their left (which would be your right foot) and continues on. The sections of this book flow in this order: Love, Law, Wisdom, Liberty, and Knowledge. Other individuals or groups have Knowledge and Wisdom switched and therefore may possess different insights and perspectives.

Just as the Pearl Pentacle points grow forth from the work of Iron, we speak about the process of how pearls are formed to illustrate this visceral and emotional magic. A pearl in nature—without human interference—is formed within a mollusk such as an oyster when a foreign particle of organic material or a parasite wounds or irritates the animal. In response to this irritation or wound, a substance known as mother-of-pearl or nacre is secreted and layers over the wound or particle. Over many, many moons, this process forms a luminescent pearl that humans consider valuable. In the process of trying to isolate and push out a threat, something beautiful arrives—a treasure that other animals on earth marvel at! Out of the intense and often irritating or aggravating process of Iron Pentacle work, we come to the wonders and harmonies of Pearl.

Human histories with pearls are deeply haunted by imperialism and colonialism, as most of our histories are. Pearl Pentacle calls us to be with, examine, and work for repair in all things, and so as a magical act we turn our attention to this. For centuries, pearl hunting and diving has been a dangerous life- and health-threatening endeavor. As human covetousness of these pearls grew, human labor—usually the coerced labor of Brown and Black people—was exploited in order to retrieve and harvest pearls from oysters on the sea floor. This is part of the horrifying history of pearls and humankind. It needs to also be noted that the mollusks—the very animals that form the pearls—are taken, ripped open, and killed for the very thing they had originally been trying to isolate and recover from.

PEARL AND IRON PENTACLES

Pearl Pentacle work is not easy, comfortable, or seamless; the work of relating to others and developing community and collectivist ethics can be arduous and difficult. Once again, we reflect on the mystery that

Iron and Pearl are not actually different pentacles; they are versions of one another. It is impossible to work with one of the pentacles without engaging the other, so in working with the Pearl Pentacle points of Love, Law, Wisdom, Liberty, and Knowledge we end up discovering other dimensions of Sex, Pride, Self, Power, and Passion.

Through the Iron point of Sex and intimacy with the life force of existence, we are immersed in the force that in the Pearl Pentacle we name Love. In turning up proudly and taking up space in our lives and the world with the Pride point of Iron, we come to meet the Pearl point of Law that defines reality and how we navigate relationships. Emerging from an experience of the Iron point of Self is a reflection of the Pearl point of Wisdom. As we engage with and critique processes and systems of Power as a point in the Iron Pentacle, we may feel the responsibility of and call to Pearl Pentacle's Liberty, or liberation. When Iron brings us home to our Passion, perhaps we are reminded of the Knowledge within Pearl that we possess and can offer to the world.

Not only do these Iron Pentacle points teach us something about the nature of the Pearl points, but Love-Law-Wisdom-Liberty-Knowledge can reveal secrets about Iron. What does love teach me about sex? If I bring my experiences and sensations of feeling loved and cherished and of beholding another in this sacred way, how does this then determine how I arrive to erotic interchange with another consenting human?

What about the Pearl Pentacle point of Law? What does this reveal to me about the nature of human pride? If Pride in the Iron Pentacle is about feeling right-sized within myself and the sensation of turning up or occupying presence for oneself and one's commitments, then perhaps Law reflects how, when, and why someone might turn up, act, or engage.

THE WORK OF LIFETIMES

A human lifetime can be felt to include so many stories, eras, and threads. Our childhood and teenage years . . . the becoming of an adult and all the adventures that guide and provoke our becoming. Our first loves and heartbreaks, successes and wins, friendships and initiations, the birth of children and their lifetimes, much of which we might never know anything about. Lifetimes inside of lifetimes. And then, spiraling out into our connections with other humans and beings, we merge with the possibility of learning so much more than we imagine possible. In the marriage and dance of lifetimes, we deepen into the rich realms of love-law-wisdom-liberty-knowledge.

If Iron concerns one's relationship with one's own internal landscape and how this expresses in our life, then Pearl is often experienced as the dynamism and challenge we experience in the world and in community. If the work of Iron is considered to be a deep and rigorous shadow-stalking that helps us investigate how we are blocked or twisted up in our complexes, then Pearl is turning that work outward and into the interpersonal domain. Or perhaps we are not fully responsible for turning that work out into relational webs, as we are for simply occupying the processes and magics of Iron Pentacle and allowing them to work through us, revealing the Pearl. If working with the Iron Pentacle points assists us in occupying our sense of sovereignty—that we are whole and complete unto ourself and know that—then the Pearl Pentacle points might aid us in reaching out to one another and deepening into what is most real and alive in being human. Love, Law, Wisdom, Liberty and Knowledge are aspirations, values, and treasures we can seek to embody and become.

HOW TO USE THIS BOOK

There are five main sections in this book, each addressing one of the Pearl Pentacle points of Love, Law, Wisdom, Liberty, and Knowledge. Each point is explored in-depth from philosophical, magical, political, personal, and social perspectives. Just as with the Iron Pentacle, these points are neither considered nor expected to be an easy ride. Love sounds wonderful, but as anyone who's been in a love relationship knows, it offers many of us the deepest challenges we may meet in our lives. Law comes across as both dry and clinical, yet when we delve into it, we discover the entire numinous and earthly realms laid out before us while we hover somewhere within that web, wondering how to behold its truth. Wisdom may seem reserved for elders, specialists, or mystics, yet within the Pearl Pentacle it is revealed as a layer of reality we all have continual access to. And Liberty—ah, liberty—the point that brings us (the authors) undone every time. We invite you into Liberty's rich currents. Finally we meet Knowledge. This point arrives on many levels. It offers concepts of specialist, worked-for knowledge, as well as secret initiatory knowledge. And it holds the route back to the beginning point of Love.

One of the most exciting aspects of this book is that ten amazing Reclaiming teachers, authors, and priestexes have each contributed their thoughts about an aspect of Pearl Pentacle that has a special resonance for them. We have Alex Iantaffi, a noted gender scholar and author, contributing an essay on gender liberation in the Liberty section; Irisanya Moon, a prolific author, offering an essay on the knowledge of a tradition; Willow Kelly, a death doula and a teacher of ecstatic arts, writing about how a community can hold death within the Love point; and Starhawk, an elder of the tradition, famous for her book *The Spiral Dance,* first published five decades ago and currently focusing on permaculture and earth activism, interviewed within the Law section. These ten varied and specialist contributions offer a depth and breadth far beyond what would be possible with only two authors, and the expertise brought to these essays as well as these individual voices are part of weaving the magic of community, as envisioned within the very nature of the Pearl Pentacle.

As well as these deep explorations, within each section of the book are four original rituals, spells, processes, or activities relevant to that point of the Pearl Pentacle, inviting the reader into the work in ways that may be variously supportive, challenging, refreshing, or consolidating. These offer ways to step into the magic of the Pearl Pentacle and explore its meaning personally, as well as examine how the points relate to our existence in the world and within community. Each of these processes offers clear guidelines and instructions. However, it is perfectly within the spirit of the book—and Reclaiming tradition magic and the Pearl Pentacle itself—to make them your own. Perhaps the instructions are to work with a white candle but you are drawn to red; or the suggestion is to spend an hour with a process or ritual but you want to devote a whole day to it; or a topic is addressed as a discussion but you feel called to enter into trance with it. Please do this—follow your heart, your guts, your instinct—and make the work of the Pearl Pentacle your own.

At the end of the book is Dawn Isidora's work on the bridges between the two pentacles. There is also information on foundational magical and ritual practices that may already be familiar to you: acknowledging country, grounding, and creating magical space. Included in this end section are also instructions on running the currents of both the Iron and Pearl Pentacles and aligning the triple souls. You might choose to begin by reading all of this section and thoroughly familiarizing yourself with the use of these tools, or this section may function more as a reference that you turn to when you have need of that information. For example, a process or ritual may suggest you begin by acknowledging country, grounding yourself, and aligning your souls.

Within Reclaiming we often work in small groups—classes, covens, study or discussion groups, organizational cells, and local rituals. Pearl Pentacle, and the structure and content of this book, are ideally suited to be worked with as a group. There are different ways to do this, but the simplest is that a group of people agree to work through the content of the book together over five or six months, meeting once a month for a half day or twice a month for a few hours each time. Each month the individuals read through the three essays offered for one of the points—starting with Love—and set aside one or two of the processes to be done as a group, doing another one or two solo during the month. Each person also runs the Pearl Pentacle current on their own, either daily or whatever frequency works for them.

When the group meets, they can discuss the content of the essays, branching out into personal reflections and discussions on what the point (of Love, Law, etc.) means to them personally and the challenges and insights offered them by that point. Maybe the group will also consider what that point offers them as a group. One or more people— ideally different people each time—facilitate several of the processes, rituals, or spells for the group, either as detailed in the book or ones that they have devised, inspired by the point. The group would also run the Pearl Pentacle current together, exploring different ways to do this—for example, in a trance, as a dance, silently, with different people speaking to each point, or with each person layering words as the pentacle is run.

This book and the Pearl Pentacle are also powerful solo works. Sometimes we travel deeper and further in magic, personal growth, and intellectual challenges when we are outside of a group container, with only our journal and our gods as witnesses. Like the Iron Pentacle, it is never imagined that we would visit this material once in our lives and then move on; rather, its introduction is considered a living thread that—while it may come and go in its prominence and inspiration—will always be available to us once we have deeply met it. Thus over time we may explore Pearl's points and the material offered here solo, and at another time with a group or with one other person, and possibly also attend a Pearl Pentacle class or a Reclaiming WitchCamp or gathering held by Pearl Pentacle work.

You can read and work through this book as it is written, beginning with the introductory section and then progressing through each of the Pearl points in turn, referring as needed to the ritual basics and Pearl Pentacle tools at the back of the book. You might choose to do this over a set period of time; for example, six weeks or six months. To do this you would devote each week or month to one of the points, progressing on at the end of that time to the next one. The final week or month would be spent integrating the pentacle as well as working with the related Iron points and Dawn Isidora's bridges between the two pentacles.

Another way to journey with this book is to read it all the way through and then decide how to approach its contents. There may be certain points that call to you as being most appropriate to your life right now or particular exercises or rituals that you want to do regardless of the order they appear in the pentacle and the book. You might instead read in-depth about each point, leaving the processes until later. Or you might approach the book mainly as a piece of reading, doing only those processes you feel called to.

The work of the Pearl Pentacle can be both excruciating and also deeply rewarding, as anyone who has been active within a community or communities will know. Some points of the pentacle may seem easily accessible to us while others confront us, seeming stuck, closed, or unavailable. This can change over time and as we continue to show up to the work. Sometimes our most favored points are those that originally gave us the most trouble and challenge. Both of us have traveled the ups and downs through the grit and the shine of Pearl over the past ten years or more, together and individually. The promise of Pearl is the shine and beauty of community, which is reflected in each individual. We know of the grit lying within each one of us that has been honored, cared for, and polished through the grace and work of Pearl's points of Love, Law, Wisdom, Liberty, and Knowledge.

RECLAIMING'S PRINCIPLES OF UNITY

The Reclaiming Principles of Unity are agreed upon as the Reclaiming Tradition's guiding ideals to navigate our rituals, classes, communities, and WitchCamps, and are referred to in the essays that form the body of this work. They are printed here with the permission of the Reclaiming Wheel based in San Francisco.

My law is love unto all beings...
—from *The Charge of the Goddess* by Doreen Valiente

The values of the Reclaiming tradition stem from our understanding that the earth is alive and all of life is sacred and interconnected. We see the Goddess as immanent in the earth's cycles of birth, growth, death, decay and regeneration. Our practice arises from a deep, spiritual commitment to the earth, to healing and to the linking of magic with political action.

Each of us embodies the divine. Our ultimate spiritual authority is within, and we need no other person to interpret the sacred to us. We foster the questioning attitude, and honor intellectual, spiritual and creative freedom.

We are an evolving, dynamic tradition and proudly call ourselves Witches. Our diverse practices and experiences of the divine weave a tapestry of many different threads. We include those who honor Mysterious Ones, Goddesses, and Gods of myriad expressions, genders, and states of being, remembering that mystery goes beyond form. Our community rituals are participatory and ecstatic, celebrating the cycles of the seasons and our lives, and raising energy for personal, collective and earth healing.

We know that everyone can do the life-changing, world-renewing work of magic, the art of changing consciousness at will. We strive to teach and practice in ways that foster personal and collective empowerment, to model shared power and to open leadership roles to all. We make decisions by consensus, and balance individual autonomy with social responsibility.

Our tradition honors the wild, and calls for service to the earth and the community. We work in diverse ways, including nonviolent direct action, for all forms of justice: environmental, social, political, racial, gender and economic. We are an anti-racist tradition that strives to uplift and center BIPOC voices (Black, Indigenous, People of Color). Our feminism includes a radical analysis of power, seeing all systems of oppression as interrelated, rooted in structures of domination and control.

We welcome all genders, all gender histories, all races, all ages and sexual orientations and all those differences of life situation, background, and ability that increase our diversity. We strive to make our public rituals and events accessible and safe. We try to balance the need to be justly compensated for our labor with our commitment to make our work available to people of all economic levels.

All living beings are worthy of respect. All are supported by the sacred elements of air, fire, water and earth. We work to create and sustain communities and cultures that embody our values, that can help to heal the wounds of the earth and her peoples, and that can sustain us and nurture future generations.

Reclaiming Principles of Unity—consensed by the Reclaiming Collective in 1997. Updated by consensus at the BIRCH council meeting of Dandelion Gathering 5 in 2012 and at the BIRCH Council meeting in January 2021.

here we are at the beginning

and yes it's always beginning

but this beginning we name pearl

a seed at the heart of things

a grit, a provocation

a start point and us living beings

can't do without it, love begins us

blessed and cursed by it

we are love

LOVE

We begin the Pearl Pentacle with the point of Love, the crown of the star. Piercing upwards, it reminds us of our connection to the divine, to spirit and the stars above us, as well as offering a foundational value for the future unfolding of this pentacle. Love has evolved from Sex in the Iron Pentacle; the ferocity of immersing ourselves in the life force of everything has created this awareness of—and participation in—love. Not just love for another or love for ourselves, although definitely also those things. This is the love of the Star Goddess for each atom and being and moment of time. This is love that sweeps the tides of stars through the universe, love that births babies and saves forests and writes poems and dances the truth of the world.

Love is most often thought of as something we receive and something we give—or that we long to receive, long to give—but a deeper journey with love ignites the idea that it is something we inherently are and belong to. Each of us is an emanation of love, of atoms in love with each other in our physical forms, each breath part of a love-song kiss-of-life with the green world, and each moment an opportunity to live as love. When we run the pentacles through the human body, the point of Love rests over, through, and above the head. As we are born, tumbling into this world, we receive this invitation to live as love. The crowns of our heads are touched by the starlight from above as we receive love, the life force, and allow it to inspire the whole of our beings.

LOVE IS A REVOLUTION

Love is at the top of the Pearl Pentacle, the first point in our journey of connection in this cosmos. Love that we feel as we gaze into the eyes of our lover. Love that fizzes through us as we listen to a beloved child's laugh. Love that roots us into being when we stand on land that is sacred to us. Love—when we visit again with someone who matters to us. When we pour our hearts and souls into a painting, poem, or dance. As we immerse ourselves in the ocean, feel the deep layers of forest surrounding us, smell the incense of the temples, or gaze upon a statue, altar, or icon that represents an aspect of the divine we worship. As we sit by the grave of someone we've loved. As we prepare food for friends or family. As we release a friend, lover, or child to their own journey. As we meet with beloved community for a party, ritual, or gathering. As we gaze into a mirror and see our life's unfolding reflected back to us. Love—love—love.

But what actually *is* this thing we call love? What is it that we are yearning for—seeking, offering—that we name love? We all hope for love, try to live up to it, and notice its levels of absence and presence at different stages throughout our lives, even throughout our days or weeks. Love is sometimes viewed as a soft, fluffy emotion or an escapist, romantic ideal, but in the Pearl Pentacle we think of love as fierce, even when it is also gentle, and demanding in its requirements of presence, willingness, and compassion. Love is a call to deep integrity, to bringing the best of ourselves and asking the best of others; love is recognized by this fullness of heart.

The Pearl Pentacle arises from the Iron Pentacle, which means that the point of Love arises from the first Iron point, Sex. Sex: that gritty entry point to life that all of us experience—being born from the sex of an egg and sperm, born into a life-and-death existence that continually arcs both away from and toward union of various kinds. Only once we are born, embodied, can we experience love, so sex does come first. We don't have to learn to be born—to be alive/in the life force—but love is something we do learn, and ideally it is a life-long learning. We can also think of other ways that sex leads into or even creates love: the creation of deep intimacy through lovemaking, the birth of a child that leads to our love for that child, the inspiration to follow a particular path followed by learning to love that path.

Way back at the beginning of things—that is, the beginning of life on this planet—there were single-celled organisms who multiplied by dividing themselves: perfect replicas, asexual reproduction. Still, we can think of the sex of sunlight onto sea, of the division of self to create more selves, of the great love-light-life force beaming through this whole adventure. And then at some point sexual reproduction occurred—the combination of the cells from two different beings resulting in a third, yet again different being. Is this love, this joining of cells together into the creation of a new thing? It's in our lineage, we are created out of that, each one of us carrying this legacy of cells meeting and joining and dividing . . . love of the stars, the dust of whom are the atoms we are made of, love of sea and sunlight, love of living creatures for life, and more life, unfolding life.

We can take this even further when we consider our existence and even every breath. We have come so far from those single-celled ocean beings at the beginning of life and yet each breath we take is sustained by the green life of trees and plants, both ocean and land based. Meditating on the essential sex of plants and animals as our carbon dioxide and their oxygen comingle and affirm life—maybe even sitting with a tree for this meditation—deepens our feeling of profound belonging, connection, and love. The trees themselves are linked to other lives through the mycelial web, with a deep collective care for their whole forest or ecosystem, demonstrating to us what it is to be loving participants of this fractal of life and love on Earth.

Dawn Isidora, a Reclaiming and Feri priestess, articulates what she calls bridges that might help a person move from and with the Iron Pentacle into the Pearl (see page 248). She names the bridge from Sex to Love *Connection*. Through connecting with others in meaningful ways, even for a moment, we expand opportunities for intimacy and deepen our capacity to be loving and loved. There are multiple—infinite—connections that exist between ourselves and the world, and by meditating on these, observing and engaging with them, we may discover the love that is available to us in all moments and in diverse ways. Through connection love unfolds in ways we are not expecting or even specifically hoping for. It could be that there are people who admire and send us love simply from hearing stories about us or witnessing the impacts of our love in others. Failures and lack of connection can leave us stumbling, feeling disconnected from love and even from the life force.

When we look at human circumstances across the globe, it's immediately obvious that resources are unevenly distributed, that systems of power, oppression, profit, and war operate to divide, stratify, and privilege different countries, ethnicities, and classes, as well as genders, ages, colors, and religions. It is hard to see that anything is equally shared. Even the most basic requirements of air and water come in different qualities according to privilege, let alone other essentials of food, shelter, and safety. But love . . . what of love?

Across all human societies, some things are held in common. Moonlight falls everywhere, seeds grow into plants, flowers bloom, fruit falls to the ground and rots. Humans have babies everywhere. We have all been children, even in vastly differing circumstances. There are parents, elders, teachers, wise women, diviners of mystery. We fall in love. We worship—gods, nature, mystery. We gaze at the stars and wonder, we tell stories, we look after our beloveds. The sex-pride-self-power-passion of the Iron Pentacle are thought of as essential human experiences lived in a variety of ways across place and time. Perhaps the love-law-wisdom-liberty-knowledge of the Pearl Pentacle are essential threads of human society manifest and understood in many ways.

Anthropologists and sociologists have artfully ascribed various aspects and qualities to our species. The term *Homo sapiens* links our kind to self-reflection and sentience. *Homo religiosus* is a term coined for our species by the Romanian scholar Mircea Eliade because it seems early on in our development and each time we arrive in a new place, we develop cultic and ritualistic ways of venerating mysterious powers. We could also be called *Homo amor* for love—because we are deeply oriented to, motivated by, and nourished by love.

The concept that love is universal or that love is always the answer may seem glib, a sort of spiritual bypassing, but if we are to truly embody this ethos and live from it, then love is in the doing and relating. Love is a verb, becoming a very real and tangible force "that creates something that was not there before" (*Hedwig and the Angry Inch*) and reveals what is. All around us is evidence of love, fierce and profound love. It exists as the feasts, gatherings, and parties beloveds organize for one another, in the meal cooked by a friend and offered without a word. Love expresses as the kiss on the forehead, a magical spell of protection and safety allowing us to relax and be at ease. Entire books are written about languages of love—how we give and receive love—but love is too all-encompassing to be bound into notions of giving and receiving. Love requires a profound willingness to show up, to turn toward, to surrender into, to open . . .

But what actually *is* love? We might be asking this question all our lives, learning as life offers us different experiences, from those of childhood and adolescence through to adulthood and, if we are lucky, eldership and old age. Along the way our answers may change as we experience ecstatic union, devastating loss, betrayal, and deep self-doubt. Love is fierce in its lessons, and we continue to learn through deep realizations, healing work, and disillusionment. There are many different feelings of love we experience: love for our children, our work, our beloveds, our traditions, communities, and the divine, for nature and the planet, and our reverence for life itself. In languages such as ancient Greek, Irish, and Sanskrit, these loves each have different words describing them. Are all those different loves just variants on Love? Let's assume that our answers to these questions will continue changing and developing throughout our lives—and this exploration may be a great curiosity and inspiration for living a considered and satisfying life. But meanwhile we can find some touchstones, some words or qualities that lean into explaining and defining love.

Love requires presence, when we turn up and pay attention to another being. Love requires willingness. Love may even demand these things. We could examine other key concepts: a willingness to surrender, a presence that allows for trust, and generosity of attention. Love teaches us that we can be wrong, that we can fuck up, that we can make mistakes. Love empowers us to acknowledge these errors and through presence and willingness make repairs, thus engendering even more opportunity for intimacy and connection. If we are present, then love is possible in a way that it is not when we turn away from beloveds—and these are not only human beings. This beloved could be our garden, a cat, a watershed. If we are willing as well as present, then we are more able to listen, learn, reflect, and grow. Love may be "patient and kind," as written in the New Testament, and love also calls each of us fiercely to the work of repair and accountability, to growing trust and intimacy.

When I (JM) was in my mid-teens, I had a close friend who was unafraid to tackle the big topics. She was vibrant, artistic, daring, and always seemed to be particularly alive. We both had experienced a lack of belonging, security, and trust in our birth families, but while I had retreated inwards, she had gone in the other direction. I vividly remember her determined breaking down of my uncertainty and doubt around receiving love. She sat on my bed with me and said, *I love you. I love you, Jane. I love you*, repeatedly, for ten minutes or more. I couldn't have explained what was happening within me, and certainly I couldn't answer her, but by the end of it we were both crying. Experiences of love—both giving and receiving—can be so powerful they don't just break down our walls; they rewrite the ways we turn up to experience our own potential and our desires and capabilities. My friend did that for me.

There is an enduring concept in our society that parents leave an indelible mark on how their children experience love. A well-known psychology trope is the notion that a parent deeply influences our internal sense of self, our connection to reality. On some level this appears to be undeniably true, but it is only one of many threads of influence, a factor in something much more complex and mysterious. Our friends show us what love is; our animal companions, mountains, flowers, and lakes show us love. Teachers, colleagues, other children— all reveal experiences of love. The practice of magic and the ability to evoke and move into ecstatic communion, which many of us experience as children, is an ancient human practice that connects us with this phenomenon we name Love in the Pearl Pentacle. All this is true, yet the shapes or forms that we expect love to take, such as idealized romantic love, are directly influenced by the social conventions and attitudes of any prevailing time.

Beyond the instruction we received or failed to receive as a child, as adults we move into wider realms of pursuing our passions, the world of work, the realm of intimate relating, and our chosen communities. Some of us will follow spiritual, magical, political, or artistic paths and be taught, re-taught, and hopefully inspired about the parts that love can play in our lives. Within the construct of the Pearl Pentacle, we don't just turn up to a preordained version of what love is (either the one set down in our childhoods or the one marketed by mass media and capitalism); instead, we turn up with deep inquiry, curiosity, and a willingness for love's revolution.

Jane Ward's book *The Tragedy of Heterosexuality* is an incisive critique and re-examination of contemporary heterosexuality from queer and feminist perspectives. It casts fresh light on the monochrome and standardized transactions that are broadly portrayed as love in mainstream heterosexual society. Ward suggests that the queering of love results in broader, more vibrant and personalized relating, with more fun, pleasure, and equality within intimate relating for all, not just those who actively identify as queer. Queerness and other marginalized social positions, such as that of polyamory, relationship anarchy, the kink community, and conscious relating, open up the whole realm of love and intimacy beyond prescription. They invite each person and each intimate relationship to start from a basis of mutual desire, exploration, consent, and negotiation.

Queerness as a radical concept of self-identification and orientation within the realm of human relational experience invites the deconstruction of concepts considered inherited and inviolable. Heteronormativity casts queerness as being only about sex or sexuality, as well as a state of suffering or deprivation, which is largely conditioned by society's treatment and apprehension of its queer people. Queerness is as asexual as it is sexual, as related to romance as it is not. To *queer* love, then—which might be the central reality of queerness—is to acknowledge the boxes and instructions we are issued with and maybe even to inhabit them, but ultimately to set them aside and experiment with the myriad roads of being human. Within this context we respond to our own impulses, wonder about them, embrace pleasure and eros if we desire, unpack traditional notions of family and marriage, and forge forward step by step, breath by breath, casting the witch's spell of creating the world we desire all the time, day by day. Queerness is radical—of the root—and ultimately it is nourished and fed by love.

Not so long ago, I (Fio) was gifted a ticket to a queer dance boat party organized by members of the emergent Australian Ballroom scene. Ballroom is best known in popular culture for one of its key art forms, the dance style known as vogue. The history of Ballroom can't be easily tracked, but we do know that it existed by the 1970s in New York City, with roots that stretched to the late nineteenth century in the United States. At the end of the nineteenth century, there existed drag balls in which Black and Brown people would defiantly and joyfully crossdress. This was illegal at the time and could have you arrested and assaulted by police. Contemporary Ballroom culture arises directly from the experience of being queer and Black and Brown in a time and place in which either or both together might have you homeless, jobless, and in danger of being assaulted or murdered. Ballroom houses emerged in the 1970s and 80s, led proudly and joyfully by queer men, non-binary people, and trans women of color. These houses would often be centered in community homes in which new queer families evolved that offered care, mentorship, camaraderie, and safety.

This boat party was my first visceral experience of a radical welcoming to my queer-non-binary-trans-brown body. I spent the hours of that Autumn Equinox afternoon in awe at the beauty, celebration, and freely offered love I could feel drenching the space around me. It said: *You are holy and wonderful. You are worthy of pleasure, joy, being seen, admired, praised, and held. You are welcome here for yourself, as yourself.* This wholly encompassing queer love can alter one's perceptions and assessments of what we might expect or desire for ourselves and our lives. Fusing art, play, and politics with being human and being deeply queer, Ballroom breaks the boundaries of what we might hope for in the world. Ballroom culture has already transformed the world and continues to do so all the time.

Ecstatic or devotional experiences of existing within a dynamic flow of love—whether from the stars, a divine source, or our own experiences—remind us continually that love is not static but ever changing and ever renewing. Every time we open our hearts or engage our hearts, we are inviting heartbreak. To ignore the inevitability of this or seek to avoid it means we limit ourselves because the full depth of heart-offering includes awareness of both the fragility and resilience of our capacity to love. Hard lessons are learned again and again as relationships change and sometimes end, as things dear to us are ripped from our lives or die quietly, when our longings are not met or we disappoint ourselves. When we let love flow through us, rather than attempting to hold on to it, we meet both heartbreak and heart fullness with more presence.

There are some stunningly beautiful—and reality rearranging—ideas concerning the nature of love and the deep romances that humans whisper to each other through the generations. Inanna and Dumuzi's love poetry from four thousand years ago is one instance of this, where they celebrate each other as aspects of nature: *My love is lettuce, planted by the water* and *Who will plough my vulva?* Solomon's *Song of Songs*, Sappho's love poetry, Rumi's mystical poetry, and the devotion of nature writers such as Henry Thoreau, Annie Dillard, and Mary Oliver—all resound with powerful, life-changing, revolutionary love. Entire magical traditions are predicated on the mystery of reincarnating through lifetimes in entwined groups of lovers-beloveds. Many traditional Wiccans will say that their mystery tradition is a reincarnation cult. They magically desire and aim to meet, know, remember, and love again. This reminds me of something my (Fio's) mother said to me about the love between her and my father.

I have long wondered how the nature of my parents' relationship has influenced my own ways of loving. My sister and I were largely raised in so-called Australia by the hand and heart of my mother. My Balinese father did come with us to Meanjin (so-called Brisbane), where my sister was born, and lived with us for several years. Out of fierce love—the kind that allows you to let someone go—my mother suggested that my father return to Bali. They remained married, and my mother, sister, and I traveled to Bali each year in September; my father would come to us earlier in the year. This was the rhythm of my family. I have wondered how this might have fucked me up and raised it with a friend in California, a couples' counselor. She offered to me that perhaps the way I grew up, with my parents sustaining their relationship at a distance overseas, might have actually expanded and deepened my capacity to love people. So if, as my father wrote to my mother early in their falling-in-love, *You and I are written in the same book*, then perhaps there are powers beyond our comprehension that also help sustain our connections on levels we might not realize.

We have both experienced enriching and powerfully life-expanding loves in our lives. Maybe you have as well. These loves are not only the societally endorsed or desired romances, but also friendships in all their aspects. Love of land, place, cultures, traditions, magics, beings . . . great loves that heal, repair, inspire, and open us to Love itself. If love is the answer, what is the question? It is any question: Love is the answer to every question, or it can be. At every crossroads, when any choice is to be made, there is an opportunity to feel into how love moves here, how love inspires us to behave, respond, initiate. Love in the Pearl Pentacle is a cosmic, worlds-birthing, realities-affirming love. It is also that quiet love that holds us in our aloneness, cloaking us in a presence beyond our assessments.

In a world in which the choices made for us are based on corporate interests and the bloating of billionaires, it can be hard to perceive how love might even be an option. Love expresses as defined boundaries and *No* as much as it does in surrender and *Yes*. Love dissolves binaries and generates new and uncharted realities. Love and art, love and change, and love and death are twins supporting the nourishing and deepening of all things rather than the notion of perpetual growth.

As soon as we entertain the thought that love is all, we start to meet with challenges, conflict, illness, death, natural and human-wrought disasters, hatred, and the existence of evil. How can we say that love is everything when these things also exist in the world? Non-dualistic thinkers and philosophers tackle just this question. Writing from the perspective of radical contemporary Jewish Kabbalah, Jay Michaelson reassures us

> That which we regard as evil is actually that which awaits incorporation into the divine; the content of evil is the mistake of thinking that it exists.[1]

He further explains that although suffering exists, it is our job as humans to transform it, and this is the mending of the worlds; in Hebrew this process is called *tikkun olam*. If the world was already mended, entire, and complete, there would be no role for us within it.

Although we tend to assume that our definitions are absolute and correct, definitions of evil and the ethics concerning this change throughout time and within place and culture. My (JM) working definition of evil is *human actions and intentions of deliberate cruelty*. Evil remains part of our world, and when we define God, or Love, as the whole, the resolution of evil with love requires our active participation. "All the world is but a cloak for God . . . there is nothing that is not part of the system."[2] We could even posit that the presence of evil creates a space, a demand to be met with love, and thus may be actively involved in the creation of love. When we are confronted with evil, what choices will we make? Will we do nothing and so collude? Or will we draw on our individual and collective well of love and step forward?

In this time of human-created climate crisis, we are faced with these choices and complexities. Where do we contribute to what could be termed evil—corporate greed, unsustainable destruction of natural habitat, species extinction, use of fossil fuels—and where do we draw the line and bring forth actions from love: of ourselves, of the planet, of life itself? Do we become a low-impact composter and home gardener? Raise our kids to be aware of sustainability and regeneration? Become a Red Rebel or a school striker or an activist in the Black Lives Matter or Aboriginal Land Rights movements? Will we give our magic, our money, our time to these efforts? Perhaps this evil has catalyzed

---

1 Michaelson, *Everything Is God*, 74.

2 Michaelson, *Everything Is God*, 99.

deeper and more conscious love, shared by more. Thus we can stretch our minds to concur that evil is not separate—from us or the All—but plays a part, whether it wishes to or not, in the actions of love.

When addressing love, we also have to address crimes committed in the name of love, such as domestic violence, rape, incest, pedophilia, coercive control, and abuse. Writing that list it seems starkly clear that none of these have anything to do with love, but often they appear in contexts where we are expecting love, the perpetrators are people whom we love, and love is cited as a context—or even reason—for the violence. This is a piece of mind fuckery that adds to the confusion, pain, secrecy, guilt, and trauma experienced by survivors, victims, and sufferers. Even though in the greater sense, on universal and divine levels, we can speak of love as being everything and within everything, on the micro human planes we need to distinguish.

A basic bar for determining if actions are an experience of love or not is: Does this action nurture and support me as a human being? Feeling into this question, we can identify some challenging behaviors that still might meet this criteria—a friend, beloved, or colleague asking us to improve our communications or interactions, for example. That is still supporting us as a human being, calling upon us to grow into a better version of ourselves. Being struck, violated, or abused does not meet this criteria. And either way, if we're not certain, the safest thing to do is retreat (at least for now), ask for support from a trusted source, and spend some time reflecting and considering our options. Even concepts of consent can be challenging in this context, with many victims giving an appearance of consenting to the abuse. It's worth remembering that true consent can only be given between equals, and these situations of abuse rely on an essential inequality. If you are in an abusive intimate relationship or living situation, most likely you will need resources beyond yourself to get out. Please reach out for help.

Love can be tough to do. Getting up for the third time in a night to comfort a crying child, supporting someone through physical or mental health challenges, pursuing our dream of art, adventure, or changing our lives, negotiating relationship difficulties—all of these are tough. But they do not seek to diminish our worth as human beings or grant one human adult power and control over another. Children, of course, are another matter, yet children require adults to take responsibility for them; essentially, adults are granted power and control over these younger humans. Back we come to the criteria of *the actions of love do not seek to, or result in, the diminishment of the worth of the other as a human being.*

Love is a verb, a doing word, an action word. I (JM) first learned this from David Deida, author and teacher, who taught that we think that receiving love is what we want. Oddly, that's not when we feel love the most. Try this experiment: remember or listen to a loved one telling you that they love you, maybe even elaborating on that theme a little— why they love you, how they love you, the flavors and joys of loving you. Really focus on receiving this, and register how you feel. Now switch around and tell the other person, aloud or in your mind, about your love for them. Expound on it—put the emotion into your expression of this love. How do you love them, why do you love them, what is it you love about them? Focus on delivering this as clearly as you can. Register how doing this makes you feel. Filled with love—even though you're busy giving it away? It's when we love, in the act of loving, that we feel love the most strongly.

The presence or experience of love sometimes translates as a deep desire to serve, to dedicate our awareness or capacity to whatever it is that has given so much to us. This may manifest as the journey of initiation into a spiritual tradition or adopting a series of practices that keep us in alignment or lineage with a group of people we feel held by. This devotional love moves us outside of self and into ecstasy. Love for a deity, for example—not just a name, an icon, or an image, but a constellation of lore, mythos, feeling, sensations, and histories—can be hugely impactful. This love has formed and birthed entire religious movements that then impact migrations, diasporas, and the downfall of empires, as well as the formation of coercive cults and colonization of sovereign lands.

To create devastation in the name of a god has been the cause of much suffering. While acknowledging this, devotion and dedication remain a timeless source of the expression of love, the private nurture of love, and the social cohesion of shared religion and spirituality. We experience the Reclaiming tradition and international community as a powerful declaration of various threads and rivers of history, action, magic, and desire all linked together through Love. One of the possible etymologies of *religion* is to re-link—we would say to re-link us to the truth *My law is love unto all beings*. This quote from the *Charge of the Goddess* opens Reclaiming's Principles of Unity.

Love is the revolution, the invitation, the way it is, and, more importantly, how it could be. How we could be. Love is the answer. Love is the law. Love challenges everything, changes everything, rewrites us even as we are rewriting our lives, placing love at the center. It is the great expansion invited by the Pearl Pentacle, and in this expansion we touch back to the core of connection, connectedness, and the sex of all things. We are born from sex, with sex, into sex, and we always reach out, yearning for and creating love. As we love fiercely, queerly, and in the deep flow of change meeting doubt, fear, hesitation, and even evil, we reach out again and again to the sources of love that are both within us and in the world around us and in our relationship with the divine. Love is the law. Love is the revolution.

LOVE POEM

Love poems can be arcs of longing, sweet memories sent to a beloved, spells, or abstract dissertations on the nature of love. Perhaps you've written many of them in your time or possibly not since you were a teenager or maybe never. The thing about poetry is there aren't really any rules; any rules you can come up with can be broken by the very next poem. Sometimes they rhyme. Often they don't. Often they're written in the first person, or sometimes the third person, or even the second person. They have jagged lines down the page or perhaps they are a prose poem, like a paragraph, or maybe they're a concrete poem, where the words form a shape on the page to represent what the poem is about. Perhaps they have formal punctuation, but often not. They're free. They flow. They take the shape and form that is needed to express their material—like love, one hopes.

Who or what would you write a love poem to? Your favorite park or lake or forest? Your sister, best friend, your child, your god, your cat? Your beloved, a future or past beloved, maybe yourself? There's no limit on the subject of a love poem, just as it's not constrained by form.

But to write a poem about love or offering or expressing love, we need to have some idea of what we think love—this particular love—is. Maybe we will express it in metaphors, of flowers and deep rivers, or in a recitation of our lover's attributes or as a deep tide of emotion. Perhaps we'll recount a memory or outline a future wish or plan—but whatever we do, we will want the reader of the poem, even if that is only ever ourselves, to be able to feel, just momentarily, the love we are expressing.

This Is a Challenge

The challenge is to set down this book and not continue reading or working further with the Pearl Pentacle until you have written a love poem. Write it on your phone, in your journal, on a scrap of paper, the back of a chocolate wrapper. Write many drafts or just let it flow out of you or wait for the words to drip, like a good coffee, slowly onto the page.

We've included a few samples here as prompts, but let your love poem be as free and varied as your unique love.

If words are just totally not your thing, that's fine. Please do create a photo montage of a love poem, or a dance or piece of music or a necklace. Just do it now as your entry point into the deeper work of Love in the Pearl Pentacle.

Sample Love Poems

RIVER

There's an underground river

in me, of desire.

You lead me there.

I am familiar with this path,

carved rock walls, the sudden rush

of moisture, seeped from earth

the darkness, leading down.

I have walked here alone—

how do you know the way?

And the river, its twisted currents

no one knows how deep

the water a cold, ice-burnt heat

to shock the skin, dissolve

all barriers, turn naked flesh

into formless force, the distant beginnings

of a universe;

you want me to swim there.

SACRAMENT

she took from me the sense of needing to possess purpose

instead she sang to me of the sacrament of longing and desire

of the fleshiness of need

of the arresting cadence of unbound hope

the melody of rapture

the rhapsody of motion

heresy in the eye of a beholder

a beloved

beauty unmarked yet offering

willing

to be touched and to unbind

bacchic in our losses

our triumphant mourning

that makes mountains weep

and stars seek human hearts again

human

in that way we forgot once upon a time

human in that accidental joy

in that happenstance praise

of something so simple

so everywhere

as love.

OPENING TO LOVE AS A CURRENT

Love is something that can be felt: at times palpably, deeply, painfully, ecstatically, easily. It might be an overcoming presence, an expression of the divine, or perhaps what happens when two or more beings turn toward each other with praise and honor, or when the self falls and rises into the self with gentleness or rapture. It seems that love is endlessly mysterious and complex, just as it is simple and intrinsic.

Many modern witches, pagans, and mystics consciously create rituals and magical workings to court love, open to love, perhaps even conjure a lover or a partner. These kinds of rituals are probably as old as any form of magic and are valid, especially when they draw upon synchrony rather than coercion. This ritual is designed for you, the worker of magic, to open to the experience of love as a current we can feel, sense, and be touched and changed by.

> » You will need: a quiet and safe space with room to move if possible, a playlist of an hour's worth of music that inspires love in you, a bowl of water
>
> » Time: 60–90 minutes

Before embarking on this ritual, you might consider cleansing your love receptors.

I (Fio) first learned this practice at a Reclaiming WitchCamp in a Pearl Pentacle path that Dawn Isidora and SusanneRae were co-facilitating. We did this cleansing with a kundalini yoga practice known as "breath of fire" that Dawn had been trained in. The idea is that sometimes our receptors get clogged or obstructed, and we might need to smooth open the way once more. Sometimes we become contorted in our own complexes or affected by unconscious or hidden narratives about love: whether we are worthy of it, if we are even able to love or know how . . . With this practice we gathered and focused vital force—which in yogic traditions is sometimes named prana—and allowed it to work through the receptors in all the layers of our being that welcome in the current of love. We did this so that we were able to more fully experience the Love of the Pearl Pentacle.

The magical act of cleansing these portals and thresholds is a spell to reorient to the reality that each of us is a being of love, deeply worthy of experiencing this current.

The Ritual

Enter into the space you have chosen for this working and place the bowl of water in a central place. Pause and acknowledge country, ground and center, then align your souls.

You might wish to cast a circle or set up a magical container in some other way or perhaps not at all. When you are ready, activate the musical playlist. As an alternative—for example, if you are Deaf—you might have your computer or another device on with scenes and images that delight you and remind you of love.

You might be laying down the entire time, or sitting, or—if you are able and desire—you could be moving around the space.

Focus on the images or the sounds of inspiration and allow them to move into you but also through you. Each of us is a vessel for love, and love moves into us and out of us constantly. Perhaps you imagine or visualize this as a spiraling force of color or textures or tones.

Pay close attention: What are you scenting, noticing skin-wise or muscle-wise, in your bones, saliva, blood? How does love manifest and express through your vital organs, nervous system, lymph, genitals, brain? Allow yourself to daydream, even wildly, about this current of love courting you, dancing around and with you . . .

Once you feel in the momentum or flow of the experience, do your best to surrender into it.

We can either go with or against a current. If we go with it, chances are we will find it easier to experience what it has to teach us. If we try to battle against this current, we may experience difficulty, discomfort, or even pain. Surrender requires trust, and trust is often paired with love. Sometimes witches say *Perfect love and perfect trust*, and this is often meant as an aspiration, something to work for and from, an ideal, or a promise.

To experience this current of love and surrender into it, do you need to trust yourself, the experiencer? Surrender even that thought, even that question, give it to breath and movement, rhythm, music, and art . . . give it up, and let in love or imagine letting love in.

This could go on for quite some time, and you might feel in rapture from the experience. There is a possibility that this ritual could also provoke or activate old wounds or stories. As best as you possibly can, surrender these as well. If you need, there is the bowl of water to dip your hands into and allow anything stuck or overwhelming to flow into.

After you are finished with this particular ritual experiment, acknowledge the space you have created and perhaps dissolve or change it. Then pour the water onto the ground or down the drain with a blessing. Ground. Eat and drink something. Record the experience in your journal if you wish.

You may also wish to integrate this practice in other ways in your life: while walking your dog; at your altar or shrines in the morning or evening; while cooking, cleaning, or organizing books on the shelf . . .

LOVE IS ART

PANDORA O'MALLORY

Love is art.

By this I do not mean that love is an art, though it is; that lovemaking is an art, though it is; that caretaking is an art, though it is; that any of the actions we call love are arts, though they are.

I mean something much simpler. I mean A equals B. I mean that love and art are the same thing.

I know this because I have been taught that the Love point of the Pearl Pentacle is the metamorphosed Sex point of the Iron Pentacle. The vexed and fundamental eroticism of the first point of the Iron Pentacle moves from our own bodies into the community through the even more vexed and more fundamental devotion of the first point of the Pearl Pentacle, and this involves channeling sexual energy, which is creative energy, through oneself and outward.

Well, what is creativity moved outward other than art?

If we think of love as art, Love as we know it in the Pearl Pentacle becomes even richer than it was before. Calling the first point of the Pearl Pentacle love is scary enough, since love is so complex and mysterious, but if we had called it the art point it would have been even more problematic. There are those who do understand deeply that love is art and would be immediately empowered by that label. A friend reminds me that years ago when we were teaching the Pearl Pentacle class together, she confessed that she did not understand the Love point whatsoever. *Oh honey*, I said, *it's easy. It's art. It's the force of creativity moving through you.* And that fixed it for her. She's an artist. It made sense immediately.

If we had labeled the first point of the Pearl Pentacle *Art*, however, holy hell would have broken loose.

We are told, often, by very well-meaning people, that anybody can be an artist, that we are all capable of art, that we are all creative. This is true, but not in the way it sounds, especially if we are in the process of being encouraged to make art. If I am creating something and it is not up to my standards, it doesn't help my mood much to be told that everything is okay because all creativity is art. I'm noticing that my own art is not up to snuff.

But if art is love, if love is art, as I posit, everything changes. Because then it is not just that we are all artists, it is not just that we are all lovers, it is that we all exist, and that existence is both love and art. The force of creation—the Star Goddess spinning herself out and creating all that is—is an act of love and desire, and is, very obviously, an act of art. We are her acolytes.

Even without adding in the idea of art, love is very big. Love is infinite, in fact, beyond even the idea of big, beyond any of our concepts of it and certainly beyond any of our rules for it. What we tend to notice are the ways in which our love violates the rules and structures for love that we have come to believe in. We notice the ways in which we ourselves do not behave as we think we should. We have inherited and acquired notions of what romantic love is supposed to look like and how we are to act if we find ourselves in it. We have inherited and acquired notions of what communal love is supposed to look like and how we are to act toward members of our family, our neighborhood, our homeland. We have inherited and acquired notions of what global love is supposed to look like and how we are to act toward the members of other countries. And we may want to keep all of these notions—or some of them—but we can't know that unless we know what they are, and, if possible, where they came from.

This is also true of art, which is exactly as infinite as love and lives in even more vexed territory. Almost all of us believe that we are capable of loving, being loved, and, by birthright, worthy of love, but a great many of us believe that we are not capable of art. It's as if art resides in an ancient tower surrounded by deadly thorns, and only very special people are able to hack their way through to the sanctuary of the studio. Everybody else is wounded and maimed, either stuck on the thorns, unable to move, or wandering around outside of them, trying to ignore the whole damn thing altogether.

Nonsense.

In the same way that clearing the Sex point of the Iron Pentacle involves finding our own creativity, sexuality, vitality, the Love point of the Pearl Pentacle involves finding our own constructions of intimate love, community love, global love. And if it is, as I say, the Art point, those constructions are what make us not only lovers but artists. We create intimate, communal, global art. Continually, without ceasing, spinning out into creation, whether we know it or not.

This constant creation transcends the fact that making dinner is love and art, though it is; that driving the car is love and art, though it is; that nurturing the young and the elderly is love and art, though it is. All of these are conscious acts, and we can notice them, change them, infuse them more strongly with love as we understand love and art as we can understand art. But this constant creation also transcends the conscious acts of love and art we embody and conceive. It resides also in the realm of what we are not conscious of, of what we cannot see.

Our cells divide and multiply. Sex, obviously, but also love. Also art. The matter of the rocks, the trees, the water, the air, fluctuate in the quantum vacuum. Sex. Love. Art. The Star Goddess spins through all of this, fluctuates through all of this. Sex. Love. Art.

I know that if I take my integrated sexual self and move it out into community—that is, into connection with beings and things not myself, outside of myself—I become more fully present in erotic sexual relationships. But not only that: I also join the infinite panorama of created and imagined beings. The universe. Beyond the universe.

Love and art abide, always, forever, within sex and beyond it. And it's a matter of consciousness—and therefore choice—as to whether I feel this tripartite energy or not, act on it or not.

The complexity of all this creativity is both confusing and enthralling. It's hard enough to understand love. The kinds of love that the Greeks articulated don't begin to cover it: *sexual, playful, charitable, lengthy, personal, maniacal, familiar, soulful, mature.* There are myriad ways we love humans. And that's just the humans. We also love, in myriad ways, animals, plants, the physical world, spirits, deities.

When we define love—oh, as best we can—we know, we always know, that we are giving limited definitions, that we have caught an aspect of love but not love itself.

Infinite aspects of love, infinite recipients of love, and of my loves become me. Knowing my loves, my desires, shows me myself. Who and what I love is what I am. The more numerous my loves, the bigger I become, more connected, more multifarious. The more conscious I can be of this, the more I am able to infuse all of my creations with energy. And I might add that no matter how I continuously strive to create myself—my better, more loving, more useful self—I don't do it alone. I say this as an extreme introvert; if anyone would be able to exist alone, it would be someone like me. But I don't. I am created by my loves and the ways that I love them. This requires interaction.

I've been in love often and continually in my decades on the planet. I've been in erotic love that was brief and raging like a forest fire. I've been in romantic love that was long and slow and graceful. I've been in love with beings that loved me back. I've been in love with beings that didn't care much about me at all. I've been in love with humans. I've been in love with animals. I've been in love with ideas. I've been in love with histories. I've been in love with books and movies and television shows. I've been in love with gods and goddesses and incorporeal beings of all sorts.

As I write this, Blanca, a white Goffin's cockatoo, is running around the floor of this studio. Occasionally she runs over to bite my shoe or pull on my shoelace or nip my ankle. She is happy; her beloved human—not me, my partner, who is beloved by both of us—has been in the room trying to make the printer work, so Blanca has been able to get some cuddles. She likes cuddles. She does not want cuddles from me, however. She wants me to be in the room, sure. The flocking birds consider themselves in danger if they are alone. She doesn't want me to cuddle her though, and she bites me when she can. She is a one-woman bird.

I love her. She belonged, for her first years, to a human who loved her—we know this because of the cuddling and petting that she wants—but when that first human died she was shunted among his grown children, from house to house of people who did not like her and did not want her. I understand that part, actually; since she is a cockatoo, she bites and screams, and she would have done that a lot because she was unhappy, unloved, and in grief at her loss. She's not easy to be around. Who knows what happened to her, even beyond the neglect and dislike? She may well have been badly mistreated. She began to lose her mind. She pulled out her feathers. Her chest is still bare, and some of her wing feathers are still missing. When she was finally given to the parrot rescue, where she was treated well, she had also started obsessively circling inside her cage, over and over. Over and over. Screaming.

We had gone to the parrot rescue to get a different cockatoo who also needed a home, who was not so raggedy, wasn't screaming, and wasn't obsessively circling her cage. But Blanca sat on my partner's shoulder, stopped screaming, and groomed the edges of her hair. We said *nobody is going to take this difficult bird*. And we took her home.

She has been with us for a year and she is happier. She still screams, sometimes like a fire engine, repeatedly, but not as often as she did when she got here. She does not circle her cage obsessively. She does not pull her feathers out. She plays with her toys (with cockatoos, this means either destroying them if they can be destroyed or screaming into them if one's beak can fit into them). She is naughty, nipping the dog's tail, nipping me, and looking very happy while she does it— and naughtiness is to be expected with cockatoos. She has a home. She is safe. She is a major pain in the butt, but she is loved. We love her because she is feisty, because she becomes more and more herself while she is living with us, because she is alive, because she needs us. And she becomes happier, more herself, more feisty, more alive, because she is loved. The circle builds on itself. We love her because she is happy being loved. She creates herself out of love. We create ourselves out of love.

I love my broken and neglected cockatoo, and I watch her heal and blossom. I love the child I bore, whose lifetime I have spent supporting and letting her go so that she can flourish on her own. I love my partner, who has consistently required honesty from me and who has allowed me to witness her growth and courage. I love the spirits and deities and elemental beings who surround me and interrupt me and help me and encourage me. I love the histories of the humans, naughty though they may be, and I love the Old English language, with its strong alliterative stress in the poetry, its kennings—*seahorse* for ship! *whale road* for ocean! *voice bearer* for human!—and the way it echoes throughout the language I speak daily, its surviving words, hundreds of them, that existed before the French Vikings changed the language forever. Foundational words: *earth, bean, night, thorn, cow, yes, no, day, year.*

My loves create me. This is who I am.

And when we are together, we create ourselves through our love for each other, the ground on which we stand, the ancestors and all who have gone before, our deities, our bright planet, all of us lovingly spun from the desire of the Star Goddess, who teaches us by example to love and desire ourselves.

Rituals are works of art, not only a manifestation of our love and our desire for the beings we know and engage. Sometimes we incorporate art itself into rituals, in the altars or in our dance or in our song. Priestessing itself fulfills my love of theatre. But my favorite example of art as ritual—or perhaps it was ritual as art—came one WitchCamp week in British Columbia when I suggested to the camp that we have a week full of mummers' plays. Throughout that week we performed scenes from beloved myths or became deities or spirits we loved in unscripted times and places. We surprised each other that week, during the whole of the long sacred space of WitchCamp, with embodied art.

I had been thinking about the ways in which, in the European Middle Ages, actors often performed in outdoor common areas, and how the community would be part of the productions in those shared spaces, the only distinction between the actors and the audience being the fact that the actors had lines and costumes. It meant that when the crucifixion was played, the audience became the citizens of Jerusalem; when the play of Mary Magdalen was enacted, and Mary Magdalen sailed from Jerusalem to Marseilles, the audience became the ocean; when Mankind was played, the little demons coerced money from the audience to see the devil, implicating them in Mankind's fall. I wanted to see how that dynamic might play out in a pagan WitchCamp, within a community that shared different stories and deities than those medieval audiences did.

It succeeded well. If Persephone got dragged away from a circle, if the Norns showed Odin the runes while we were standing in the dinner line, if Brigid walked through the camp distributing apples, we were all part of the drama. Not just an audience, but Demeter's attendants, Odin's ravens, Brigid's beneficiaries. We would never know when we would find ourselves part of their realms. It was a reminder of the constant presence of the unseen spirits, deities, active all around us and through us, manifested in time and space by the fellow campers who were channeling themselves into art, into love. It was a representation of what the spinning universe is: matter imbued with spirit, spirit dancing through the stars and planets and creations. Sex. Love. Art. We are all creative, we are all artists, dancing our stories through the world.

Moving from the Sex point of the Iron Pentacle to the Love point of the Pearl Pentacle helps me create myself consciously, more and more, and create all that is outside me consciously, more and more, though there will be levels I may never consciously know. Oh, electrons. Oh, galaxies. Oh, art. Oh, love.

It's that simple. It's that complex. Love moves through us and creates. Art moves through us and creates. Same thing.

But I must be honest and say that though I am often aware of multitudes of loves and creations, even to the level of the tiny particles of matter and the large galaxies of matter, I am not always in that state. I have to turn my mind and heart to it. We say that understanding and integrating the Love point of the Pearl Pentacle takes several lifetimes. Well, certainly so. And with that we know that we are not required to integrate it fully, that we cannot. Not right now. Maybe later. Lifetimes of all our loves crafted together. Maybe an infinite number of lives and loves to get it right.

After pondering the Love point of the Pearl Pentacle so that I may share my experience, strength, and hope concerning it, I have decided that I am a very young soul because I really know nothing about love.

All that is created and that creates, love and art . . . they are not a feeling. Feelings change, though some of them do show us a way toward love in its infinite greatness and art in its infinite creation. Neither are they actions, though acts of kindness, helpfulness, charity, and invention can connect us to and reveal love and art. They are a force, a force that moves without ceasing through the known world and the unknown world, that moves through all the worlds. And they are trustworthy. And worth knowing.

CHOOSING LOVE

Many years ago, someone told me (JM) that all actions came either from a place of love or a place of fear. At the time I scoffed at it as too simplistic, and I still think it's simple—but now I think it's basically true or true enough. Actions come from a place of love or from somewhere else. We can call it fear, or it might be doubt, past trauma, convention or tradition, pain of one sort or another, lack of freedom or power—but not love, essentially. Actions that come from love we can suppose to be furthering love's cause. Maybe that love is self-love or maybe it is love for another, of a community, or the earth. Actions that come from love follow my yearnings, desires, heartfelt responses, inner truth.

This experiment is to look at our own lives through this lens, this provocation: *What if all my actions were to come from a place of love? What would that even entail, and what might my life look like if I were to do that?*

> » You will need: journal and pen; quiet place (inside or outside) to reflect
>
> » Time: 30 minutes to an hour

Begin by grounding and centering. Take a few moments to check in with your body and breath, noticing how they are today. You might want to introduce the word or the feeling or the concept of love to your breath and body, and notice what happens. Perhaps your belly relaxes or your throat tightens, your toes clench or your spine straightens. There's no wrong or right way to be with love, but we can choose to welcome these reactions and feelings, maybe observing through the space of a few more breaths what happens with our continued attention.

Ask yourself what the current challenges are that love brings to your life. There might be challenges within various relationships, health or self-talk or other personal situations, challenges about living up to your values and beliefs. Take up your journal and pen and make a list. It's fine if there are only one or two items on it—but there may be five, ten, or more. Make the points as specific as you can, so rather than *self-talk* write *I put myself down with my self-talk*, or instead of *work*, write *I'm working in a job that I don't love.*

Then put aside the journal and pen and allow yourself to relax as fully as you can, letting go of all thoughts and constructs for the moment.

When you are ready, imagine the crown of your head opening like the petals of a flower. You might even imagine a lotus, rose, or some other flower. At the same time, become aware of the stars and the Star Goddess, whom we can choose to recognize as Love. Allow this love to flow down, as it naturally does all around you, even into the crown of your head, the point of Love in the Pearl Pentacle when we run it through the body. Imagine this as a refresher dose of universal love pouring down into the container of yourself.

Spend some time feeling and breathing this in. Perhaps you will experience it in sensations—a flowing warmth, a sparkling effervescence, in colors—warm red, glowing gold, cool blue—or as an image, such as letting your whole self become that flower, or in some other way entirely. Perhaps you just breathe it in and know it in your mind. Spend five to ten minutes with this until you can really recognize the difference and feel it is established within you.

Imagine that when an action or decision is required from you, some of this love, sourced from the Star Goddess herself, can flow through you as the conduit and into that decision or action. You might want to try opening your mouth and imagining this love emerging with your breath into the world. Perhaps words will come or you will want to move your hands and imagine the love flowing out through your palms and fingertips. You might try walking a few steps in this flow, imagining you are treading in the path laid down by love. Breathe into this a little longer, leaning into the idea of being sustained by this love that flows as endlessly as starlight.

When you are ready, pick up your journal again. Read the first of the challenges you wrote down. Imagine this force of love that is within you flowing out toward this situation. You can ask yourself questions such as:

» What would love do?

» If I were actively loving myself and all beings,
  what would happen here?

> » How can I hold love as a central attribute in this
> situation?

You might want to jot some notes down before you move to the next challenge on your list and do the same thing. Let the love flow through you and into the situation. Breathe deeply while asking yourself some questions. Take notes if that seems useful.

Depending how you are feeling, you might wish to pause this exercise after two or three of your challenging situations or you may be on a roll and want to examine all of them! Do what feels best.

Before you complete the exercise, list several action points—things you will actually do—for each of those situations. Action points might look like:

> » I will only ring my mother when I am feeling
> centered and grounded.

> » The next time I'm asked to stay behind at work, I will
> say I have to leave at the usual time, but I'll start on
> what needs doing first thing the next morning.

> » When I hear the critical voice in my head, I will
> thank it for its vigilance and tell it that I will handle
> the situation.

> » When my partner says something hurtful, I will say
> I can't continue the conversation, and I will take steps
> for self-care.

You may notice similar themes or action points arising from one challenge to the next—or maybe not.

When you are done, for now, take some time to rest, quietly breathing. You might thank the Star Goddess, and even though you may still be aware of Love, and the love that is flowing through you, you can allow your attention to widen to other things as well, such as the quality of the breeze, thoughts of what you are doing with the rest of the day, or something else.

Over the next several weeks, continue to return to this process of breathing love in from the universe, flowing it through you, and asking how it can inspire and support your actions and decisions. Let yourself explore and test out what changes, how it feels, and what happens as you lean into these choices, allowing love to be the guide.

LOVE POTION

One of the ways in which the ancient Romans characterized witch-craft was as *veneficia*. This term was used in a derogatory way to refer to the makers of poisons and potions in order to coerce or enchant others. The root of the word veneficia is connected to the name Venus and experiences of love, lust, and desire. Many of the philters, potions, and spells created in these times by magicians, witches, and sorcerers were about love and the procuring of it. Certainly the love spell or love potion has a lot of gravitas behind it, and at least in Rome—and with its huge influence over many nations—was linked implicitly and directly with witchcraft.

>   » You will need: A container/vessel big enough to
>   comfortably stir the plants, oils, and herbs below
>   with your hands. Some of the following: rose petals,
>   a few drops of lavender essential oil, one drop of
>   ylang ylang essential oil, jasmine flowers if they are
>   in bloom, one drop of cedarwood essential oil—
>   please add whatever you are genuinely called to, and
>   also consider your allergies and sensitivities as you
>   curate the herbs and oils you will be touching. Fill
>   the vessel halfway up with water. The largest red
>   candle you can find.
>
>   » Time: 60 minutes

As you mix this potion, you are invited to imagine or open to sense and feel these ancient witches conjuring up their spells, magical oils, brews, and incenses. We are linked in a great spiral of magic makers across cultures and times who desired to open to love, to call to love.

This love potion is for you and only you. It works through you and magically may bring potential lovers, partners, and friends your way, but this is not exactly the point. The point is to enchant yourself, fall in love with yourself, and carry that in the waking world.

The Spell

Acknowledge country. Ground and center. Align your souls.

Set aside your working space or go to your altar or circle if it is more permanent. You might also do this in your kitchen, your bathroom, or a private space outside.

In this space you might feel like casting a circle or invoking the presence of spirits and allies who might aid you in your magic. As you invoke, let them know—say it aloud—why you have come to make this love potion. Speak your desires and yearnings for connection, intimacy, self-love, ecstatic communion. Hold up the vessel you will mix the oils and plants in and declare it to be the container for your magic for this spell. Place it down safely and then light the red candle as a signal that you are stepping further into this working. You might say:

> I light this red candle here and now. I light it to call
> the powers of love and wonder. I light this candle
> to conjure forth a powerful feeling of love—that I
> may be drenched in love and that love may spiral
> throughout and about me. May I be held in love.

Bring your attention now to the vessel of water and your plant and oil friends. One by one, drop in the oils and plants and name aloud the qualities or virtues you are invoking with these allies. With the rose you might say *love, loyalty, truth, beauty, joy*—with the lavender *purification, dreaming, soothing, happiness, peace*—and so on.

Keep naming aloud virtues and properties until everything you have brought is in the vessel. You may also place in blood, sweat, tears, saliva, or your own hair if you desire.

When you feel ready, ground and center your awareness once more, then dip your hands into the water and begin to mix. As you mix, you may wish to chant. You might chant the following:

> With hands of love I mix this spell
> I mix it now, I mix it well
> By all the virtues invoked herein
> A loving potion for me I win!

Chant or mix—or both—for as long as it takes to feel and raise the power and then release it into the water and the oils and plants.

Honor the spirits you called, unravel the space if you cast one, and clean up after yourself.

Your options now could be to strain out the organic matter and then use the enchanted water in a bath and soak in the magic for a while or decant the liquid potion in a bottle to use for anointing over the coming weeks. You might place the vessel on your altar for a week or so and then pour it onto the earth in thanks for the love magic that is unfolding now in your life.

WHAT IS REMEMBERED LIVES

WILLOW KELLY

I dedicate this essay to Reclaiming ancestors Colleen Cook and Copper Perse-phone. Beloved and Mighty Dead of the Craft, thank you for initiating me into the magic of living, dying, and death, and for showing me my purpose. Thank you for the wisdom you taught us all about love and how it can manifest in community through your living and dying; that being human is messy and we aren't going to do it perfectly, but we can do it lovingly. Thank you for choosing to die consciously in our Reclaiming community, initiating us all, and for your generous service in life and death.

> **Colleen Cook**
> (May 26, 1968–July 8, 2019)
>
> **Copper Persephone**
> (September 22, 1962–June 28, 2020)
>
> **WHAT IS REMEMBERED LIVES.**

Death magic in Reclaiming has been a master class in love. Colleen, Copper, and Reclaiming set me on a path I didn't know I was seeking. The love of community changed the course of our collective magic, our relationship with dying and death, my life, and their deaths. We'll never do it perfectly. Life and death are messy. We do the best we can and hopefully forgive or unburden ourselves and each other for the unintentional harm we cause as we learn to do better and grow together in love.

My story begins exactly seven years ago in 2016 on a sunny spring day in Minneapolis. I came to co-teach a workshop for the Upper Mississippi River Reclaiming community. My friend Colleen (pronouns she/they) had been living with stage four cancer for about a year and a half and had been very open about her journey. She invited us along on the journey through poignant communication, connecting more intentionally with me, friends, and family, frequent social media posts, and regular updates.

On this beautiful spring day, we were walking through the alley toward their house when they asked if I would be their death midwife. That moment planted a seed of magic that would change the course of my life forever—magic that took root and grows still in the fertile soil of Reclaiming love. Colleen explained how they had taken on this role for a beloved friend who died in the same house where they lived now. She wanted to show me the space and talk about logistics, challenges we might face if I accepted the role, her intentions and definitions of a good death, her family, community, and the unknown emotional, spiritual, physical, or psychological situations that could arise.

I was on the precipice, the Fool about to leap into the unknown, to begin a new journey with no idea what I was getting into, what it was going to look like, or what would be asked of me, while feeling a visceral, profound, resonant YES rippling through me.

I leapt. Reclaiming and the Great Mystery caught me.

Colleen was committed to all forms of justice, and as part of that commitment held the intention that I would be compensated fairly and sustainably for my time, energy, travel, and expenses, even though they did not have the means to do so. It was the least of my concerns, but Colleen wouldn't let it go. They would quote the Principles of Unity, reiterating our community values of being justly compensated for our labor. She decided to give community the opportunity to show up and make it happen.

I felt weird about it. I wasn't sure how to navigate this or define what just compensation was as a death doula for a beloved member of my community. I knew I needed travel and expenses covered; I was self-employed on a tight budget. Colleen asked for my permission, then went to work inviting witches in our Reclaiming community to support us. The witches showed up. They showed up for her, for me, for us as a tradition in this great experience of doing death magic collectively.

Community love poured out, glistening like pearls on an intricate web of connection, holding us throughout this process over the next three years. Funds started to come in consistently, always enough to cover the next travel costs or expenses with a bit more, sustainably compensating me for my time. People showed up to organize mundane tasks, trips to doctors, a wild string of epic fiftieth birthday parties for Colleen, rituals, gatherings, supporting the supporters, food drop-offs, planning, cleaning, strategizing, resource gathering, checking in, and so many other innumerable voids that were filled with loving service by Reclaiming witches. You were exquisite to behold. Thank you.

Colleen wanted to lift me up, to show the world that I was fabulous and deserved recognition, support, and value for my gifts. They spoke of me as someone doing essential magic with them in service to community and decolonizing the dying and death experience. They saw and believed in me what I had not yet seen or come to believe in myself but learned to, not only through their eyes, but through the eyes of many in our beloved community who said YES to Colleen and to me in this role.

Then there was the YES from the Great Mystery. Well, more yeses than I can count, but this one falls into the mythic category and is just so Colleen. No doubt the magic of the multiverse sang through us both as we grew along this path.

Part of Colleen's mission to elevate my service and do the magic of decolonizing dying and death was to share our story with anyone who would listen. Colleen wanted us to do podcasts, reality TV shows about death, or any kind of interviews that would catch the public eye and give us a platform. She had sought out some opportunities to feature our work together, but nothing came of them until the spring of 2019 when a reporter from a small town in Virginia where I was living at the time asked if he could interview us.

Jeff Schwaner was writing a feature story following death doulas and their clients with several interviews over a handful of months. We all got chills and shed a few tears when shortly after we began our work together, Jeff learned that his father was dying too. Jeff's dad and Colleen would journey toward the gates of death, passing through them within weeks of each other.

Later that fall, after their deaths, Jeff wrote a heartbreaking and powerful article about the growing trend of engaging with death differently, end-of-life doulas, and the ways we are bending the culture of dying and death back toward healing and wholeness. The online version of the article featured photos of Colleen's journal and the series of paintings they had done shortly after learning of their diagnosis. At the end of his article, he wrote that Colleen was "the first person I met who made me think there really was an art to dying."[3] I knew she'd be happy about that.

Through these years with Colleen and my desire to learn more of my craft—and with a lot of Reclaiming support—I became certified as a professional end-of-life doula. My passion inflamed, I immersed myself in learning, sharing, and co-creating death-positive culture. I became a home funeral and green burial guide and began the process of launching a local volunteer organization to provide resources. Knowing that home funerals were legal in every state, that we needed radical change in the modern funeral industry for the sake of the environment, and that psychologically we needed to connect with dying and death in love, I joined in the magic of reweaving this broken web in our culture through advocacy and education.

I heard of the National Home Funeral Alliance's conference in October 2019 in Chaska, Minnesota, from other death priestexes in Reclaiming who were involved and presenting. The themes were ritual and funerary art. I hadn't been back to Minnesota since officiating Colleen's funeral in July of that same year. It seemed like years ago and yesterday.

As I was crossing the state line into Minnesota, I got a text message from Jeff stating his article had been picked up in the weekend edition of *USA Today*. He wasn't sure how much of it was published or if it was intact so he couldn't guarantee we would be in it, but he wanted me to know. I stopped at the first gas station and the story was there on the front page and printed in its entirety. I could feel Colleen's YES!

Love, community, and death continued to forge me. Earlier that year, in 2019, Copper Persephone, another beloved community member, teacher, and mentor, asked me to be her death doula, and in the summer of 2020, the call came. She was in the hospital and soon going home on hospice to die within weeks or days. The world as we had

---

3   Schwaner, "The Art of Dying."

known it was upended by a global pandemic. Government offices were shut down, businesses were closed, flying was unpredictable, and travel restrictions seemed to change hourly as updates rolled in from news sources around the world. Preparing to travel across the country to California with agreements and consent from those I'd be exposed to on either side of my travels, despite the instability and unknowingness of the times, I felt just as much of a YES then as I'd felt with Colleen three years earlier.

Again the Fool, I leapt. Again Reclaiming and the Great Mystery caught me.

I headed off to California filled with uncertainty. The ensuing weeks were grueling and exhausting, as end-of-life care can be, but with the added complexity and intensity of navigating COVID-19 within a community that thrives on connection. The air was full of negotiations, support, making schedules, blowing off steam, conflicts, mediations, resource gathering, food wrangling, collaborations, learning, mentoring, ritual, magic, caregiving, planning, self-care, sleep deprivation, impossible tasks, figuring out how best to connect as a community while keeping people safe, seeing people show up in amazing ways, and so much more.

Once again, I witnessed the stringing of community pearls of love as coven mates and beloveds made great sacrifices taking caregiving and vigil shifts around the clock, adding magic and ritual from their hearts to every precious moment. Logistical support witches helped to prepare and bring food; financial donations from people around the world covered my expenses and compensation once again. Unexpected support emerged around every corner, from the mundane to the magical. Beloveds provided sacred music and poetry, sending in recorded spells, well wishes, and songs from around the world that we played for Copper as she lay dying. A heartbreaking duet that Galen, a Winter WitchCamp beloved, had mixed using a recording of Colleen's voice was among the treasures.

Copper had decided on a home funeral and green burial in a plot near another Beloved and Mighty Dead of the Craft, Lizann. That choice proved to be a beautiful invitation into an expression of community love. We were initiated collectively, overcoming challenges, refining what matters, gathering power and strength from deep within and all around, submitting to the Great Mystery and all the unknowns, trusting we would come out the other side transformed, healed, and empowered. Amidst breakdowns and breakthroughs, we were tasked with collaboration and dedication despite the messiness and imperfection we'd face.

Yule—a member of Copper's beloved family of choice—and I were trained as home funeral guides but with no hands-on experience. We were ready to figure it out, to learn as we went and reach out for support. Coyote wove a coffin of bamboo reeds with a 3D model of the tattoo on Copper's back crafted on its lid. Gwydion brewed sacred plants, resins, and oils for tending Copper's body and spirit after death. Hilary made a magical shroud covered with runes and earthy art with dozens of tiny pockets around the edge to hold offerings, and many more witches than I can name brought their magic and art to these moments. We came together to carry her body from her deathbed to the temple, to tend her there for three days, to carry her to her final resting place, and then surrender her back to the earth she so passionately loved, ready to join in the magic of mycelium.

I knew an indescribable sense of wholeness reconnecting a thread in the web of life, death, and rebirth as we tended Copper during her dying and after death. We made space for community to be with her in death and witnessed the care from many. We were truly held in love. It was messy and hard and maybe as perfect as an initiation gets.

Before there was a contract for this book, Fio and Jane had asked Copper Persephone to write this essay on love, death, and community. I wish I could read what she would have written in preparation for this, but instead I am picking up a task that she set down, hoping I can do it justice.

Some of the most powerful lessons I know about the magic of love for living and dying I've learned from Colleen and Copper: act in alignment with our integrity; ask for what we desire and hold ourselves accountable for our choices instead of blaming others; establish, maintain, and respect boundaries because as Prentis Hemphill, somatics teacher and political organizer, wrote, "Boundaries are the distance at which I can love you and me simultaneously."[4] There were lessons: the art of compassion and how to extend it to our own and others' humanity; how to dance with imperfection knowing it is inescapable and will teach us much. Their wisdom continues to teach me, to open me to learning the ways of love more intimately.

Colleen often said the biggest task we had to do, the most that was being asked of us, was to just show up. They talked about how this can be challenging, uncomfortable, anxiety producing, inconvenient, and about a million other things that can divert us from action, but this was what mattered most. They often said in our discussions around death, death magic, legacy, and becoming an ancestor, *I want to be remembered as the ancestor who made mistakes.* Then added, *And was deeply accountable for those mistakes.* This is the legacy Colleen hoped to pass on: *Show up. Be accountable.*

And, if we show up, we're going to fuck up. We can't avoid it. Colleen often said the hardest part of showing up was knowing we would make mistakes. It's painful to have good intentions and still fuck up terribly, causing unintended harm. People with good hearts wanting good things for others can still cause unintended pain. Colleen knew she would make mistakes—a lot of them. She knew it was inevitable that things were going to get messy and hard, and that it was still worth it. She invited us often to let go of the idea of getting it right, looking good, or making a good impression, and to instead cultivate a loving, real, raw, human, accountable presence.

Cleaning up is hard but sure feels good when it's done. The second most important thing, Colleen would say, was to be deeply accountable for our impact. They were adamant that it was necessary in the process of healing our collective and individual wounds to create containers to listen and respond to how our choices impact others, to learn to do better, to do our best to clean up any messes or unintentional harm, and to allow others the grace to do the same. We are tasked with learn-

---

4   Prentis Hemphill, "A Reminder," Instagram post, April 5, 2021, https://www.instagram.com/p/CNSzFO1A21C/.

ing the nature of a true apology, where we do not seek to justify our behavior or compare our pain but to come with an open and willing heart to the hearth of love.

We are immersed in a culture of intolerance and contempt. We are in danger of it taking root in us, making it less safe to be in our community; to speak our truth, get it wrong, mess up in public, learn, apologize, and do it all imperfectly. We have a challenge, an opportunity, to choose whether we allow opinions, wounds, traumas, and judgments to be our law or if we will take on the magic of the Pearl Pentacle with love as our law, anchored firmly at the top of our magic as we continue to create the world we desire.

We are humble, human, and imperfect. To know we can surrender into that and trust a community not to exile us for our shortcomings and missteps, but to hold us accountable and allow us to clean up our messes—that is the most precious pearl of our love.

For our future generations, we work to decolonize dying and death, to build more connection, community, compassion, and compost. We step in where others are stepping out and invite them back in. We work to reform the modern funeral industry that is both devastating our environment and economically unjust. We engage the magic of mycelium as we move away from institutionalized death practices toward taking our rightful place in the natural cycle of tending each other in dying and death, returning our bodies to the earth that we worship in a final act of love.

Death cracks open hearts, creates more space for grace and tolerance, nurtures gratitude for the simplest pleasures, and builds compassion for the toughest among us. Death has the power to dispel great and small resentments, encourage us to let go of what is not essential, and help us prioritize what truly matters: our purpose and our connections. When we embrace death and give it a place of honor in our experiences, we cultivate gratitude and forgiveness. We don't sweat the small stuff.

Copper and Colleen both showed us how to do death consciously. They chose connection and engaging the magic of our collective web of support as they entered the mysteries of dying and death. My journeys with them and many of you have been epic, rich, powerful, challenging, hard, transformative, initiatory, love-filled experiences; love given and received, life-changing lessons learned as we co-created the end-of-life experiences for which our beloveds asked.

I believe we can and are co-creating a community of love that invites us into belonging with the full scope of our humanness and gives us opportunities to learn, do better, clean up our messes, seek repair and reconnection, and offer the same to others, but we still have a lot of work to do. Show up. Fuck up. Clean up. Show up for people, relationships, hard conversations, friends in need, justice; just show up. And when we fuck up, let's grab our brooms, witches, and get some loving done!

Sweet, fierce, impeccable love, continue to teach us your mysteries and open our hearts. May we learn, enact, and share your law. These pearls and so many more, strung together over time, adorn our community in love.

What is remembered lives.

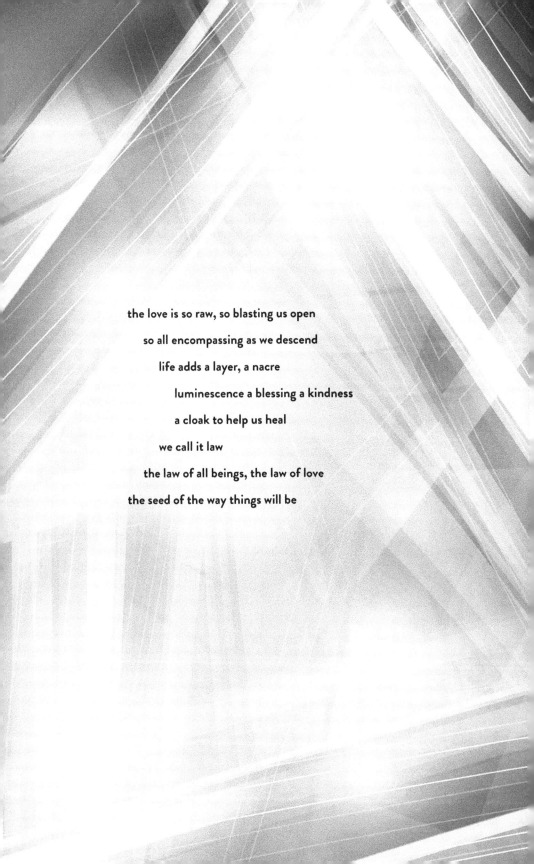

the love is so raw, so blasting us open

so all encompassing as we descend

life adds a layer, a nacre

luminescence a blessing a kindness

a cloak to help us heal

we call it law

the law of all beings, the law of love

the seed of the way things will be

The second point of the Pearl Pentacle is the point of Law. Grounding downward into the earth, it reminds us that love is just the beginning, the seed of grit within the pearl, and there's many layers yet to come. In Law we fiercely examine the truth of the way things are—both the way they have to be within natural law and how we have arranged them to be within human law. In the Iron Pentacle, underlying and informing the Pearl Pentacle, this second point is Pride. In the fires of finding true pride, we burn away the dross of self-doubt, of keeping up a front or saving face, and come to know ourselves deeply—our strengths and our challenges. This right-sized pride allows us to step into the complexities of law, showing up for what we believe, for who we are and what we will stand for.

Law in the Pearl Pentacle is not a depository of books detailing historical court judgments and acts of congress or parliament. Like love it is a living thing, continually unfolding in the way the planets dance about each other, the ways stars form and blaze and eventually die, in the beating of our hearts and the intricate balance of ecosystems, in the code of our DNA and the makeup of atoms. As we map the pentacles over our bodies, Law is held in the right foot, reminding us of putting our best foot forward, stepping over the threshold, and placing ourselves on the line. What are the laws you hold sacred? What are the laws you will live by and die for? Where will you put your body and being as we fight for justice? Law burns like a flame, illuminating our actions.

LAW: THAT WHICH MUST BE

Law is the second point of the pentacle as we move from Love, deeper into the mysteries of Pearl. Perhaps here we can come to an understanding about how Love might actually *be* the Law. To do this we have to know what Law is. Clearly the word law refers to laws created and enforced by societies and the impacts this has on us as individuals. The law is the formal contract we make between individuals and society. If we were to choose to act with love as our law, that would mean making a conscious choice to center ourselves within love, to act with love, asking ourselves at every step *What would love do?* We might envision utopia, imagining how it would be if a whole clan or tribe or village, a whole town or city or country—a whole world—were to make this choice. Love is the Law: what if this referred to the greater-than-human law, the laws that underpin, create, and structure the entire universe?

If we choose to embody *love is the law,* then how does this direct our thinking, feeling, and behavior within the web of our relationships and in the world? *Love is the answer* is a sentiment or trope sometimes graffitied on buildings or posted as a social media status. *Love is the law* is similar; they both imply something fundamental about reality and the cosmos. Although these phrases may come across as glib or reductive, perhaps their provocation is enough to create a bridge for our thinking, a way to begin imagining into *What are the laws that love writes?* If we lift up our heads from the page and look around us, perhaps it begins to become self-evident that law exists as the shining threads that infuse all of nature, creating the systems of the universe.

We wish to acknowledge that law is a complex and charged term that is often evoked in legal and state-sanctioned ways to actively oppress and fragment entire communities. Law enforcement is a term applied to police and other officers of the law. Police violence, the prison industrial complex, and punitive systems are part of the law and legal systems. It's possible that you may right now be in prison or have previously been and therefore experienced worlds that we, writing these words, have no insight into. This writing on the Law point of the Pearl Pentacle is intended to broaden and deepen our perspective on how humans engage with and understand law, as well as to unschool and unravel some of the ways human societies internalize the overculture's paradigms of lawfulness.

I (Fio) am writing these words a week before January 26, 2023. This year it will have been 235 years since the first fleet of eleven ships arrived in Gadigal and Bidjigal country—so-called Australia—into what was then named Sydney Cove by the British naval captain Arthur Phillip. Here I have to drop the colonial indoctrination I was given from age five (when I started school) and interject with the truth. The British Crown invaded sovereign lands and then over many years stole and colonized land, seas, river systems, and raped and murdered the First Peoples of many proud Nations and Clans. These inflicted horrors dispossessed Indigenous people and their descendants of their languages, ceremonies, and cultures.

I want to cry out that *they broke the law!* These commandeering agents of the British Crown sailed across vast stretches of ocean over eight months, bringing hundreds of convicts taken unwillingly from their own countries, homes, and families, to break the law. This is the law that is country: the deep multidimensional and sacred truth of being in, coming from, and relating to one's place, home, and ancestral land. Whenever I have had the privilege of listening to First Nations elders and community members, I have heard that *the law that is the land cannot actually be broken.* However, it can be disrespected and outright denigrated. By now there are so many systems that are out of their original harmony. We are faced with many consequences of colonization and imperialism: rivers drying up, weather patterns disturbed and changed, children stolen from families and culture degraded, genocide, and rapid and rampant mass species extinction . . . This level of violence to law far exceeds even the strategic impacts the original perpetrators were intending.

We humans often think of ourselves as distinct from other animals. Creation and culture stories spell out the pivotal moments in which humans become set apart with the power of naming: *crocodile, tiger, swan;* or eating fruit and being changed; emerging out of the trees. We may even believe that we have transcended our instinctive and biologically determined programming. Human civilizations create art, war, cities, and societies that develop and decline. We innovate and employ technology to the nth degree, and arguably we are becoming ever more intricate and absorbed in these arenas, to the point of precarity.

Many who have dismissed religious doctrine and theology have embraced secular humanism—or science—as the arbiter of all truth and reality of the law. A popular assertion for science is that we are not bound by anything except our ambition to discover more and more. The discovery of natural laws and their dynamism is one of the marvels of scientific inquiry; however, the paradigm of science as the great authority that answers only to itself has often bolstered those with corporate and financial interests to hijack science for technological advancement in contraindication to natural laws. One of the best examples of this is nuclear power, as this is arguably one of the most ingenious ways of producing energy, and yet we must mine the earth for uranium and dispose of the radioactive waste. Both of these activities come perilously close to breaking the law if, in fact, they did not already break that boundary.

Laws have always been something humans have sought to observe, understand, and describe in order to make sense of the world. We need to understand the laws of the animals and plants we are dependent on, of the seasons we exist within, and the functioning of our human bodies. From philosophical as much as scientific perspectives—and the two meet and run parallel—we want to understand the laws of why we are here, how we got to be us, and what's going on around us in the solar system, the galaxy, and the universe. What are these laws we are subject to?

The whole scientific endeavor of humans—all the history of it that we know or can imagine—has been dedicated to discovering the laws that govern our existence and the reality we know, as well as the origins of the universe. These laws are not decided by ourselves or those that study them. Instead, through the painstaking work of hypotheses, observation, experiment, and reasoning, they are pieced together and proven, or revealed—sometimes only partially, until the next hypothesis evolves.

In *A Universe from Nothing*, Lawrence Krauss states, "I was brought up on the idea that the goal of science was to explain why the universe had to be the way it is, and how that came to be."[5] In other words, science—and I (JM) would add, philosophical inquiry—is directed toward discovering and describing Law. In the preface to his book, Krauss explains that the three key principles of science and scientific ethos are:

> (1) follow the evidence wherever it leads; (2) if one has a theory, one needs to be willing to try to prove it wrong as much as one tries to prove that it is right; (3) the ultimate arbiter of truth is experiment.[6]

These are the laws of scientific inquiry.

All of our descriptors, formulae, charts, and experiments are designed to explain not how we wish the world was, not (usually) how it might be at some future point or under different circumstances, but how it is. The periodic table of elements is a motif of this concept. Maps of the earth's surface, of the night sky, of the human body are drawn and redrawn as we continue to discover the details of the law. We postulate mathematical equations of energy, the speed of light, the planets' orbits. Experiments are conducted in labs and backyards and out in the stretches of dark space as humans seek to discover traces of the oldest galaxies, reading imprints left over from the hypothetical big bang. Humans search for microorganisms that might eat the plastic littering our seas; we seek to cure cancer, discover why Christmas beetles are disappearing, track and learn and understand a thousand thousand things. The law. All of nature offers us this without ceasing—a second-by-second reading and enactment of the law. Of *that which is* leading our understanding toward *that which must be*.

Humans love to imagine that we are all so different from each other; each one utterly unique and almost incomparable to the others. Yet take a look around. Although each red cedar is slightly different than every other red cedar, none are actually identical; they are all similar enough that without much difficulty, on meeting a red cedar we've never seen before, we can recognize it: *Oh, a red cedar*. I (JM) can easily

---

5 Krauss, *A Universe from Nothing*, 175.

6 Krauss, *A Universe from Nothing*, xvi.

imagine that each new baby pademelon is quite distinct to its mother, but watching them on the lawn it's not really distinguishable to me from all the others. So with a tawny frogmouth, a dianella, a strangler fig tree. They are not that different from all other tawny frogmouths, dianellas, etcetera, and only rarely are the differences between them the important factors.

If this is so for red cedars, pademelons, strangler figs—in fact, for every species we could name—how could it not be true for humans? We are all fundamentally human, and so it follows that all of our differences from each other are minor and usually not what's important. Watching the pademelons or the red cedars, I can easily see that they follow what could be called *red cedar law* or *pademelon law*—that is, it's impossible for them to do or be anything outside of what is a red cedar or a pademelon. They are the living law of red cedar, of pademelon; so, then, it must be for humans. How could we ever act outside of the law of what it is to be human? We cannot suddenly fly or breathe water. We cannot give birth to our babies in eggs or hibernate or spin cocoons around our bodies to dissolve all our cells within.

Fire also follows the law, the law of fire. The winds, tides, moon, and tectonic plates follow the laws—their own laws and the laws that govern where they intersect. A wildfire that runs rampant and burns down forests and human dwellings, takes lives of animals, plants, insects, birds, still is following the law—not just a law of what's possible but the laws governing its nature. We say that humans are unusual in having the capacity to act with cruelty or make choices or destroy our own habitat, but other species do have these capacities. Some dolphins are judged to be mean or violent (by humans) in their behavior toward other dolphins, but we don't imagine they're outside the bounds of what it is to be a dolphin.

When the numbers of a species get out of control, it can result in the destruction of its own habitat regardless of the impact this might have on any future generations, just as we are busy doing. And while human free choice might be a vexed concept, believing ourselves superior to the rest of the natural world, any animal or even insect makes choices all the time: this flower or that, to stay perched on this branch or fly off somewhere else, to flee that loud noise or decide it's no threat just yet and remain. We like to imagine our own choices have more volition than that of an insect, that we are not bound by the same constraints that others are, but that's ignoring the evidence.

It is true that humans make errors and are capable of what we designate as evil. Therefore this potential for evil thoughts and actions must be within the law of being human or it would not be possible. Early cultures and their mythologies try painstakingly to contextualize the origins of evil within humans, as well as to steadfastly implement human-agreed-upon laws that mimic or reflect the greater natural laws. These help hold the boundaries and contain or limit that potential of human evil. The laws also impose agreed-upon restrictions and punishments for those who deliberately, and sometimes even mistakenly, break them. This is one of the central theses in Indigenous law, as addressed by both Tyson Yunkaporta in *Sand Talk: How Indigenous Thinking Can Save the World* and Marcia Langton and Aaron Corn in *Law: The Way of the Ancestors*.

It is also within the laws of being human that we offer compassion and witness to one another, that we feel empathy and desire fairness and diplomacy in our societies. I (Fio) think of how the Hebrew word for sin, *khata*—that biblical sin so often discussed—means something like *to miss the mark*. We are able to bring each other back into harmony and solidarity through asking questions, listening, challenging, reminding each other of our agreements—social and emotional laws—enshrined in tradition or custom. Traditional religious law can over time become removed from its roots—its context—and wielded against people and persecuted groups or entire lands to dominate and subdue. This is encoded in the Hebrew Bible with stories of God smiting those among his chosen people and those outside of that group haphazardly, as well as the church or Christianity endorsing doctrines of discovery and manifest destiny, which have provided leverage for colonizers to invade Indigenous land and commit genocide.

These forms of violence are ideological and insidious, removed from the natural accountabilities of law as enshrined within the land, the sky, the rivers, the ecosystems at large. Tyson Yunkaporta in *Sand*

Talk speaks on the place of culturally sanctioned violence in Aboriginal communities, where skirmishes between individuals or family members of the same age and same gender, held by certain known rules that may include things such as no knives, may be witnessed in the streets. These conflicts emerge and disappear and may seem to the white reader especially as uncouth or violent. Yunkaporta remarks that violence is always present within human societies and provokes the reader to consider how violence in western colonial systems is sanctioned by the state and enshrined within the police force, the military, and, some could argue, the courts. Humans and our dance with violence is complex and ancient. We have always attempted to work with the law in order to curtail the worst of it and protect the most vulnerable from it. Unfortunately, it is also true that the law has been wielded against the most vulnerable, marginalizing and oppressing these groups even further, creating ongoing and intergenerational trauma.

Laws can appear to be paradoxical, as with the balance between cooperation and competition. Competition is often described as the law: the strongest or fittest survive, those who can adapt survive, those who can find and utilize resources best survive. The law of competition puts different species in conflict with each other and different members of the same species similarly competing. Just as in a dense forest trees may compete for the available sunlight, sending out branches as wide as they can, putting out as much leaf as possible, humans design whole social systems based on competition. Yet survival is not only in competition but also cooperation; however contradictory these two things seem, finding the synergy between them is what creates success for the individual, the group, and the ecosystem—and in this model, a city is also an ecosystem.

As well as the law of those who compete best survive, the law is also that those who cooperate survive, and it may be that those who cooperate best survive the best. Humans cooperate with each other, even with strangers: one person grows vegetables, another transports them, another sells them. We cooperate in joint ventures: creating a government, school, hospital, even a large scientific experiment. We cooperate with the laws we live within—most people pay taxes, follow the traffic regulations, and observe the labor laws without volition; we live cooperating with law. Competition and cooperation may have different weightings within each family, culture, nation, and historical time, but both always exist as they do out in the wider world beyond the human realm, and the balance of them is always acknowledged as important.

If we consider that ecosystems can become unbalanced, either within themselves or due to outside intervention, we can see that the laws of that ecosystem might get broken. The internal arrangements and functioning of these ecosystems become damaged as one or several species has its numbers severely increased or decreased, placing stress on other species and perhaps the entire habitat. Within an ecosystem there may be a self-correction—in the following year as the weather changes, for example, or as predators increase in response to higher numbers of their prey, or whatever it might be. So systems can self-correct, returning to their original harmony or finding a new one over time. Thus the law has not been permanently broken but, more accurately, challenged.

There are also larger corrections that occur within natural law, for example, as cities are built some species adapt and thrive, while others may become scarce or die out. We are in a time now of looking at whole planet corrections, wondering how natural systems can respond to a human-created climate crisis. What will happen if the Gulf Stream disappears or the Amazon rainforest can no longer function as the lungs of the planet or the Great Barrier Reef is unable to replenish itself? A simple self-correction might be that if the planet warms too much for us delicate humans, the troublemakers will be extinguished, leaving the whole system to reset or adapt without us.

So as these laws do get broken, part of the law must allow for breakages, adjustments, and resettings. The law is both *that which is* and also *that which must be*. *That which is* can be challenged, changed, broken. But *that which must be* will assert itself, as inevitable as the architecture of the stars. The law is kept every day and broken every day and reset every day. This type of activity shows us that law is not static, as love is not static. The law is writing itself every day—we are writing it every day as we live our human lives, struggling to recognize and live within the laws, with law, and as law.

In the meantime, we do our best to explain the law to each other.

Myths have always purported to explain profound truths, to convey the law. To the myth tellers and myth readers, the story of a myth is only the first layer, a vehicle to reveal progressively deeper meanings. We use stories because they're easy to remember, because they're vivid and exciting, and because, at the heart of it, complex and even para-doxical truths can be embodied within story. Myths operate with an internal logic where they are both following laws and creating their own laws. They are like a great mystery story—when the denouement comes, we realize we have had all the clues all along. Thus the ending makes perfect sense, both structurally within the myth as well as to the listener. The deeper myths—those that last and last or turn up in differ-ent places, times, and cultures—may be conveying more than human law, which is local and varied.

There's a Greek myth of the goddess Artemis bathing nude in a woodland pool with her attendant nymphs. A human, Acteon, is con-ducting a stag hunt with his hounds in that same forest when he spies the naked goddess. The law is that he cannot live, having seen her. Because we can imagine that perhaps the sight alone would be enough to kill him, his death need not be a revenge or punishment that Arte-mis undertakes but simply the way things must be. The law. Forests and stags and hounds are sacred to Artemis, so when Acteon is turned into a stag, and therefore hunted to death by his own hounds, it makes perfect sense. Thus is the law of stags and hounds in forests. We can read the myth forward or backward: by becoming a stag, he has been claimed by Artemis, and all that has happened is he has become closer, bound to and bound by the law of the goddess he already worshiped—or else what was he doing in her forest with hounds, seeking a stag? The vision of the goddess was granted him as a gift in exchange for the offering of his life.

In the Sumerian myth of Inanna's descent to the underworld, she passes through seven gates. At each gate one of the objects she wears is taken from her, but they are magical objects, as each confers powers upon the bearer. At their loss, she loses also those powers. Yet as we lean deeper and deeper into the myth, perhaps asking ourselves what those objects were or what they mean, what we discover is each one was exactly what she could not pass through that gate carrying. It was impossible to pass unless she no longer had it. The object she loses at the first gate is her crown, or what makes her a queen in the upper world, and thus the myth says that a queen of the upper world cannot pass through the first gate on the way to the underworld unless she is no longer queen.

The ways of the underworld are perfect and may not be questioned, as Inanna is told seven times in this story, once at each gate. The ways of the underworld are the laws of the underworld, perilously close to the laws of death. Once a queen is dead, she is no longer the queen. One leaves queenship and all the powers of the living on the other side of those gates. These are the laws. And it's not so much that they may not be questioned—certainly Inanna questions them at every gate—but that the questions make no difference; questions cannot change anything. The laws are the laws. Inanna's myth is also a revealer of another law as she, like Jesus Christ a few thousand years later, dies for three days and three nights before returning to the upper world: exactly what the moon appears to do from our position on earth. From anywhere and everywhere on earth, this is the law.

Reclaiming tradition, a distinct form of modern feminist witchcraft, often calls itself anarchistic although its organization and functionality is quite different to what anarchy is assumed to mean, as there are many structures, defined roles, and suborganizations within it. Briefly, the history of Reclaiming stems from the Reclaiming collective whose public rituals and political actions in the early 1980s attracted more and more interest, leading the group to eventually dissolve the collective into a broader tradition. Before it dissolved there were several years devoted to discussion within the wider community and networks—via classes, covens, and camps—in order to discover what Reclaiming-identified people considered central to their expression of the tradition. From this outreach, discussion, and debate, by 1997 a document known as the Principles of Unity (see page 13) was written.

These principles create a great deal of freedom for folks belonging to or identifying with the tradition, but also define our common unity: community. The Principles of Unity are a manifestation of the Pearl Pentacle's Law within the tradition.

Inside of and revealed by the Pearl Pentacle point of Law is the Iron Pentacle point of Pride. Pride and Law might not seem obviously connected and yet they are intimately interwoven. When we consider pride the way that many societies do—as equal to arrogance or a form of hubris—then we might wonder how at all this is relevant to law except as a warning. Pride in the Iron Pentacle is often experienced as being in right relationship and right action with oneself and the world. Pride is being within and as the threads of harmony that link all things. If we allow ourselves the space to drop into our breath and ground through our body, we might feel a sense of deep purpose anchoring us into connectedness. In this way, as we align with the latticework of these perfectly arranged threads, we are enacting Law by simply existing. Pride could be the personal realization that we are in alignment with law. The Pearl Pentacle points so often reveal more about the Iron Pentacle points, and Law shines a light on the nature of Pride as an awareness about being in right relationship.

In Reclaiming we often discuss the points of the Pearl Pentacle as being especially manifest in the interactions we have in community, as a series of webs of relationship. In Reclaiming and Feri there is a saying, a proverb even, that is often attributed to Victor Anderson. Pandora, one of the mothers of Reclaiming, is in fact the origin of this quote: *Iron Pentacle is the work of a lifetime, and Pearl Pentacle the work of many lifetimes.* I (JM) like to think that those are many concurrent lifetimes rather than sequential, and that just by existing within community we are already showing up to the work of Pearl. Effective and dynamic communities are comprised of many lifetimes—people— who come and go in cycles and seasons, but who form familiarity and intimacy with one another and each other's relationships over time.

In the 1990s a British anthropologist Robin Dunbar theorized that the average number of a socially coherent human community is 150 individuals. This was put forth after research into other primates, specifically their brain sizes relative to their physicality, and cross-analysis of anthropological, historical, and behavioral data. Beyond this number, the complex capacity to recognize and be related to individuals meaningfully and know about others' relationships diminishes noticeably. The basic premise is that primates, including humans, have an essentially limited number of individuals they can create social coherence with.

We began discussing this number on a walk through the intense raw beauty of the Blue Mountains west of so-called Sydney, and we arrived at the idea that beyond such a number you can no longer rely on knowing and trusting everyone to be responsible for communal law tending. We conjectured that perhaps this is when a society enters the domain of requiring law officials to do this on our behalf. We notice a deep discrepancy between how many Indigenous, clan-shaped, elder-anchored, smaller societies who know one another function, compared with complex, vast cityscapes in which laws have to be created and enforced by elected and paid officials.

The more deeply we immerse ourselves in Law—learning about and opening our awareness to *what must be*—the more we understand not just what governs our lives but the very nature of what it is to live within the field of Law. The laws scaffold on each other—the makeup and behavior of atoms, the formation of atoms within star systems, the composition of the universe—and like a kaleidoscope or a mosaic, the shifting, forming patterns of these laws add up within us, eventually, we hope and aspire, to some sort of wisdom. We begin to understand not just individual laws as separate things, and not just the layers of laws as they intersect and affect and determine each other, but to have a sense of Law itself, and thus an ability to move within, know, and be responsive to and responsive for the living law.

The people who do this most deeply not for themselves, but for their village, tribe, culture—for all of humanity and for all of the planet— we consider wisdom keepers. These people we regard as living embodiments of *love is the law*. Even when love and law might seem paradoxically opposed to each other, we trust this intention, of love *is* the law, to show the way. In more secular societies, these roles of eldership and authority may be held by High Court judges, as well as more informally by artists, poets, and passionate truth seekers and truth sayers. And even if we never seek to hold that role of being the living embodiment of law for more than ourselves, still in this approach to law as we deepen and deepen within it, we begin to meet the next point of the Pearl Pentacle: Wisdom.

If the law is alive and we are all living it—we are living instances of law—perhaps it is unfolding along with us within each of our lives and our collective living. White cockatoos are always learning to do new things, expanding what their law covers, and then they teach each other. Many living things adapt to changing or new conditions. These laws, at least, are not static as the law is broken and remade in every moment. Understanding this is what leads us into wisdom. Unfolding law as a verb that we live, individually and collectively, we recognize that it's not done or finished in the way finite human laws lead us to think of law. It's like God, it's like love, it's like life. Law is the poem that describes in adoring detail each stroke of color in each petal, the position of each atom and electron, each beat of each heart. Even the laws of the universe are dynamic as we watch another shelf of the cliff sheer off to fall into the valley, as the inflation of the universe slows and the percentage of helium in proportion to the whole gradually lessens. As everything gets further and further away, Law is what holds us together, leading us back to the acknowledgment of Law as that which must be. This supports our deep collective health and need beyond our individual desires.

LAWFUL BOUNDARIES

One of the most significant parts of relating is through acknowledging, respecting, and affirming one another's boundaries. A boundary is an edge that communicates needs, desires, preferences, and realities.

A boundary is often thought of as verbally communicated—and it can be—but they are also sensed and perceived, culturally ingrained or created, and sometimes we magically catalyze them through our own personal work. At times we navigate boundaries through understanding our deep values or what we hold to be immeasurably and irrevocably sacred. These are my boundaries of law, or lawful boundaries.

This process is a magical working for you to affirm your lawful boundaries. First you will need a container of time to do some deeper investigating. A distilled but spacious amount of time might be a traditional month, from one new moon—first sighting of the sliver of a crescent—to the next. In this container you will be invited to consider—with mindfulness practice, observation, and divination—*What laws do I require myself to live by? What must I swear by?*

Examples you might arrive at could be: *I live my life by respecting the web of relationships, therefore I will no longer eat meat that comes from factory farmed or killed animals. I will only eat animals I know personally and eat fruit and grain from this region.*

Another might be: *I will anchor into compassion and curiosity for myself and my actions and the actions and responses of those around me.* And yet another: *When I feel hesitation or doubt to a proposed activity, I will say no.*

> » You will need: a working space that is quiet and private for the duration, a new pillar candle that feels solid in your hands, a beautiful stone, a feather, a cup of water
>
> » Time: 45 minutes

The Ritual

Begin by acknowledging country, grounding, and aligning your souls. You may want to cast a circle.

In Reclaiming witchcraft we regularly adore and praise the elements of life: earth, air, fire, water, and spirit. Take the stone in your hands and as you drop your attention into earth, ask this element to help you affirm your lawful boundaries. When you are ready, say *Earth is sacred.*

Take the feather in your hands and perhaps move it through the air or trace it over your skin. Through the feather, enquire of air; ask that air help you clarify and communicate your lawful boundaries. When ready, say *Air is sacred.*

Light the candle. Feeling the heat of that flame, ask the fire to help invigorate and radiate your lawful boundaries. Say *Fire is sacred.*

Hold the cup of water and drink some if it's good to do so or sprinkle it around with your fingertips, offering some to the land. Ask the water to deepen and hold your lawful boundaries. Say *Water is sacred.*

Spirit or mystery will help you feel the intimacy and connection between all of the elements and take you deeper into the ritual. *Spirit is sacred.*

Ideally you have spent a moon cycle affirming, clarifying, invigorating, and deepening into your personal understanding of your own lawful boundaries. *What laws do I require myself to live by? What must I swear by?*

As with the examples above, it is time now to speak aloud the lawful boundaries you wish to live and swear by. You may include a time boundary too. You might say *I do this for a year and a day.* We recommend something that is as substantial as a year but not too much longer. You could renew or transform these boundaries each year as some people do with their relationship agreements. You may do so upon and with the elements, but you might also now invoke other spirits and beings such as ancestors or gods to witness you in this work.

When you feel you have come to completion for now, cast your awareness through the magical space and begin to hum or tone to raise the power to bless and seal this work. You may dance around the space if you are able or clap or play out a rhythm with your hands on the ground or your legs or chest. Sense into your lawful dedication and commitment to these boundaries and to the container they set for your life. When you can sense or imagine that the power is peaking, release it up into your god soul and then let it go and ground yourself.

When you feel complete, honor the elements of life and other mysterious ones you have invoked to witness you. Release the circle or dismantle the space you have created for the ritual. You might like to journal reflectively about what you have done and what you have agreed to—what boundaries you are going to keep lawfully for this time in your life.

LAW KEEPER, LAW BREAKER, LAW MAKER

However we might choose to regard the point of Law, the law, or even the laws we live by, we are always in dynamic relationship with them. Consider the laws you grew up with and notice what has changed. Many of us come from families—even whole lineages—that have an almost unbreakable law about staying silent, keeping certain things hidden, and valuing social nicety over truth, especially hard truths. The laws of the land we live in are often taken with a grain of salt—we keep the traffic laws (mostly) when anyone's around, but who has never done an illegal U-turn when there's no other cars on the road or silently sped down a deserted country road?

Some laws we feel it is almost, or perhaps actually, our duty to protest or even break—laws about blocking traffic for political actions; unjust laws that enable the state to imprison, torture, and even murder people; laws that allow mass clearing of native forests or logging of irreplaceable old growth trees. In some countries the very expression of who we are and our personal freedoms—as women, queers, immigrants, refugees, Indigenous, witches—may be imperiled, illegal, or unprotected in law.

Other laws we keep rigorously—perhaps the agreed-upon laws of a community or within our relationship or friendship circle. Our own ethics that we refuse to step outside (those same ethics that can lead to us breaking other laws). We also make laws—perhaps relationship agreements; contracts we sign at work, in finance, or other situations; rules for our kids; and, if we are privileged enough to live in a functioning democracy, laws (and law makers) that we implicitly or explicitly vote for.

Each of us at different times and in different situations can be a law breaker as well as a law keeper and even a law maker. In the previous exercise we were invited to deeply consider what laws we choose to live by. That provides a basis for the first part of this exercise, as well as a foundation within our personal relationship to Law.

» You will need: journal and pen; it is preferable to have done the previous exercise already, on page 77

» Time: 40 minutes

Law Keeper

In your journal, list the times and ways that you are a law keeper.

Perhaps you are a law-abiding citizen who pays your taxes on time. Perhaps you are the law keeper for a formal or informal group—the treasurer or secretary of a local neighborhood center, the person who organizes your coven, the conductor of a choir—or your job requires you to uphold company or state laws. Perhaps you try to stay within laws of sustainability, moderation, or even replenishment and nurture of the planet. Perhaps you speak out for justice, human rights, against ecological devastation, or other issues.

Law Breaker

Now list the ways or times that you have been a law breaker.

Maybe you are an activist who deliberately challenges or breaks laws that you disagree with. Perhaps you take illegal drugs, park your car in the wrong places, operate in the cash economy, or drive while over the alcohol limit. Perhaps you've broken laws you've grown up with—cultural, religious, or unspoken laws. Maybe there are times in your life where you have broken the laws of the state or the country you live in and paid a price for that. Probably most of us at some time have broken an agreement within a relationship negligently, deliberately, or accidentally.

The more deeply and carefully we consider ourselves as a law breaker, the more we will find ourselves inside the vexed depths of Law. Sometimes laws come at cross-purposes—the inherent law to defend a piece of land versus the law to follow the directives of the police, for example. Sometimes laws feel so wrong to us that breaking them is almost irrelevant, it is so necessary to our personal code. But there also may be moments we have broken our own laws—to be honest with our loved ones, for example, or always speak up for injustice or separate out the recycling properly.

Law Maker

Finally list the ways you have been, or continue to be, a law maker.

Perhaps you are the one setting boundaries for your children—literally creating the laws they live by. Possibly you facilitate the making of group agreements for organizations and activities you participate in or relationship agreements between yourself and loved ones. Certainly you make your own laws, consciously or unconsciously. And maybe your job requires you to make laws—for the organization, for employees, or in another realm. Finally, we are all law makers as we participate in the greater social and political realms. Our activism can cause new laws to come into force, old ones to be expelled, and the very choosing of those who make laws on our behalf.

Completion

Read back through everything you've written. Perhaps you will make additions or adjustments.

Contemplate your dynamic relationship to the point of Law, the law, and laws. Perhaps you will write a concluding paragraph, trying to sum up this position. Be aware, as you move through your day and the work of the Pearl Pentacle, of this ever-shifting and seeking relationship with Law. Perhaps you will find it speaking back to you as you refine your awareness around it.

If it feels right, and perhaps at some other time, you can take this work into a ritual, a piece of art, a dance, a poem, or open a conversation with others in your life about where, when, and how you are each (or collectively) law keepers, law breakers, and law makers.

MY LAW IS LOVE UNTO ALL BEINGS

STARHAWK

This conversation between Starhawk and Jane Meredith was conducted in Glastonbury, Somerset, England, Northern Hemisphere, on Lammas, July 31, 2023.

JM: *How did discovering the human laws of your land impact you as a child or as an adolescent?*

SH: I guess there are two sets of laws. It just seemed like there were always laws . . . and as a child it was not always clear what's the law of the land and what's the law of your parents. As an adolescent there were certain laws of the land which I consistently broke. But there are other laws like stopping at red lights which you tend to keep because you know it's to everybody's advantage.

I also became an activist fairly young. That didn't always involve breaking the law, but sometimes it did. The first time I ever got arrested I was fifteen. I got arrested with Santa Claus, who was a Vietnam veteran against the war, and a friend of mine for handing out balloons in Beverly Hills that said *Peace on Earth— Stop the War in Vietnam*. We were arrested for soliciting donations without a permit, at gunpoint. The police waited till we were starting to drive away, pulled our car over, poked guns in our faces. It was very dramatic for essentially a minor thing. The scariest part of it all was dealing with my mother, who had to come pick me up.

JM: *So did you experience that as being on the other side of the law?*

SH: Definitely! There's nothing like having the cops pointing a gun in your face to make you feel like an outlaw. Martin Luther King talks about the ethics of civil disobedience and when it is okay to break the law. He talks about the difference between a just and an unjust law. An unjust law is a law that applies to people without their having a say in how it was made, and that's what justifies breaking it.

JM: *Were you aware of those kinds of theoretical arguments when you were doing this action or were you going more on a gut or heartfelt instinct?*

SH: I don't think I was aware of that saying of Martin Luther King's, but I certainly was aware of the civil rights movement and the example of people like the Freedom Riders and people in the South because that had all happened just a few years before. My mother's best friend had a daughter who was mixed race, and we were very good friends. I remember we would sit there and watch what was going on in the South and the beatings. We'd say, *We wanna go to the South!* They would say, *You can't do that! You're twelve years old!* I was very much aware of that level of civil disobedience. Although when we were handing out balloons, we actually had no idea we were violating the law.

JM: *There's a powerful story of you hearing the Charge of the Goddess as a teenage college student. What laws did you hear in that Charge?*

SH: In my first year of college, my friend Patty and I decided we were going to teach a class on witchcraft in the experimental college, although truthfully we knew nothing about it. But we learned. We researched and read and we got everyone together and said, *Well, this is not hierarchical; we're not experts on this, clearly.*

Through doing that we met some witches who were part of an American Celtic tradition, and they came and started teaching us. I remember when they read the Charge of the Goddess, it was so illuminating. *Oh yes this is what I really truly believe in my heart.* I think the part that struck me was *My law is love unto all beings.* I think that is the core of the Goddess tradition. In permaculture we talk about having basic principles and ethics; to me they're very much the same as the principles and ethics of Goddess religion and they go back to *everything is interconnected, everything is interrelated.* As humans we're called to respond to the world with love.

Law represents the core law of love unto all beings, but it also represents the idea that the world works through certain laws. We talk about the law of gravity, the second law of thermodynamics; nature has laws or patterns that it really behooves us to be aware of and follow because if you decide that the law of gravity doesn't apply to you, you're likely to get seriously hurt.

I'm also the adult child of two psychotherapists. My mother would tell me about her clients instead of bedtime stories, and I was very much aware that human beings worked according to certain laws of our own nature that were often invisible to us at the time. That's always fascinated me. And the thing about law is that law applies to all. There's a lot of discussion right now in the US about *are we going to be a country that respects the rule of law or the rule of men?* Having been an activist for so much of my life, I was never a great fan of the law.

I understand it now that when you are in a country that is ruled by man—and I say man judiciously—it's the rule of a dictator, the rule of the person who happens to be in power, then the law does not apply to all. One law for the rich and one law for the poor; one law for the powerful and one law for the powerless. It's a big fight right now to say *no, we need to be a country ruled by the law that applies to all without fear or favor; that doesn't prejudice you against the poor or give certain privileges to the rich.* Even Trump, though he was president, is not above the law.

JM: *So much of early Reclaiming was formed by protests, civil disobedience, and nonviolent direct action. Do you view this as part of Pearl Pentacle Law?*

SH: I think being a witch—being someone with a deep commitment to the Goddess—means that you have a deep commitment to this world and its protection and nurturance. At a time when so much is threatened and when there's so much injustice, you have an obligation to stand up to that, and sometimes that might mean civil disobedience. It might mean other forms of activism. Not everybody needs to go out there and blockade on the front lines, and that isn't always the most appropriate response to what's happening at the moment. My own feeling right now in the US is that so much of the battle is coming down around electoral politics that it probably makes more sense to put energy into working in that realm than in just protesting against it. But both are really necessary, and both can work together.

JM: *What in particular in Reclaiming do you feel is drawn from those early protests?*

SH: I think a lot came into Reclaiming, and I think Reclaiming brought a lot into the movement. One of the things that came into Reclaiming was that we had always said we worked by consensus, but we didn't actually have any training or know how to do it until a whole bunch of us went down to Diablo Canyon and actually learned how you do consensus and how to facilitate it. Our style of organizing, our model of having different cells that send representatives to spokes councils, *that* came directly out of those movements and how they were organized.

JM: *So—internal law structuring?*

SH: And Reclaiming has had its own dialogues around violence and nonviolence, as has the movement as a whole. I think that core ethic of nonviolence, of understanding that the Goddess is in us, that there is a divine spark in every human being no matter how loathsome they may actually be—I hope that that never gets lost in Reclaiming. I think that is part of that core underlying law. When the Goddess says *My law is love unto all beings,* she doesn't say *unless they behave really offensively.* You can love them in that more cosmic sense and still understand that maybe the most loving thing that could happen for them in the world would be for them to be stopped in their actions.

JM: *Permaculture and earth activism trainings are a big part of your work currently and have been for some time. How does that work that you've really chosen to make central come out of or feed back into this Pearl concept of the Law?*

SH: I came to permaculture after many years of doing Goddess spirituality, and it seemed to me that permaculture was the practical side. When we started Reclaiming we saw it not just as something we were doing for fun or for enrichment, but really as part of our attempt to change the overall culture. The shifting from a belief in male gods—who even though they were supposed to not have any sex or gender or form were male gods—to re-embracing the Goddess . . . moving from a sky-centered *the sacred is out of the world* kind of worldview to one that says that the sacred is embodied in the world and the divine is immanent in the world . . . that was a powerful way of addressing the social injustice and the environmental catastrophes that we saw coming back when we started in the late '70s and early '80s.

A couple of years ago I heard Andras Corban Arthen saying how they started EarthSpirit with the same idea of changing culture and he felt like they had not done that. I feel the same with Reclaiming; that we've done a lot of really great and wonderful things, but we have not changed the overarching culture around us. Maybe fifty years is way too short a time to actually do that. But it also began to feel to me like the spirituality—if it wasn't actually rooted in how we live our lives and how we get our food and how we treat the land—was like a hobby. It wasn't really something that moves and shapes your life in the way that it does in a traditional culture. I never have stopped teaching Goddess spirituality—I very much weave it into the permaculture—but the focus became a lot on the practical end.

JM: *You have been involved in supporting or learning from Indigenous communities, elders, and wisdom in colonized and stolen lands in Turtle Island. What have you learned and integrated from Indigenous law in your life and work?*

SH: One thing I've learned is the importance of gratitude, thankfulness, honoring. I have shifted somewhat from invoking elements to honoring elements. The Haudenosaunee peoples have a Thanksgiving address where they begin by thanking everything in the universe. Sometimes this can go on for nine days. From all the elements, all the animals, all the plants . . . and giving thanks for that and how important it is to have that kind of attitude. I think gratitude is one of the things that counters those little cycles of self-pity and feeling victimized that we can all get into.

Another thing that has struck me, especially now that I'm older, is how much that attitude of respect for the elders carries through. It's really quite nice if you are an elder. People treat you well; they're always offering to carry things for you or they bring you a plate of food or let you go first in line. I remember that at one of our very first WitchCamps we had a revolt of the crones, and all the crones came into the dining hall banging their sticks, saying *We are the crones, we are the crones, first in line for the showers, first in line for the food.* And we did let them go first in line. I realize now in Indigenous cultures that would have gone without saying. It is nice because when you are a crone, it's hard to stand around for a long time at the back of the long line.

Of course we were the generation that rebelled against all of our elders; we said *Don't trust anyone over thirty.* That's a big shift, but now that I am in my seventies, I can see that it would have been good if we'd had the foresight back when I was in my thirties to build in more respect for the elders.

JM: Thinking about those protests . . . obviously there's a clash between what we might regard as the law and what is in the courts regarded as the laws. What's it like choosing often to respect what we regard as sacred law rather than those laws that are written down in the constitution or wherever?

SH: While I was at Standing Rock—I was only there for a very short time, and when I was there none of the horrific violence was happening—we did a women's action in which we went up to the barricades. I got to hear a couple of the elders—Cheryl Angel and LaDonna Brave Bull Allard—just basically talking to the police. It was some of the most powerful nonviolent activism I've ever seen, hearing LaDonna say *Hey, we grew up together, we went to school together, this is your land as well as our land that we're fighting to protect; why are you on that side?* I would watch the faces of the police as they did that; seeing these stony faces, there'd be a little twitch and a little eye movement and they'd gradually soften and eventually allowed us to do what we wanted to do, which was go to the river and make an offering. That was very powerful.

JM: So it's interesting that I asked you about a clash and instead you're telling me about a communication. I'm just going down that track and thinking where that point of Indigenous law or land law or sacred law or Pearl Pentacle Law meets those other laws—those written-down ones—that perhaps you're telling me that maybe the most effective thing is not a clash; maybe the first most effective thing is a dialogue.

SH: I have had plenty of clashes, and I'm thinking of one time in Cancun when we were protesting the World Trade Organization meeting there. The first day there was a big march to the barricade and there was a group of Korean farmers, and one of the farmers went to the barricade and committed suicide . . . So many farmers around the world were committing suicide because of the policies of the WTO.

We were coming to the barricades in another march. We always go with a buddy, and my buddy was Andy, a Korean American and a great activist and very funny guy. Our method was to wade into the middle of the trouble. We had activists all around us shouting and yelling and cops on the other side of the barricade. Behind us there was a group of the Revolutionary Communist Party who were always unwilling to abide by any laws. They like to go in, throw a bunch of rocks, and then run away.

So there were rocks flying over our heads and there was tear gas flying and I just remember looking at Andy and he says, *How do you think we should work the energy here?* I said, *We could try grounding it,* so we just stood there grounding. As soon as we did that, the Mexican activists leapt up and started juggling. Suddenly it all turned into juggling, and the tension dissolved, and the Revolutionary Communist Party went away.

A couple of times when they tried to pull someone out of the group, we puppy-piled them. In Egypt when we were on the Gaza Freedom March, my friend Lisa led us out to block all of the traffic. The police came in and grabbed Lisa. You do not want to see your dearest friend dragged off by the Egyptian police. I puppy-piled her—I threw myself on top of her, and fortunately others trained in nonviolence threw themselves on top of me, and the police backed off. They weren't prepared for that solidarity action.

JM: *I'm hearing the narrowness of the written-down laws compared to the breadth and depth of the actual Law that we're trying to live. What are some of the laws of activism in your opinion?*

SH: I would say for me one of the first laws is around nonviolence. You are dealing with other human beings, and if you dehumanize others, you end up dehumanizing yourself. I am not a 100 percent pacifist. I would not tell the Ukrainians that they should be out there singing *kumbaya* to the Russian soldiers at this point, but you can fight if you need to without turning your enemies into something subhuman, and to me that's an important thing to remember. If you do have to use violence, that violence comes at a cost, and the cost is partly what it does to you.

I guess another law is the law of solidarity. When you are in a group and you are acting together with other people, you have a responsibility to each other and to do what you can to keep each other as safe as possible in a dangerous situation. If you're practicing nonviolence to your opponents, you better damn be practicing it with each other, and that includes emotional nonviolence and kindness. We often are not kind in political movements; we tend to be extremely judgmental.

I think we're in a phase right now where people are so influenced by Internet culture that their idea with anything disturbing in the group is often to cast people out. That is a terrible way to organize. In organizing you need to be building coalitions and bringing people in—bringing people in who don't already agree with you and who aren't perfected in their political correctness.

JM: *Is there anything else that you'd like to say around the intersection of human law, natural laws, and lore?*

SH: I think lore is often the record of how culture has discovered these laws. We pass them on through story and myth rather than through a set of rules or instructions. In how many fairy tales is the motivating factor someone's jealousy and envy? You could say one of the laws of human relations is that jealousy is bad. Jealousy doesn't make for good relations with yourself or with anyone around you. The universe rewards those who are generous and courteous and brave.

JM: What is your personal experience and view of working Law in community?

SH: I think that there's a very crude way of applying law, and the idea is making rules. There's a very punitive way of applying laws, and I don't think that works well in community, at least not in ours. It throws us back into a hierarchical power-over mindset and it undercuts our ability to actually hold each other with kindness and with love even when we make mistakes. I think there's an interesting challenge in how do we hold each other accountable for our actions without simply making laws and rules? I think that has to go back to that question of relationship. How do we build and strengthen our relationships and develop the kind of honest communication and feedback systems that can deepen those relationships?

I like restorative justice as a model, where when somebody does something that harms someone else, it's considered to be a harm to the community, and the goal of that justice is to repair the harm, not to punish the offender. I think the more we can work out of that model, the stronger we are as community. So in that model there's often a restorative justice circle where people sit together, where the harm is communicated, where the person who's created the harm has to face the person that they've harmed or their representatives and where they come up with a plan to make reparations. I think there always needs to be a path back.

JM: You've talked quite a lot about the connection between love and law. Do you want to say anything about the connection between law and wisdom?

SH: I think wisdom is in part that recognition that you are not above the law, that the laws of nature apply to you. I've been thinking about the talk I'm supposed to give in a couple of days on the lessons from my cronehood. I think that's one of the core ones: that you will get old, you will die, your body will change.

I remember in my younger days being so impatient with my mother and all the different pairs of glasses she had and how she was always trying to change one to the other and asking me to go find one, thinking *I'm never gonna be like that.* Then you get into your forties and your eyes change and you realize there's no damn thing you can do about it except adjust. So I think part of wisdom comes from that. They say knowledge is knowing what to say and wisdom is knowing whether or not to say it.

TUNING IN TO LAND, INDIGENOUS COMMUNITIES, AND TEACHINGS

I (Fio) offer this as a so-called mixed-race person of Balinese, Irish, Scottish, Welsh, and English heritage. I write this as a child of my father, who is native to his Indigenous lands and practicing his culture proudly, and of someone who descends from settler-colonizers, some of whom are deeply complicit in colonialism and others who resist it. I contain within myself all of these paradoxes, and likely you do too. When you reflect on your heritage and ancestry and who you are made up of, do you feel shame, guilt, sadness, anger, joy, pride, wonder? All of it, likely. These feelings are yours, and some will be incapacitating and some constructive.

» You will need: yourself
» Time: the rest of your life

I was born in Bali, an island in the Indonesian archipelago. I was raised in so-called Toowoomba, the stolen and unceded lands of the Jagera, Giabal, and Jarowair peoples.

We've already begun the work of this ongoing exercise. I've acknowledged that the land my settler ancestors moved onto is stolen and unceded sovereign land belonging to the Jagera, Giabal, and Jarowair peoples. This is part of what we call *acknowledgment of country*, which you can learn more about on page 255.

Many of us reading this book will be residing in the invaded and stolen lands of Indigenous peoples. Each of these peoples comprise their own nations, tribes, clans, and kinship systems. They belong to, steward, and are responsible for their vast network of sciences, ceremonies, languages, philosophies, ethics, governing structures, law, and lore. If you live in the so-called USA, Canada, Brazil, Australia, or New Zealand, you and I are living in the traditional lands of peoples who still exist and are living in postapocalyptic worlds, strangers cast out in their own lands.

Breathe. Drop in. This is a fact. Perhaps you are a First Nations, Aboriginal, or Indigenous person. Perhaps you know this better than I can write or speak or think it.

Many witches and pagans consider ourselves to be earth-centered, land-based practitioners of animistic or continued or revived ancestral traditions. These traditions are often fragmented or syncretized with various forms of Christianity, Buddhism, Hinduism, Islam, and Judaism. Many of us feel dispossessed of our own heritage, and perhaps this is part of the greater issue at hand. Indigenous elders are constantly encouraging non-Indigenous people to enquire into their own family histories, ancestral lineages, and cultures, and this can feel confusing or disorienting to some who identify as "just" Australian or American or who feel unable to access those root cultures because they no longer speak those languages (some, like Welsh and Irish, were actively subjugated) or live in those lands.

I present this to open up a space of compassion and empathy for the Indigenous communities who are not dealing with foreign, imperialist, and colonialist occupation in the distant past, but now and ongoing. Our struggles and histories are interlinked, and we can and need to be in solidarity with one another.

We have already begun this exercise.

How can we turn into the lands we live in—especially if we are settlers and descend from the recent colonizers (I certainly do)—of those sovereign, unceded lands? And how do we respectfully turn toward the wisdom of the First Nations, Aboriginal, and Indigenous elders and communities where we live?

I am told it begins with listening: not just to the humans—yes, to the human elders and communities—but also the rivers, the trees, the stones, the clouds, the fungi, the animals, the little ones, the whole web . . . aren't we as witches and spirit workers completely aligned to this work? Isn't this what we say we do? So we listen and we let go of overlaid cultural narratives about what we think might happen. We listen and we don't get in the way, and then we really listen. So if you are able, go for a walk or read a book or access a resource (please see our essay on page 99 and the exercise following this one), and then keep listening. Every day make a commitment to keep listening.

And then we turn up. We access and engage the public ways out there in community and society where Indigenous folk invite non-Indigenous people to be in solidarity and celebration. There are public powwows throughout Turtle Island, there are Blak markets (markets run by First Nations peoples) and Survival / Invasion Day marches in Australia, protests, and places to come together and be in grieving, rage, ceremony, and the beauty of dance, art, laughter, and food. There are policy makers to write to and schools and places of work where we can combat racism and white supremacy, both in ourselves and in our surroundings. We remain diligent, and we listen.

We align our souls, and we dedicate that time to listening to the land and then wondering what we might do that day, week, month, or year to offer pragmatic aid to Indigenous resistance and liberation. We write in our journals. And the whole time—if we are non-Indigenous people—we practice not centering ourselves and our feelings as part of this larger law-affirming justice work. A Munanjali elder and lore-woman once told me that all I needed to do was go out in Country, sit under a tree, and listen; deeply listen. *The Law is there,* she said. So I continue to do this. I continue to listen. This is the Law.

What you decide to do with all of this makes all the difference. Meditate on the law that is land and the land that is law, and remember you carry the land within you. How will you offer the best of those lands you carry to the land you are now in? And perhaps you live exactly in the place that formed and birthed your ancestors, and perhaps we still all listen to the Law. And we do the best we can each day. ♡

LAWS OF THIS LAND

This process was first developed in collaboration with Bernadene Sward.

The laws of the living land—that is, the laws that govern how things operate within nature—are all around us and happening every moment. The laws of the red cedar are immutable; every red cedar is bound to them throughout its life and death. However different we might perceive individual red cedars to be, still each one is within the red cedar law. The same is true for pademelons, for igneous rock spat out from volcanoes, for the lomandra, for the summer breeze. They cannot operate outside their law. I (JM) think there's a good argument for saying, if this is the case, then clearly humans cannot be separate from that sort of law—but unlike the pademelons and red cedars, we seem capable of forgetting that.

If the laws of the land are all around us, displayed in every moment, what would it be like to return to awareness of that—not just acceptance of the concept, but a living awareness in each moment of the existence and interplay and story of those laws? I think to have this consciousness is probably Eden, the original Garden, Paradise, and that our great longing and experience of this underpins much of paganism and pagan magic. Once we perceive parts of the law, we are able to move more gracefully within it, both in our everyday lives and also when making magic.

A wonderful example of this is David Abram's self-reported experiment to investigate shadow in his book *Becoming Animal*, where he stood in one place for twelve hours and observed his own shadow. One of his observations/realizations was that shadow, which we usually think of as something flat, two-dimensional, a cut-out, is actually three-dimensional—the whole space between his body and the ground was in shadow, thus making it larger (or taking up more actual space) than his own body for most of the day; he saw this as he watched insects flying into, through, and then beyond the shadow his body was casting. He then began to dream into the metaphor of this, as I am doing now . . . What if our shadows, metaphysically speaking, are quite vast and three-dimensional, casting effects onto all those who come within reach of them? That is, we can't contain them in the way we usually imagine ourselves capable of containing or repressing our shadow selves.

> » You will need: preferably an outside space, although you can do this exercise through a window or with a pot plant or indoor pet; journal and pen, coloring things (all optional)
> » Time: 30 minutes minimum; potentially all day

Take yourself to a place where you can observe part of nature for twenty minutes or more uninterrupted. This can be a tree in your local park, the waves at the beach, a window where you can gaze at the sky, the grass or earth in your backyard. You can take your journal and pen (and even coloring things) with you if you want or leave them behind if you just want to be present with nature and the Law.

Settle yourself—maybe you will be standing, seated, squatting, or lying down.

Offer an acknowledgment to the land you are on. Maybe this will take the form of naming the Indigenous peoples who live or have lived here and their names for the land, or some other form.

Then let your focus come into your body and your breath. Stay with this for a while, allowing other things to recede from your awareness as you become more and more present within the breath and body.

In your own time, allow your awareness to expand beyond the confines of your body to what is immediately around you. Notice the qualities of the ground beneath you . . . of the air . . . of the presence or absence of moisture and water . . . the sources of light and heat, and their qualities. Perhaps you can sense the life force, spirit, aether, or the very presence of the gods or the earth as Goddess.

Let your attention be drawn to one thing. Perhaps it will be the seedpods hanging from a tree, the sound of birds from a nearby bush, the tiny flowers in the grass, or the way the wind is moving across the sand and waves. Perhaps you picked this location for its magnificent trees but instead find your attention caught in a spider's web or insects on the bark. Let your eyes and focus choose what they will; you can always come back another day.

Allow yourself to be present with whatever it is that has taken your attention. Observe it. Notice its connections and interactions with other things around it. Be curious about it.

After a while, start to ask yourself or the thing you are studying, What are (some of) its laws? You might observe the way laws such as the law of gravity or the law of the seasons play out in relation to it. You might observe its own laws: the way ants move through grass, the way a crest of a wave starts to break, the different stages of a seedpod.

Sometimes we might observe these laws without being able to frame them into words or concise descriptors. Other times we can clearly express laws we are witnessing. Here are some examples: the law of the baby pademelon is *Stay close to mum.* The law of the Banga-low palm is *Let the old fronds drop away.* The law of the shell is *We are on the way to becoming sand.* You might come up with three or four laws (or more) for just the one thing, a few laws for different things you are observing, or just one law.

When you feel complete, for now, return your attention to your own breath and body, bringing the laws you have observed with you. You might choose to record them in words, drawings, or both. You may choose to reflect on them: How do these laws apply to me? How am I on the way to becoming sand? How good am I at allowing my old fronds to drop away? What is my equivalent of staying close to mum?

Ideally this type of process can become an ongoing practice as we learn to fall deeper and deeper in awe with the laws of the living land.

A PERSONAL RESPONSE TO THE COLLISION OF COLONIAL LAW AND INDIGENOUS LAW

This writing was completed in the week that the majority of Australian citizens voted no in a referendum to change the constitution to recognize the First Peoples of Australia and the Torres Strait and to establish an Indigenous voice to the Australian parliament. The referendum failed. October 2023.

. . . I (Fio) want to begin with this ellipsis. I want to throw my hands up and sigh, moan, break down, cry. What is written here is raw and messy, but it's a start.

Isn't this all obvious? Isn't it painfully clear that the legacy of Rome and of empires preceding and proceeding from them carry out violence to this day? Destroying culture, oppressing sovereign peoples and nations, declaring your gods are our gods or denying or demonizing them altogether? Later on Rome became the Holy Roman Empire and the Roman Catholic Church committed similar atrocities throughout Europe, the Western Islands, and then the rest of the world.

I write this as a thirty-five-year-old brown child of a white settler woman born in so-called Australia and a Balinese Hindu man born in that island—as was I—in the village of Kintamani, which is perched above an active volcano. Jane Meredith is a cis woman in her fifties who was born in Australia of two lineages: her maternal line of French settlers and paternal of Polish Jewish refugees, both arriving in this land three generations back.

When first considering the essayists for this book, we invited an experienced Reclaiming teacher to write on Law and Indigeneity. Our brief was short:

> We are wondering if you would be into writing an essay on the point of Law from Indigenous perspectives and how this can be or could be relevant to Reclaiming.

When this person thoughtfully declined, we asked another experienced Reclaiming teacher, and they, after deep exploration and much reflection, also declined.

What was brought to us in these responses was something that I as a person of color understand intimately and Jane Meredith recognized as a deep and potent cry, a call to action and solidarity.

We decided we needed to take on this burden: not to ignore it or bypass it or keep searching for someone else to take it on. The burden of this precarious position of speaking unpalatable truths, of positioning ourselves as potential targets from all or any sides in the debates and conversations around racism and privilege, which occurs even within pagan communities and amongst those working land-based magic. The questions of what this all means and where our magic comes from is part of the potent discussion we **must have** about how we can exist with authenticity and love within intersecting realms of Indigenous Law and western-based magical practice.

We are aware that we might or will or have already fucked this up. We could read back over this in five months or two or five or ten years and wish we had done it differently or not done it or done something else. In writing and publishing this piece and our opinions, we open ourselves to critique and feedback both within our own traditions and from wider afield, but right now we see no other genuine, lawful way to act. We cannot approach a third writer of color with ties to Indigenous communities to do this labor, emotional and otherwise. Really, it's our concept to have this piece here in the first place, and this is our book. We will take this on.

We acknowledge that we do this from a place of privilege. We are known both within Reclaiming and the broader pagan, witchcraft, goddess, and magical realms as authors, teachers, and facilitators. This offers us a degree of social power from which to take a stand on a sensitive and contentious topic, one that carries the potential to deeply challenge the status quo. We also acknowledge the material and emotional impacts that occur for people of color and specifically Indigenous people when these topics are taken into the public realm. We have the power and privilege of a platform from which to do this, and perhaps be heard; thanks, Llewellyn. We are also calling upon the grace and potency of the Pearl Pentacle to be supported as we are called to our own work within Law.

Reclaiming as a tradition and movement of witches, pagans, and activists did not emerge out of a vacuum. Real-world compounded histories and colliding paradigms and systems catalyzed the tide of Reclaiming's emergence. Early on in the Goddess movement that began to come together with fierce energy in the '70s—fueled by second-wave feminism—there was much discussion and critique concerning the place of both women of color and trans women within the broader sisterhood. Many Black and Indigenous women did not see themselves represented in what they felt was white women's middle-class solidarity with one another. Similarly, though Reclaiming witches have been predominantly female and white, there have been notable Reclaiming leaders of color. Several of these folk have left the tradition for a variety of reasons, and others have died.

I (Fio) came into Reclaiming thirty years into the development of the tradition. I was drawn in by friendships with a young person of color, Abel R. Gomez, and a white woman, Jane Meredith. Retrospectively I can see in a crystalline way how reflective of my life experience this really was and continues to be. I entered Reclaiming already deeply involved in Wildwood witchcraft, as a curious witch deeply interested in feminism, queer politics, and intersectionality. I was hired as a first-year student teacher at the inaugural Australian Reclaiming Witch-Camp. I had great mentors and guides in the tradition, and whatever foibles or mistakes I made (and still make), I had genuine and caring feedback. I became woven into an established and ever-evolving web of community with elders, teachers, initiates, initiators, and beloveds.

I also experienced racism and the impacts of white supremacy. Racism exists everywhere I go. It exists everywhere you go as well.

Racism and white supremacy are powerful historical and social constructs within which all of us are entrained to think, act, respond, and behave. If the majority of people in a group are white and cis, let alone able-bodied and middle-class, certain blindnesses and prejudices will be predominant. Often the voices and perspectives of people of color are viewed through white lenses as more harsh and confrontational than they might actually be. The racist trope of the angry Black woman who takes no shit is a strong one that almost all of us reading this will understand immediately. We are trained to fear the presence of people of color and especially to fear men of color. We have been taught that men of color pose a threat to white women—and this, of course, is under the cloak of white cis-het patriarchy—as if women must always be in the company of white men to be safe. Alliances between white women and men of color—the alliance I am born from—is proscribed and one many of us are taught to fear.

Racism and white supremacy in Reclaiming often look like white people willfully or subconsciously twisting and misunderstanding the context of magical practice and spirit work in communities of color. This can manifest in group fear of trance possession, which is often tied to African and Southeast Asian cultures, as well as the selection of myths and deities considered viable to work with. A contentious debate occasionally shows itself regarding the place of cursing and hexing in witchcraft, which are both traditional and established. The willful misinterpretation of the place of cursing in the Craft is both a dualistic and Christianist reaction. It does not allow for nuance or for the deep reality that witchcraft has always been the magic and myth of the oppressed.

It's obvious by now that I (Fio) am the front voice of this reflection, though it was really Jane Meredith's idea: that we as the invokers, compilers, and editors of this book had to take on responsibility for this writing after two experienced Reclaiming folk had decided against it.

And what is *this*? This is the reality that the vast majority of us in Reclaiming—as with many or most other so-called western magical traditions—are doing our magic on stolen country, that we are complicit in sidelining Indigenous wisdom, that we could all do better at turning toward and listening to First Nations perspectives. Most people in Reclaiming need to remember that Indigenous people are us too; that Reclaiming witches are Black and Indigenous, Brown and refugee, Asian and light-skinned people of color. Our life experiences and families form the warp and weft of our identities in the world and our internal and magical law. As people of color, we bring this wherever we go and cannot leave it behind.

Dear reader, you have gotten this far. By now, or even from the very beginning, you might be asking, *But what can I do about this?*

Our answer is to offer a list of resources, prompts, and ideas below. These are not prescriptive but rather invite you to engage in ways that make sense to you and in places where you reside, work, and travel. Risking making mistakes is part of showing up, part of learning, part of following the path of love that leads us to law. When we make mistakes, we also need to be accountable for those impacts and open to receiving feedback. This path leads us into this thorny, painful, provocative, deep, incredibly rewarding work of learning about law from and with living traditions, law makers and keepers, that have survived and are surviving. This work may even inform humanity to support our planet in keeping its own laws and thriving.

List of Ideas and Actions

» Ask for and potentially provide an acknowledgment of country at any class, ritual, and gathering you attend. A guide on how to do this is on page 255.

» Learn the Indigenous names of the lands and places where you live and work and where you travel. Use them as you explain to people where you are and as you address meetings, give speeches, organize events, post photos on social media, and in other ways.

» Ask questions at the gatherings you organize and attend. How would this content/format/ presentation be for any First Nations or Indigenous people who attend? Are we merely tolerating or tokenizing First Nations and Indigenous people who might attend or do we want to actively welcome those peoples and cultures to our gatherings? Are there broader accesses we can offer? What can we learn here?

» Ask how your magic—individually, and in your traditions or groups—might be appropriative, colonizing, or disrespectful of First Nations and Indigenous knowledge, culture, law. Where can you do better? How can you learn, adapt, and change?

» Bring these conversations into broader fields—not just with the organizers of an event but with those who attend. Not just to the publishers of the magazine or podcast but with the readers and listeners.

» Form a study group with your coven, family, or friends. We recommend choosing a text—for example, we did this with Tyson Yunkaporta's *Sand Talk*—and framing each meeting around discussing one or two chapters. Other modalities and processes apart from discussion you might want to utilize as you explore the concepts and ideas presented include creative expression, dreamwork, silent contemplation, walking the land, and trance.

» If you have kids attending schools, ask those schools if they invite local Indigenous elders to come and speak with the children. If not, is this something they would be open to? How can they reach out to make this happen and make it financially viable for these elders?

» Consider tithing from paid events—classes, gatherings—to local Indigenous cultural centers and programs or asking for donations from those present.

» Educate yourself. Turn up to local events with Indigenous speakers, presenters, artists, or elders. Read books and listen to podcasts.

» Listen.

List of Resources

Law: Way of the Ancestors by Marcia Langton and Aaron Corn (Thames & Hudson Australia, 2023)

This is the 6th book in the First Knowledges series edited by Margo Neale. It is focused entirely on Law from Aboriginal and Torres Strait Islander perspectives. It dives deep into the intricate ways of ancient and innovative knowledge and relational systems that guide and guard Indigenous law in the various countries that make up so-called Australia and the Torres Strait Islands. Both authors are scholars and work within academia and also have deeply rich and personal relationships with Indigenous communities. The First Knowledges series is written for a popular audience by experts in those fields.

Sand Talk: How Indigenous Thinking Can Save the World by Tyson Yunkaporta (Text Publishing, 2019)

This book rippled and struck like lightning through intersecting communities all over the world. It's a recent book with a giant and perhaps irrevocable impact. *Sand Talk* challenges, provokes, and dismantles assumptions, popular tropes, and narratives of how we are taught in western societies to think of images, art, ceremony, story, landscape (and even that very list of words), let alone belongingness and Aboriginality. Yunkaporta lays out his own shortcomings and failures while reminding us that when we can shift our consciousness—parallel to how many in Reclaiming think of magic—rich dynamism opens to us. We belong to life and each other. The through thread of this book is the Aboriginal device of yarning and co-learning with a variety of people who inspire and challenge him.

Becoming Kin: An Indigenous Call to Unforgetting the Past and Reimagining our Future by Patty Krawec (Broadleaf Books, 2022)

I (Fio) read this book during a journey in Turtle Island. My friend Abel R. Gomez quoted from it during a meeting on Indigenous solidarity at California WitchCamp and encouraged us all to read it. I bought the book and read it cover to cover, drinking in its beauty and power. Patty Krawec is an Anishinaabe/Ukrainian writer and thinker. In this book she lays out the painful and tragic history of invasion, occupation, colonization and indoctrination, child removal, and the tearing apart of the fabric of Indigenous ways of relating to one another and the Earth. However, Indigenous people survive and resist colonization. This book is a testament to the spirit of reverence, lawfulness, faith, and wonder that guides people like the author to invite the non-Indigenous reader to remember who we really are and who we could all be.

Bangarra Dance Theatre, bangarra.com.au

Bangarra is a contemporary Aboriginal and Torres Strait Islander dance company that was birthed by African-American dancer Carole Johnson, who helped found the National Aboriginal and Islander Skills Development Association along with Rob Bryant and Cheryl Stone, who were both involved in NAISDA. I (Fio) used to be an active student of contemporary dance, and I have been a willing participant in the witnessing of Bangarra performances ever since high school. Bangarra breaks boundaries and brings audiences into rich and cosmologically profound experiences that arrest the senses and the heart. Their exploration of the consequences of colonization, the deep pride of Indigenous peoples in their law and culture, and the sophisticated artistry and skill of First Peoples is brilliant and bold. Bangarra performs all around the world and also has produced films and documentaries.

Dark Emu: Black Seeds: Agriculture or Accident? by Bruce Pascoe (Magabala Books, 2014)

Dark Emu challenges the hunter-gatherer and nomadic designation of Aboriginal peoples used from Captain Cook onward. With extensive historical research, Pascoe lists and quotes from an exhaustive set of accounts by early colonist-settlers and white explorers, as well as more recent scholarship. He puts forward the case that Aboriginal cultures included building, agriculture, and aquaculture, as well as astronomy, engineering, and other arts and sciences, and that prior to invasion, the land now called Australia was farmed and managed, and that early white settlers recognized this and documented parts of it. As the invasion and settlement of Australia always relied on the theory that the land was only barely inhabited and certainly not farmed, owned, or cultivated, this work in effect casts Britain's claiming of the land as a crime, under even their own laws. It was both welcomed and highly contentious for several reasons at the time of publication.

Living on Indigenous Lands: (Re)Considering Relations with Occupied Lands by Abel R. Gomez (July 2023, https://contendingmodernities.nd.edu/theorizing -modernities/living-on-indigenous-lands/)

Abel R. Gomez is a scholar who identifies as a non-Native person from an immigrant Central American and Mexican family born and raised in the San Francisco Bay Area. In his writing he explores the deep and nuanced ways that settlers, migrants, Indigenous, and non-Indigenous peoples can explore relatedness when we center the realities of invasion, occupation, and willingly move into the behavior and responsibilities of being guests in Indigenous lands.

Starbook: A Magical Tale of Love and Regeneration by Ben Okri (Random House, 2007)

This novel written by Nigerian-British poet and novelist Ben Okri is a magical tale of love, art, and destruction. It's a fable, an allegory, and a history. This book reimagines historical literature with enormous grace and power, refusing to conform to Anglocentric historical mores, instead dancing through its subject matter with such splendor and confidence that it's impossible not to fall in love with the magic and artistry of the almost utopian society evoked and not have one's heart broken as one realizes: this is history, not fantasy, as the end times come.

My Place by Sally Morgan (Fremantle Arts Center Press, 2021; first published in 1987)

This autobiography was explosive and pivotal in the reimagination of the personal history of Australians. Sally Morgan grew up not knowing her Aboriginal heritage, which had been denied and buried by the shame her mother had; Sally's mother had always told them she was Indian. Uncovering the truth as an adult, the author undertakes a personal journey of discovery as to what this means for her and her family and find her own relationship to it. The effect of this book was to haul the conversation into the mainstream about what it meant to be Aboriginal and to have Aboriginal lineage and ancestry. Challenged was the convention of passing as white or nearly white, if at all possible. The laws of lineage, the emotionally devastating consequences of colonization that continue on, and the law of kinship and return are invoked.

And the art, provocation, healing, offerings of endless resistance warriors, leaders, elders, law people, healers, activists, and children of parents—known or unknown, stolen, taken away, or remaining in the wreckage of colonization yet strong—who live for their cultures, lands, and peoples. A fierce and potent example of an Aboriginal leader and Reclaiming teacher is Raphael Lavallee, whose work in decolonising spiritual practices and activist art they share with many: www.instagram.com/bogongmothart.

These resources are just a beginning. You could listen to the profoundly healing music of the Yolngu man Gurrumul, who died in 2017, or the fierce resistance music of Bobby Sanchez; start here. Listen to words you may understand or languages you've never heard, that you might never speak or sing in. And I'll close here for now by offering something of the Indigenous wisdom of my father's culture.

Each time we pray in Bali, wherever we go, we bring the incense, the flowers, the holy water, and the sacred rice. We offer to the spirits of the elements, we offer to the sun, the ancestors, and the gods in their secret places . . . but before all of this, we first ask for permission to pray here, in this place, in this time, to be in gratitude and communion here. Remember to be humble, to not assume, to walk even as a guest, taking such precious care in the lands that grew you to celebrate, dance, laugh, sing, make ceremony, remember, and honor the mystery of this remarkable existence and web of relating.

in the interstices we turn and deepen

wisdom, call in wisdom

another layer like a veil

the heart still shines through, love

cloaked by law now wisdom

the pearl is forming deep inside

us, our fleshy raw beating selves

we're starting to shine here, to shimmer

pearlescent

WISDOM

The third point of the Pearl Pentacle, the way it is worked in this book, is Wisdom. Wisdom is informed and supported by both Love and Law. We might say wisdom can only exist within the context of love and law. Like these earlier points, it is not so much a matter of inventing it but of discovering it, of paying attention and showing up and allowing Wisdom to unfold. With each moment and each breath we take, if we bring our attention there, we can see the world through the eyes of wisdom, experiencing the ever-existing love and understanding how the laws operate within that. Witnessing the intricate interaction of love and law, we allow the breath of wisdom to touch us and breathe through us. Ah, we understand now, and from that understanding we drop deep and open wide, allowing wisdom to blow many things away, revealing essence.

The Pearl point of Wisdom lies over the Iron point of Self. We hold these in our left hand, often considered the hand of magic, the private hand, the less important or less obvious hand. We may hold our wisdom close to ourselves or we may allow it to be seen, just as we learn to allow our self to be seen when we do the work of the Iron Pentacle. Wisdom lies in the land; it exists in children, elders, all of us—it is found everywhere and anywhere but only by those who seek, who listen, who are patient and true and present. Wisdom can be found in a village and the poorest community as well as the grandest library or most esteemed university. The wisdom of the forest or the ocean or the mountain is available to those who study the laws, the patterns, and allow them to speak.

THE PEARL OF WISDOM

We walk along the trail in the wide landscape of the Blue Mountains National Park in Darug and Gundungarra country. We are immersed within the wisdom of the land, and each step takes us farther in. These are not really mountains but a huge tableland formed millions of years ago under the ocean and eventually pushed a kilometer up above sea level. In the intervening time the land has been worn down into deep and often twisting valleys edged by escarpments and shaped by wind, water, and fire erosions. This land carries layers of experience, layers of wisdom—from the sea, the uplift, the wearing away, from the life and growth that cover it now. We are talking about wisdom as we walk the narrow track, how its presence is right here and all we have to do is pay attention—enough attention—to realize it and begin to taste it, hear it, see it.

When we take a turn and begin to descend the escarpment, everything changes. The landscape both opens up before us—in depth, intricacy, intimacy—and narrows ferociously. Breadth is hidden from us and now all that can be seen are the details up close. Suddenly the waterfall—which has been distant, muted—is immensely louder, and waves of sound crash off the rock walls, vibrating through us. We can no longer see the horizon. We have no sense of the generality of where we are—only the particulars, up close, are revealed to us. That wide landscape no longer exists; now we are all verticals as we climb down wide stone steps, further down by narrow metal ladders, along a track under an overhanging cliff, then more ladders. We are within the land.

Reaching the waterfall, we witness a wisdom revealed. Here is the water, spooling off the cliff face to fall into the pool below, and it is Law—the way things have to happen. How else could this water travel than along the channel carved out for it by the waters that came before and, reaching the cliff edge created by this precedent, what else can it do but fall? Wisdom lies in observing these vastnesses: tectonic plate shifts and their consequences, erosion, the patterning of the land, the continued forces still creating. Perhaps, we say to each other, Knowledge is to do with the particularities of how this plays out in each time and place. Liberty could be the element of choice, when someone or something makes a change such as the choice to build a path to this particular waterfall, of all the waterfalls. These choices add dimensionality and difference to the endless unfolding of the laws, to the layered strata of the wisdoms. And all of this together, as the water pours and falls and pounds into the pool—all of Law, Wisdom, Liberty, Knowledge—adds back up to Love.

Our journey into the conversation about wisdom and our journey down into the land to the waterfall shows wisdom as implicit, unfolding, revealed—you don't have to try for wisdom, it's there all around us. Wisdom is there, though we might be too busy talking or paying attention to the ladders and rocky way underfoot to notice what is spread all around us. It's completely available—the strata of the geological shifts laid out in front of our eyes, the lessons of the waterfall constant and unending, but we might not notice it. There's something here about turning up, paying attention, being willing for wisdom. About trust, really. When we open, listen, and surrender, there it is. Wisdom. It's been there all along. We need to be schooled and practiced enough in the preliminaries—showing up, being present, staying grounded, opening our senses—to receive what was always there.

Along with being the first point of the Pearl Pentacle, we can see Love as the seed, the original spark—that starburst explosion that begins the world as well as that moment when sea and sunlight first create life together. Law becomes the extrapolation of this—as love and life unfold, patterns are created and followed, systems emerge, and exponential complexity is born through myriad forms of life, atomic arrangement, and structure. Meeting first the all-encompassing simplicity of Love, followed by the inherent complexity of Law, this point of Wisdom arrives into the Pearl Pentacle as a distillation, a synthesis; the place where love shows us what to make of law or how to keep the law.

Wisdom is notoriously tricky to claim, define, or reach consensus on. In contemporary western society, we flail around when deciding what wisdom will guide us as a collective. Will we let our politicians decide this for us? That brings us into an adversarial system with vital matters such as how to approach the climate crisis or justice for First

Nations peoples and communities coming down to political strategy and maneuvering, where the voices of vested interests have a disproportionate say instead of leaning into any accepted or accrued wisdom. The churches, then? It seems redundant to consider that for even a moment as organized religion becomes increasingly stultified, minoritized, and reliant on inherited and, in some cases, rules of conduct that have not been critiqued, rather than any living wisdom. What about the universities? The old people? The young people? First Nations peoples? What about the latest wellness guru or manifestation expert? Perhaps if we just keep following this path down the escarpment, through the layers of the landscape, we will find wisdom there.

Whereas there is some consensus on what love is, and perhaps quite a lot of consensus around what law is, wisdom appears to be another matter. Have the white-dominated societies of invader-settlers—those separated from their own lands and lineages—lost touch with wisdom? The wisdom that guided our peoples, that held our lineages, that governed our relationship with land and community—we know it existed. It was held and in some cases is still held by the druids, the pagans, the travelers and nomads, farmers living untold generations in the same location, fishing communities, and others. There have been mystery traditions linked with land and place and passed generation to generation, but we left it behind. We put it down somewhere along the way—not always voluntarily as there were wars and clearances, starvation, poverty, purges, inquisitions, forced conversions, slavery, as well as economic necessity and sheer survival—and now that we need it, we don't know how to find it. But wisdom never left. There are wisdom cultures everywhere if one only looks, turns up, and listens.

With our earlier forays into both love and law, we eventually realized they were there all along—they do not have to be fought for or earned, as much as awakened to, received, offered. Perhaps this is indicative of the Pearl Pentacle—that at least half our struggle with these points is within ourselves and once we let go, show up, open to what is present—there is love. There is law. There is wisdom. If we say that wisdom emerges from love and law, then it becomes not so much a matter of going out to seek it but more about deepening our awareness, capacity, and willingness to become aware of it. While pieces of wisdom can be found within politics, law, and the lessons the current gurus and established religions offer, perhaps there are simpler, more immediate accesses that don't require wading through a whole lot of irrelevant and divisive content to arrive at a few gems of (possible) wisdom.

Pearls and wisdom are often linked together; not casting pearls before swine from the Bible, as well as the Chinese dragon's pearl of wisdom, usually held just out of reach of that snapping mouth. Both these images equate pearls with value and rarity. If we remember each mollusk creating each pearl, we can imagine that impulse to protect life—this force we often name love—as being the instigator of the coating of nacre over the grit particle. Then law would be the process as the layers continue, and wisdom where we arrive at the oyster now protected, the pearl formed. Wisdom is the pearl that is received when we do the work of Love and Law.

We seek wisdom in order to know how to live our lives—what choices to make among the unending possibilities within the law. Wisdom offers guidance and support and a living tradition of understanding and being within the world. Wisdom is constantly unfolding, arising, arriving. And we are arriving to Wisdom, evolving to become wiser beings as we receive and act upon these wisdoms. We might ask what does it mean to become wise or acquire wisdom? How would we know when we might have become wise? There's a wonderful maxim around eldership, common to many cultures, where the status of being an elder or regarded as wise is not something one can ever claim for oneself. It is a position only granted by recognition from and within the community.

Many cultures teach that wisdom comes with age, and we might consider this a wisdom of perspective, a retrospective and intimate understanding of the phases of growth, relating, endings, change, and dying. There's a particular piece of wisdom that comes only after we have experienced a loved one die; there's another we gain from falling in love, and yet another when our hearts break for the first time. Wisdom coming from raising a child, from living with grandparents or grandchildren, from working the land, from being in leadership in a community. This archetype of elder certainly carries wisdom, but it is not the only type of wisdom.

The Fool is another archetype whom we consider wise. The wisdom of elders rests on a broad depth of knowledge and experience distilled over a lifetime. The Fool's wisdom is seemingly plucked from the air or from within, like a child's might be. It is startling, subversive, the undoer of kings, and it has the grace of buying—well, if not safety, at least a modicum of preservation for its bearer. The Fool is the truth teller in a court of subterfuge, strategy and lies both covert and overt. Yet the Fool's role, clothed in comedy, pathos, and riddlery, reveals the collective wisdom: what everyone knows but no one will say, or it turns the world on its head with its upside-down logic, challenging what must never be challenged but somehow getting away with it. Usually. This aspect of wisdom—the dare of it—speaks to that element of trust we arrived at earlier. We can only be wise when we accept what is, when we go to the heart of the matter, when we show up for what is truly there. Wisdom reveals itself not in the artifice of the court or the power of the king but in the humble antics of one designated a fool, so foolish they are outside the social conventions that apply to everyone else.

What of all the wisdom proverbs we are raised with, which we might even live our lives by? These are passed on because many people over multiple generations find meaning, clarity, and importance in the saying and in the act of passing on the wisdom. Wisdom that is denigrated as old wives' tales or folk superstitions often represents age-old, multilayered, and generational experience of the sacred ecology of land, beings both seen and unseen, and human relationships with weather, food, plants, fungi, and the mysteries. There's wisdom in waiting just as there is in seizing the moment. There's wisdom in staying and wisdom in leaving.

Wisdom is multivalent and infinite in application. Some people say wisdom is knowledge applied and all the discernment and insight that goes into that application. Others say that wisdom is gained with age or perspective. Many consider children wise. Some rivers, trees, and birds. Others seek the wisdom and counsel of the gods, the spirits, and the ancestors who have infinite forms and faces. Perhaps one of the wisest things that one could say is *I don't know, but I'll look into it. I'll take time to learn and think and reflect.* In this current age of swiftly formed and reactive opinions, in which social media and society urge us to have binary ideas and dispute one another, wisdom is in the willingness to be able to appreciate and relate to a variety of perspectives, and even to hold multiple seemingly conflicting truths.

Wisdom is not an individual experience but a shared one, and sometimes it is shared by a wise person to someone in need. This is often the collected tried-and-true wisdom of many family generations or it is held within lodges, guilds, lineages, or temples. For centuries into the modern era—and in many cultures today—wise women and cunning folk were present and available for consultation. Modern witches in the West have often been linked to these magical practitioners, and certainly we have drawn spells, prayers, and formulae from them. Wisdom as a perennial stream feeds and nourishes people in all places and times. The old wisdom of plant medicine, star lore, listening and deducing patterns and therefore solutions, of working with powerful words or texts to invoke or summon the aid of great powers in the universe . . . healing by touch or stone or water, divination and the finding out of important information . . . these are touchstones for people around the globe. As Reginald Scot wrote in the infamous *Discoverie of Witchcraft* (1584), "At this day it is indifferent to say in the English tongue, she is a witch or she is a wise woman."

Humans the world over have evolved, received, and passed on wisdom traditions. First Nations traditions everywhere, Kabbalah, alchemy, astrology, Yoga, Tantra, witchcraft, Druidry, Sufism, inner Christianity, the Grail mysteries—our planet is filled with endless roads by which we may come to experience the mysteries and access wisdom. There's the wisdom of the well, of the nine hazel trees, of salmon, the rice harvest, of winds that bring change, of when and how to sow, winnow, grind, mill. Wisdom of listening to and tracking waterways, wisdom of kookaburra, wisdom of friends, elders, children, serpents . . . wisdom of how to be with all these kin on these lands; how to be part of them.

Wisdom is innate, within and all around us. In order to experience wisdom, quiet, space, and surrender—sometimes also reflection and remembering—are required. Wisdom is in all things, available to us all in all moments; how, then, do we grow wise? If knowledge is pursued or gathered or learned over time through dedication, diligence, and focus, is wisdom revealed or unfolded because we are connecting and engaging, participating in the great chorus or conversation of life? We can't do wisdom by ourselves, just as in the end we can't do love entirely by ourselves, and we certainly can't do law by ourselves. Wisdom and the Pearl Pentacle are about relating—relating with individuals, with community, with land, with the numinous. Based on a solid foundation of Iron within ourselves—of sex, pride, self, power, and passion—we flow out into the Pearl and the world of connection and belonging.

I (Fio) sit in a greenroom in a converted railway carriage works—now a venue for community arts and political and powerful solidarity with the marginalized—listening to a Sista girl (an Australian Indigenous term for a trans woman) from the Tiwi Islands. She talks of the design on her dress. I do not ask her name. I already know it, for she is renowned by queer and trans folks in this vast continent and arrayed islands, and she does not ask mine. This is common in Aboriginal and Torres Strait Islander cultures. It's common in many cultures. Listen, share story, talk about your ancestors and kin and where you've traveled from, what you are here to do (in my case, Balinese dance), but names are later, if ever. What I felt listening, rippling in this room was a deep stillness and presence connecting us together in story, culture, and wisdom freely shared. It was the weight buzzing between the words that transmitted a deep sense of wisdom, the wisdom that is waiting for us to remember it.

A long time ago, the ancestors of our settler-colonial families were Indigenous. They spoke their own embedded-in-land languages; knew the secret and sacred names of rivers and birds, when and how to hunt and reap; respected the ancient laws; and initiated the young people into clan, community, and their own gender mysteries. Many First Nations people encourage white folks to remember who their/

our own ancestors are: to turn to them, to study where we got lost or where we had our sacred traditions and laws stolen or transformed utterly. We are also urged to consider how we have become complicit in the privilege gained from being white in the system and how to relearn our own belongingness to this earth, to place, to the cycles of moon and sun and this very breath. For many of us—perhaps many of you reading this now—it has been in the remembering and reclaiming of our ancestral, ecstatic, and magical traditions.

In the practice of magic we may become wiser. In the exercise of our power in and between the worlds, we might begin to understand how, when, and why we are making a decision, working magic, discerning the way. From the vast web of threads that forms the western magical traditions, we inherit what Gwydion Logan, an elder of Reclaiming and Feri, calls *the challenges of the elements*. In Reclaiming tradition we often align these challenges and their associated elements with classical magical tools: air with the knife, fire with the wand, water with the cup, earth with the pentacle, and spirit with the cauldron. I (Fio) created the following rhyme as a mnemonic device to work with this lore:

> The knife—to know—discern the way.
> The wand—to will—the sun's own ray.
> The cup—to dare—to feel, to flow.
> The star—be silent—and listen and grow.
> And the cauldron in the center—
> to be, to love, to hold, to enter.

To know, to will, to dare, to be silent; to be, to love, to hold, to enter. Meditating on these challenges and being provoked and held by them, we may deepen into and discover wisdom.

In some lineages of Feri tradition and in some bioregions of Reclaiming, when we travel through the Pearl Pentagram as an invoking pentagram (following the star from point through to point, rather than going around the edges in a circle), the practice is to go from Love, to Law, to Knowledge, to Liberty, to Wisdom, and back to Love. The older practice—the one we present in this book—is that Wisdom and Knowledge return to their original places, so the pentacle runs Love, Law, Wisdom, Liberty, Knowledge. Both options contain wisdom. Experimenting and immersion is recommended! The challenge of Wisdom coming before Knowledge aids us in remembering that the wisdom of and in the world is not so much something we have to acquire or become; perhaps we simply listen, remember, and align with it.

Wisdom offers us something larger, vaster, deeper—like the land itself—than the straight and narrow society-sanctioned track of graduate from high school, get a job or go to university and get a degree or trade, build your career and profession, probably get married or find a partner, settle down and have children. While gathering and refining a body of knowledge implies energy, time, effort, and dedication, the Pearl point of Wisdom gifts us something that is immanent, intrinsic, innate. We don't have to go anywhere to become wise, though wisdom might direct us to travel or journey inward or outward. Wisdom doesn't need us to be anything we are not already, though wisdom may inspire us to break and transform addictive or limiting behaviors and patterns. Wisdom can show the way to healthier relationships, lifestyles, and choices, as well as open us to the numinous land, place, and time.

Wisdom overlays the Iron Pentacle point of Self. It appears so utterly different than Self—general and everywhere instead of particular and individual—and yet perhaps we can see how one flows to the other, just as Iron itself flows to Pearl, and Pearl back to Iron. Working with the Iron point of Self, it is very common to have an experience of the definitions of our self dissolving, blending, swirling beyond this self to become all selves. We may experience ourselves as facets of the All and lose or release our rigid understanding of self, other than as a point on a spectrum, one star in a sky of countless stars, one moment within time and place. Wisdom takes this up from the other side: everything is present, revealed, and available to all. Within that we can hone down to a particular moment and place—the one we happen to be inhabiting—in order to have a lived experience of wisdom.

When I (JM) hold a mirror up to my face to perceive myself—the Self of the Iron Pentacle—I gaze at this moment, myself in this moment, or myself *as* this moment. If I don't have a mirror, I gaze into the palm of my left hand, imagining it as a mirror or even seeing myself in that arrangement of skin and bone and tendon, lines and cells. But the back of my hand or the back of the mirror—is that what others are seeing? Obviously they don't see the same thing when they look at my self as what I see; perhaps they see the wisdom of me? And I don't mean the wise parts; I mean the this-is-what's-here, the vastness of context within which this singular self belongs. Hopefully that might be wise! But if they look with the eyes of wisdom, they might see how I belong to the whole; how I am intrinsically part of it. I might realize this myself when I work with either wisdom or self long enough and deep enough to trust and be shown. And one can find it from either side of the mirror, looking within at the self's intricacy or gazing from the broad sweep of wisdom.

This body holds wisdom. This body writing and this body reading—body wisdom is here, in the pulse of our blood and the flicker of our eyes and the lightning-quick calculations we constantly make, judging how and where to move, how tense or relaxed to be, where to place our focus. Just as the body is the only place we have to inhabit love, and the body is also our most intimate arbiter of law—the laws of muscle and blood, sweat and tears, birth and death—the body is also the perfect place to learn wisdom. Not just our left hand, either, though we could start there, with its reminder of Wisdom layered over the Self of Iron. But within all of our body lie its wisdoms regarding rest and nutrition and movement, its wisdoms of growth and healing, its wisdoms of sex, fear, pain, ecstasy.

We rely on the wisdom of the body in so many ways. If something smells or tastes bad, this is our body letting us know it might poison us. When we're exhausted—perhaps from exertion or illness or stress—our body is insisting that we rest, sleep, recover. When we meet a stranger, our body reacts to countless clues of scent, posture, what we read in facial muscles, hand gestures, stance, what we hear in their voice. Our bodies will immediately—instantly, it feels like—let us know if we should relax, stay wary, or flee. Our bodies know how to make love, nurture small ones, soothe with touch and tone; our bodies know how to carry loads, walk long distances, give birth.

It's not that we always trust these wisdoms of the body. Much of our upbringing and social etiquette requires us to ignore, rewrite, and disobey this wisdom. But the fact that each new generation has to be taught—again—to ignore and rewrite it shows how all-pervasive body wisdom is. And all of us can relearn these wisdoms—we're carrying the source of them around every moment—that body is us, that wisdom is ours. Intuition is somehow imagined to be an almost etheric sense, yet intuition is part of the body. Our gut instinct, our hackles rising, our heart softening or melting, our brain freezing, butterflies in the tummy; all these wisdoms our bodies offer us. The body's reactions can be so powerful that it is hard to override them regardless of all our training and all our belief that the mind is superior to the body. The mind, as we realize when we think for just a moment, is part of the body. It has a physical existence whether we are speaking of the brain or the entire body-mind, and we cannot separate out mind wisdom and say it is somehow superior to body wisdom because it's all one thing.

Bodies know when to be born. The best that science can say about what naturally triggers a pregnant woman to go into labor is that perhaps the baby sends a signal. Or decides. Or the pregnant body, still mostly one being until that moment the cord is cut and the baby breathes autonomously, is wise in the moment of birth. The body is wise in death, too; choosing for itself, when allowed, its time of leaving, which is sometimes much quicker and sometimes much slower than the medical profession predicted. It's said that often even those attended rigorously by loved ones will choose a moment to die when no one is in the room, as if the body's wisdom folds back on itself when it is no longer engaged in the world, taking us home.

I (Fio) like to write, sing, and incant the following: *All is body, we are bodies, bodies upon bodies, eating bodies, fucking bodies, delving bodies, swimming bodies, opening bodies, loving bodies, connecting bodies* . . . Body is deeper, wilder, and richer than we are taught. Bodies hold memory, bodies hold joy and wonder and the capacity for great pleasure and connection, and the body also remembers trauma. Trauma is one of those words that catches us. We hear it and we may want to dismiss it, run from it, embrace it wholeheartedly, or regard it as our one and true savior—the way to understand who we are, what is happening in our lives, and how to resolve our problems. An event can be traumatic, but when English speakers say trauma, we are often talking about what is left behind: those marks, wounds, and indelible psychic and emotional imprints.

During the year of my (Fio) astrological Saturn return, I was told by a psychologist that the symptoms I was expressing sounded like acute complex post-traumatic stress disorder (CPTSD). Though his voice resounded with certainty, it was never an official diagnosis, but it gave me an insight into what I was going through. Essentially I was so stressed—trying to engage a dance degree at university, edit a monumental book, sustain coven life, teach, mentor, and be in a monogamous romantic partnership—that when intense memories of my own sexual abuse emerged, I froze. I began to sink. My story is distinct and it is common. It was trauma that was running through my body, working itself out, processing. The wisdom of the body was that I could not fully show up in my life until I danced with the ghosts of my past.

We can learn a lot about ourselves by examining our own trauma, but modern capitalist societies also fetishize trauma. This is often sold to us in the intense violence of film and social media that loops scenes of rape, guns, car chases, genocide, and physical abuse that we can't look away from. Trauma and trauma-informed modalities teach us about what has happened in our past that is forming us now and also about our boundaries and what the remarkable poet Mary Oliver (1935–2019) calls *the soft animal of your body*. When we acknowledge trauma, not attaching ourselves to it consciously but being mindful of its impacts, which itself is a difficult and labyrinthine journey, we remember that we humans are also endless changers; we change all the time. This too is the wisdom of the body.

Beautiful art has been made by, with, and through the human body. The wisdom that sings through our words, that expresses itself on canvas, or that weeps or sighs or yearns through a poem is one of our body's ways of expressing its wisdom. Law and wisdom lie intimately together when we think of the way our hearts keep beating, our lungs supply oxygen to us, our brains keep up the countless calculations required every second to sustain this complex bodyself. This body wisdom is a whole discipline—a field of disciplines—within the medical and allied health models, and the wisest of practitioners, whether they be midwives, massage therapists, or surgeons, are those who enquire into each body's own wisdom: *What's going on in your body? What do you need? What's important to you?* Our bodies are all wise in the same ways and all wise in different ways. We follow the law of humans and the wisdom of our unique life, situation, body.

We are back at the landscape where we began: the broad plateau, the intimate descent, those twists and turns that reveal again the wisdom that was always there. This is the pearl within the oyster, this is what is hidden in plain sight, this is what calls to the questioning heart, to the seeker, and it was always here. Wisdom is the dark curved mirror of space reflecting all that is. Here in the burst of star explosion, here in atoms forming, unforming, reforming, here in the salty sunlit pools of life becoming on the shore of that same ocean where later pearls form deep in oysters, around grits of sand like the dust of stars themselves. We belong to all this: we unfold; we drink deep; we are washed by it, reformed and remade; we are the Fool borne on the waves and tides of it; under the moonlight we are both named and nameless. The pearl of us layers with each wisdom onto the self so that we become both truly ourselves and also more than ourselves. We feel ourselves part of the stars, the pearl, the All.

ANCESTRAL WISDOM

Ancestral work in the Pearl Pentacle point of Wisdom draws upon and feeds the Iron Pentacle point of Self, which lies underneath it, both of them held in the left hand when we cast the pentacles through the body.

Just as pearls are formed around a piece of grit, ancestor work can be challenging. Quite often we don't actually like our ancestors, whether that is our far distant ancestors (invaders, colonizers, oppressors) or our more immediate ancestors; that is, our parents and grandparents. For many of us, ancestor work is inseparable from the injustice and hardship our forebears suffered, which we may still continue to experience today: racism, prejudice, sexual violence, slavery, poverty, and other deep wrongs, often perpetrated through generations and affecting whole communities, cultures, and geographies. If we have emerged from that and done the work of acknowledging, grieving, healing, and integrating some of that trauma, the last thing we may want to do is more ancestor work.

All of us have ancestors who were survivors or we wouldn't be here. All of us have ancestors who passed their DNA down the threads of generations to reach us. All of us are born of lineages of people who loved, worshiped, learned, and taught what they knew to others who were part of nurturing and sustaining the wisdoms of their people in whatever ways they could. This wisdom trance invites us to connect with the wisdom of those ancestors, not in a generalized *those who came before* way but specifically our own ancestors. So in my case (JM), those who lived in France, Italy, and Poland, who were Catholic and Jewish, whose bodies and lives were built from those soils and who lived very different lives than mine.

Do this trance on your own terms and in a way that feels safe, held, and viable for you. Setting a clear intention to seek the wisdom of these ancestors—and one particular line of ancestors—is a way to steer the trance into a place of learning. If this feels triggering for you, feel free to skip this work or create an alternative for yourself, such as building an ancestral wisdom altar (see page 129).

» You will need: journal and pen; some information on immediate ancestors; a safe and comfortable place to trance

» Time: 60 minutes

Preparation

Each of us has four biological grandparents, and we may have more grandparents (for example, through adoption or remarriage).

Draw three wide columns down a page. Begin by writing the names of your grandparents, spaced widely apart, in the first column. If you don't know their names, write down what you know them as or even as *father's mother.*

Under each of their names, jot down some facts that you know about this person—where they were born, what languages they spoke at home, what order they were in their family (only child, seventh surviving), and any particulars you know about them.

Which of those grandparents can you go back another generation for? That is, how many of your great-grandparents can you name? In the second column, write what you can of this generation, your grandparents' parents. You can use arrows or lines to connect these names to those in the first column. Under or near their names, record any other facts you are able to: where they were born, their languages, place in the family, and anything else you know. Some of these eight people you may have known or heard stories about, whereas others may be a complete mystery. I know only one single thing about my paternal grandmother's parents: they were Jewish.

The third column represents your great-great-grandparents; what can you write in this column? Perhaps your lineages are well preserved and you can fill this in with ease; perhaps you have a family tree you can refer to or you know (or can guess) what country these people were born in. Fill in anything that you can for these sixteen people, all of whom are your fairly immediate ancestors.

Trance

Let yourself be drawn to one particular ancestral line. You may choose a line you are familiar with, one you know nothing at all about, or one for which you have partial information.

Begin with grounding and centering yourself, as well as doing whatever feels right to make the space and your trance safe and comfortable. This could include casting a circle, breath work, speaking your intention aloud, or lighting a candle.

You can do this trance eyes open, letting your finger trace across the page over the generations; eyes closed, surrendering to the images and sensations that arise; or with a soft gaze, mostly closed but not entirely, held at a point such as a candle on your altar.

Start with the grandparent whose ancestral line you have chosen to follow. Let a sense of this person, the shape of their life and who they are or were, arise within you. You might whisper a recognition or thanks to them as you reach further back to the parent of theirs that lies on this line you are following. For this person, breathe gently while again allowing a sense of them, their life, and who they were to arise within you. Notice your sensations and impressions. Again, you can acknowledge or thank this person as it feels right to you. Then reach back to the parent of theirs who forms the third part of this line, a person who lived not all that long ago but is four generations removed from you.

Once again, allow a sense of this person—or at least what you know or can imagine about them—to arise. This time, ask to go a little deeper. What wisdom is this person carrying? Perhaps when you ask this question, you will have an impression of the far distant past and many other generations of ancestors. Perhaps you will be offered glimpses of circumstances from which wisdom arose or informed or even offered a specific piece of wisdom. Spend at least a few moments breathing with this, even if all that arises is your own questions. When you feel ready, you may offer a thanks or acknowledgment to this individual and even to the whole ancestral line as it stretches back through time.

Then, carrying whatever wisdom you have sensed, heard, or witnessed with you, travel back to the great-grandparent who was born from this person. Perhaps you will catch a glimpse or understanding of how this wisdom ran or didn't run in their life. Then travel back to your grandparent, the parent of one of your own parents. With each of these generations, you may also receive understandings of how the wisdom was expressed, conserved, or even lost.

Completion

Bring yourself back from the trance state: open your eyes, focus on things around you in the room, maybe stretch or get up for a small walk, perhaps to get a drink of water.

Take notes in your journal of what you want to remember of your experience.

Over the coming days, allow yourself to reflect on how the wisdom of this particular line of ancestors may have translated into your life and your self. Maybe you will also want to draw something, make or add to an ancestor altar, or be inspired to find out more about your ancestors.

WISDOM ALTARS AND SHRINES

Altar and shrine making is one of my (Fio's) favorite activities. Throughout my apartment and anywhere I have lived are shrines filled with icons, offerings, candles, oils, and gifts. There are altars too, and these altars and shrines often live together in the same space. The main distinction between an altar and a shrine is that an altar is a surface upon which dedicated magical or religious ritual happens, and a shrine is made in devotion to a spirit or deity.

I have a Wildwood working altar upon which are multiple shrines to Wildwood spirits. Facing this altar across the room is my Feri altar upon which are shrines to the Mighty Dead of the Feri tradition and to the Star Goddess and Peacock Angel. In my current living space are shrines to St. Brigid, Aphrodite, Hermes, Ganesha, Kali, Persephone, and an ancestor shrine.

You are invited to make a shrine to the Pearl Pentacle point of Wisdom. This dedicated space for communion with wisdom might house or merge with other shrines you keep for mysterious ones whose wisdom you venerate. Ideally you will find a space to house both the shrine—the items that create the devotional space together—and an altar for wisdom workings.

> » You will need: a space for the shrine/altar, found and
> beloved items you feel ought to be in the shrine/
> altar, offerings for the hearth spirits in your hearth-
> hold and for the land spirits outside
> » Time: 30–60 minutes

Once you have assembled all of the found and beloved items together, move to the space in which you will begin to create the shrine and altar.

Acknowledge country. Ground and center. Align your souls. Whenever I create a new shrine in my hearth-hold, I tend to spend more time than usual acknowledging country before I begin. I will also give offerings to my hearth spirits who anchor the integrity and virtue of my home. I then go outside and give offerings to the land spirits. This is to connect everything mindfully and respectfully together. A new dedicated space to venerate or honor a mystery or a spirit needs to sing in harmony with both the land and the hearth those shrines are within.

When you feel ready and aligned, begin to sing one of your favorite wisdom chants or hum a melody you enjoy. As you are doing this, intuitively assemble the shrine with the items you have gathered.

Reflect on how you have come to hold or relate to wisdom in your life. How does the Pearl Pentacle point of Wisdom reverberate through your thoughts, actions, and ways of being with others? How does forming this shrine right now help you commune with and access the wisdom you carry, the wisdom in the land, and the wisdom of your ancestors? Take your time with each of those layers: the wisdom you carry, the wisdom in the land, your own ancestral wisdom.

Arrange the items so that there is a clear surface upon which to enact the movements of your wisdom spells and rituals. This will be your wisdom working altar. You might want to begin to pick up the focus and intensity of the humming, singing, or chanting to help raise power to bless this altar and this shrine in the name of Wisdom.

When you feel the power peaking, add in the running of the Pearl Pentacle current internally; to link to the running of the Pearl current practice, see page 271. Feel that current move from point to point within you, and each time you reach Wisdom, strengthen the blessing with that point's presence. Let that Wisdom run through into Liberty and into Knowledge, back up to Love, then down to Law, then right back through Wisdom again. At this point the power should be buzzing!

When you can't hold on to the power any longer, release it into the altar and shrine, blessing them both.

Here is your Wisdom shrine and altar. Here you can come when you are seeking insight, counsel, and advice and you need a break from the voices and perspectives of humans. Sometimes I need to get quiet and grounded and connect with the Mystery. I might recite *The Charge of the Goddess* and go into a trance state, I might drum and sing while incense rolls across my skin and ignites my senses . . . I often do this in front of my shrines and altars. By doing this, then opening to listen and listening deeply, I find equilibrium and perspective in my life. At the very least I feel more calm, less stressed, and more capable.

This Wisdom shrine and altar can remain in place for as long as you desire. This could be a week, a month, a year, or many years. It could also change: you might light candles there, mix oils, brew spells, write chants, journal, or throw cards and runes.

Blessed be, Wisdom.

WISDOM OF LAND,
LINEAGE, AND TRADITION
RAVEN EDGEWALKER

The day I sit down to start writing this essay is Beltane in the Northern Hemisphere. After a dismal, cold, typically British spring, it dawned fair and bright. The new green leaves glow against the bright blue sky and the hedges are filling with white, foamy hawthorn blossom, called May in Britain. Perfect timing for May Day. I walk to a coffee date with a friend accompanied by an elderly neighbor, talking as we usually do about the weather, the wildlife we've seen recently, and the imminent return of our local migratory house martins and swallows.

These birds are late, and we are anxious; fewer and fewer of them make the journey every year. I've watched for their return since I was six or seven. They're an important marker in the turning of my seasons. We talk about how amazing it is that such tiny birds travel so far and return to the same nesting spot year after year, generation after generation, each holding and passing the seed of a biological GPS, coded as generational wisdom in their DNA. I meet my friend for coffee, sitting in the sunny courtyard chatting and connecting, and as we do I see the house martins in the sky, swooping in to check out their old nests, made of tiny pellets of mud hung under the eaves. They've made it; their wisdom has guided them back home.

While there are many May Day and Beltane celebrations going on locally that call my attention, today was the one day forecast free of rain in a week, which means a perfect day for gardening. That's exactly what I choose. To spend the afternoon in the garden pushing my hands into the earth, feeling its cool dampness, feeling how healthy it is as a worm wiggles through my fingers and drops back to burrow into the soil. I pull out weeds, admiring and despairing at how fast they grow, and gather a basket of herbs, noticing the robin who always shows up at the right moment to snatch insects from the dug soil. I plant rows of vegetable seeds, thinking how appropriate this is to be doing on Beltane. I sink into the moment and open my senses to be present with all this growing LIFE; to listen, to be aware, to feel into the wisdom of all these beings around me.

Working in the garden, growing vegetables for food, herbs for magic and healing, and flowers to feed my sense of beauty is a part of my work in the world. It's also a potent connection to the local land and my recent ancestors. My mother, grandmothers, and great-grandmothers were all keen gardeners, and it's here, kneeling on the damp grass, where I most strongly hear their voices and wisdom reaching though time, telling me what weeds to pull, what herbs to cut, but loudest of all not to kneel in the wet grass or I'll end up with arthritis. Beyond my own ancestors I feel the connection, when my hands are sunk deep into the earth, to the ancestors who have dug and worked this land since human beings learned how to farm the land. I feel the lives of the green bloods who have grown and been nurtured in this soil and then sunk down into decay, becoming the very earth itself. This is land, earth, and soil that has been in relationship with humans through so many ages and changes, and its wisdom is woven with the history of its human stewards.

I grew up in a small, very rural village in the south of England, surrounded by the kind of lush rolling hills, patchwork fields, and woodlands that look idyllic in photographs. It was also isolated, with no public transport, shops, or many other kids. Those hills, fields, woods, and especially the garden were my playgrounds, shopping malls, cinemas, and best friends, the human kind being in short supply. My mother stuffed a trowel into my hand as soon as I was big enough to hold it, and I followed her around the garden copying her: digging out weeds, turning the soil, collecting up the snails in a bucket and keeping them as transitory pets. I later found that snails are considered to be good fortune in Cornish folklore. I developed a passion for both gardening and the natural world along the way. I was a scruffy, grubby, weird kid who was sent to school unable to read but able to identify pretty much any tree or wildflower, bird, or animal. My head and heart were, as they are now, full of the kind of local folklore that still infuses Britain and our culture if you scrape the surface just a little.

My grandmother would take me to the bottom of the garden to show me how to see the tiny fey beings that lived there. Fey with gossamer silver wings the size of wrens that flitted amongst the branches of the old cypress hedge and made incredible palaces from fallen sticks and broken cardboard egg cartons. She took me for rambles and allowed me to climb trees and paddle in streams. She told me all kinds of local lore: customs and charms for good luck; myths, legends, and folk wisdom that became part of my landscape. Trees became characters in my stories; the hills and hollows became castles and portals to other worlds. We'd nod at magpies to dispel their bad luck, blow dandelion clocks to send their seeds off to the wind laden with wishes, and tell fortunes by counting cherry stones in the summer.

When I left home and moved to London as a student, the sudden lack of green surrounding me was a shock, and after a couple of weeks of reeling and feeling ungrounded, I realized something needed to be done. Slowly, carefully, and with all the patience I'd learned watching plants grow, I began to learn the land of the city, the streets, the sounds and scents; to notice where the birds nested high on the roofs and how tenacious plants managed to grow in out-of-the-way corners. I found the dark spaces where the street lights didn't reach, what places to avoid when the pubs closed, which tube stops were well lit and safe. I sought out the stories and folklore of London, of which there is plenty, just as much as in the woods and fields even if it feels more distant and abstract. In doing so, I created a daily practice of intentional walking that I still lean into each and every day that I am able, which allows me to connect, listen, integrate, and be present with the wisdom of the land.

Perhaps because I was working hard to expand my senses while in London, I fell into a practice of tagging along on all kinds of demonstrations for environmental and social justice. These meandered through the streets at a time when concern for my beloved nature was coming to the forefront of our consciousness, and the need to do something became a loud calling. I was trying on for size spiritual practices that resembled my internal landscape of passions and curiosity when I connected, in the middle of the city, with what turned out to be another of my grand passions. My wanderings led me, inevitably, to bookshops and thus to a copy of *The Spiral Dance*, thrust into my hands in a moment of life-changing coincidence and synchronicity. A seed was planted.

The land of Britain is soaked in myths, stories, and legends. They are densely packed into these small islands. Not many miles up the road from where I live is Glastonbury with its Tor, thought by many to be the mysterious Isle of Avalon where King Arthur and Guinevere were laid to rest. Stand on the top of the Tor on a clear day and you might see South Cadbury Castle, an Iron Age hill fort also linked to the legends of King Arthur. Under the Tor, it's said, lives the King of Annwn, the Welsh Otherworld: Gwyn ap Nudd, whom I make a point of greeting each and any time I glimpse the Tor because really that just seems smart. This is the land on which I first experienced the full-blown glory of Reclaiming witchcraft. The land in which I was introduced to one of the parts of our tradition that I adore and which has taught me so much—the way we work with myth and story to create life-changing, transformative ritual.

Within Reclaiming we often work with the stories of the divine and mysterious ones as ways to connect with the mythic resonances of those beings, the wisdoms of the lands we work on, and all the unseen beings that we share these spaces with. We seek connection through the stories of these lands, to understand on a cellular level that we are also divine beings. We strive to hear the calling of our hearts, leading us to do the work that some might call the work of our gods. We work to build relationships with these beings so that they might be our guides and teachers and so that we might learn what it is to be in right relationship with divinity, ourselves, the land, and other humans.

We human beings are creatures of story. We all have stories within us of how and where we grew up, of joy, love, sorrow, despair, and hope. We tell each other stories, or pieces of stories, to build relationship and find commonality of experience in each other's words and worlds. We look to the stories of others, be they modern novels and poems or ancestral myths and legends, to guide us in our lives. We seek for wisdom in all these stories to understand and grow. Stories are part of our inheritance and lineage as human beings, part of our humanity, part of our collective wisdom. They connect us all the way back through evolution and the creation of life on earth to the birth of our universe. Reclaiming holds, as a sacred mystery, creation stories of the Star Goddess, whom we also name God Herself. These stories were passed into our tradition at its inception from one of our ancestor traditions, Anderson Feri. Stories of the universe created in love and desire and wonder by the orgasm of the Star Goddess sent forth seeds of wisdom that brought us to where every one of us is right here and right now. This wisdom teaches us that we are also divine beings, descendants of the Star Goddess.

Exactly what these seeds of wisdom are, how we access them, and how we interpret them is personal, subjective, and situational, often shaped by the stories of our lives. The wisdom may come to us in the form of a bird song, as a sign in the clouds, an overheard snatch of conversation on the underground, the scent of cooking drifting out from a restaurant, a random found object in our path. These pieces of wisdom may also come in the form of irritation, frustration, or the understanding that we need to do something different. These wisdoms speak to the grit inside the pearl that we often talk about in this Pearl Pentacle work. Sometimes we need to lean into discomfort and ratchet around until finally understanding emerges and helps soothe away our sharp edges. It could be something we've seen, heard, or been past a hundred times before, but it means nothing until we're in the right moment and present with the land in order for it to register. Sometimes we run into wisdom by chance or coincidence, but we can also learn tools and practices that will help us notice and access wisdom.

Wisdom, and learning the wisdom of a land, can feel like an alchemical process. It's a mysterious mix of passion, information, knowledge, experience, emotion, and stories coming together within us over time to mix, meld, and fuse into this thing we call Wisdom. It's a process, meandering along through life and experiences like a river flowing through fields until we realize *There it is!* We grasp it—sometimes it slips away again, slippery as a river fish, but sometimes we get a taste of it. Suddenly, then, we're not separate from the land; through this familiarity and presence, we're part of it, aware and sensitive to the small, almost imperceptible changes in the scents, sounds, and sights that are here. The Pearl Pentacle offers a structure for exploring this work, a model of signposts to help navigate the meandering river and codify our experiences as well as a language to communicate with others.

Learning to access wisdom experientially is core to my experiences within Reclaiming. We offer tools, such as the Iron and Pearl Pentacles, in our teachings and rituals. We craft experiences so each learns in their own way, rather than being instructed in the right or wrong way of accessing wisdom. We create space for the magic to happen by weaving containers out of story and myth. We immerse ourselves and find what we need in the space created by tapping into the mythic while holding each other in community and in the compassion of Pearl. We try to create space for a diversity of experiences and needs by offering models of facilitation and teaching that are not rooted in hierarchies of age or experience but are shared co-creations that offer multiple perspectives and access points. Age, experience, and the wisdom that comes with those things are honored and respected in our tradition, while wisdom is also understood to be held by many.

Reclaiming, founded in the 1980s, is very, very young compared to many spiritual traditions that have been about for millennia. As such, the lineages of our tradition are short ones. Many of us are first generation Reclaiming witches, coming to the tradition as adults. A few have grown up with one or more Reclaiming parents. Some of us have added or will shortly be adding another generation to our biological lineage, passing the seeds of wisdom along to more humans as Reclaiming grandkids. But biological lineage isn't all we're talking about. In a tradition such as ours, lineage and the wisdom that is passed on is not as simple as moving from one descendant to the next.

We teach our WitchCamps in teams of between four and twelve people. We teach classes, workshops, and paths at camps in pairs, or sometimes more. We believe that we each access wisdom in different ways, and by offering different perspectives we are more likely to be able to offer a tool or idea that creates understanding and growth for as many people as possible. More experienced members of a teaching team step into the role of mentoring those who are less experienced. Sometimes that means the younger person may be the mentor. In this way we honor wisdom and teachings from our elders as well as our descendants.

Reclaiming coalesced into a tradition from many roots and influences: anarchy, ecofeminism, Anderson Feri, and more. We talk about how we are still evolving, bringing new ideas, tools, and experiences into our tradition from many sources. We joke gently that if someone calls themselves Reclaiming, then what they offer within the container of our tradition also becomes Reclaiming, part of this magical lineage of stories and experiences that we pass along. This enriches our tradition and also brings with it a complexity of challenges as we aspire to step away from the prevailing cultures of whiteness within and without Reclaiming. Part of our work is to acknowledge and attribute these sources of wisdom, and at times to step away from those sources that have been appropriated or misused and so to move though feelings of entitlement that this process may evoke in us. The sources of our wisdom are thus not confined nor limited to what we have created ourselves, although we are a gorgeously creative and inventive tradition. I believe we are open to exploring many ways and sources to open to wisdom, even when that is challenging.

Wisdom is always around us and presents itself in many ways within and without Reclaiming: through humans, tradition, and land. All these things are so much wiser than any one human being can be alone. We strive to be present, notice, and be open to receive the wisdom when it appears. Just recently I was walking along musing about the wisdom of the land, writing this essay, and angsting if I was talking about the right stuff. I walked round a corner and saw two runes, Gifu and Algiz, in the cracks in the concrete road that I've walked over hundreds of times but never noticed before. Yes, point taken.

Sometimes the message is very clear and simple. *You want to learn this wisdom? Sit down, shut up, take a breath, and listen to the divine within and without. Feel your body on the earth, sink your hands into the soil, get out of your head and just notice. Be aware; remember that you too are part of this web of connection and in constant reciprocal relationship.*

Perhaps this sounds too simple to be true witchcraft, but in our frantic, mundane world, we don't often give ourselves the time to build the kind of slow, sustained relationships with the land and within our communities that our ancestors would have had. We need to slow down and make time. This work of Pearl, this practice and desire to access wisdom, is not an overnight spell to be cast or weekend workshop to be done once and then checked off the list. It's a process. It takes time, practice, and experience. It can be hard and frustrating. It can make us cranky and irritable, but it can also be full of joy, delight, and connection. Just like the practice of working with the Pearl Pentacle as a whole, it takes the wisdom of many lifetimes. It is not simply the wisdom of our individual lifetimes but the wisdom of all those lifetimes around us. The voices of our ancestors and descendants are woven into this work along with the wisdom of the living beings around us—and their ancestors and descendants—and the land itself; all that has been and all that will be.

WISDOM CONVERSATION

There is wisdom in everything and everyone. Each being, each inter-linked system of life, is embodied raw wisdom. Wisdom offers of itself freely, if only we pay attention.

The intention of this activity is to respectfully uncover and engage with the wisdom embodied in another living human being whom you know. There are other processes and workings, often through the arts and skills of trance, to access the wisdom of our beloved and mighty dead, plants, deities, and entire landscapes. The same principles apply, however: ground, get centered, align within yourself and the other person, drop or expand into your deep and active listening, and listen. Perhaps you ask questions to clarify, enrich, and participate dynami-cally in the journey of the conversation, but largely it's listening.

For this activity, you might choose someone you know quite well and whose wisdom you are desiring in your life right now. This could be a dear friend, colleague, parent, child, mentor, student, or grandpar-ent. Later you might repeat this activity with someone you know less well, and then with someone you've met a few times but would really like to listen to and get to know a little more. You can visit if that feels appropriate and is accessible to you both, or phone calls and video calls work well too. This person does not need to be a witch, pagan, spirit worker, or mystic of any kind.

> » You will need: yourself and someone who has
>   consented to this wisdom conversation; a journal
>   or music or paper and drawing implements for
>   reflection afterward
>
> » Time: at least an hour

STEP ONE will be asking the person that you want to have this wisdom conversation with. Tell them what it means to you and why you have chosen them. Let them know that there will be speaking back and forth, but that largely you will be actively listening. It's not an interview; it's not for anything other than listening and hopefully learning. They may ask you clarifying questions and for more information, but once you have agreed, you can continue to step two.

STEP TWO will be arranging the best time to meet and the logistics. Is the meeting going to happen in what I (Fio) call the flesh-to-breath or is it via distance?

STEP THREE is to make sure you keep the appointment, and depending on the relationship between the two of you, you might offer a pithy and potent grounding (as we like to say in Reclaiming) so that you can both turn up in the best way possible.

Grounding and centering (see page 259) is one of the most accessible magical offerings. Many psychologists and counselors offer grounding and centering practices to their clients. It is a tool commonly worked with in western styles of yoga, meditation classes, dance, theatre, and acting. When I read tarot for anyone, I will always lead the person in a simple grounding. They may be an atheist doctor, a Catholic farmer, a Buddhist chef, or an agnostic parent, and every person always loves it, so begin there.

STEP FOUR will be to start with a prompting question. For example, *When have you felt most alive in your life?* You can't just expect someone to fountain their wisdom upon you. Sometimes a wise thing is to ask a question, a discerning question, to open the door to wisdom. So you start, you offer some structure and orientation and honor the person by engaging them in this way. I personally respond well to questions that help direct me through the landscape of reality and my own experiences.

STEP FIVE. Keep listening, keep grounding and centering, and listen, listen, listen. Ask a few questions here and there. The person may ask for more questions, or perhaps the person will ask you for your wisdom. You may feel like sharing your perspective and experience as well.

STEP SIX. After the conversation is complete and you have parted, take some time to journal what you have learned. You may journal with words or with pictures and landscapes. You may prefer to go on a long walk and think and feel that way. You may want to turn on some of your favorite music and dance and move.

STEP SEVEN. Repeat this process again as mentioned above, perhaps with people less known to you. Or you might decide you want to go in the other direction, starting with someone you don't know very well, and then someone you know a little, and then an intimate beloved.

Wisdom is everywhere, in everything and everyone. Wisdom is waiting for us to discover it. Wisdom is around every corner, and we can never fully know or comprehend how much of it is awaiting us in any conversation, interaction, or meeting. Welcome to Wisdom.

WISDOM OF THE SELF

Wisdom is something we gather throughout our lives, and thus older people are often thought of as the wisdom holders for a community. But it's also common to remark on the wisdom of children as if there's innate wisdom, they're bringing it through from the other side, or they see more clearly as the layers of conditioning, propriety, and limitations haven't set in yet. People remark on the generation just coming into young adulthood—how they seem not to have to go through the same struggles we did; they have already integrated what we learned with such difficulty and struggle.

Maybe it's better if we start from assuming that we all carry some wisdom, or wisdoms, whatever our age, and so we all have wisdom that we can acknowledge, honor, and, in some cases, offer. Even if what we are carrying is a wisdom that we share with our own generation, who lived through a certain piece of history, for example, or of the culture we are part of, the family we were raised within, or the spiritual tradition we belong to, that does not make these shared wisdoms any less important. Each of us will have our own expression and unique experience within that shared pool.

I (JM) have placed this ritual within a circle, but if some other form appeals to you, please follow that. The focus is on examining different parts of our lives for the wisdom we've gained and acknowledging this in some way, perhaps by recording it in a journal.

> » You will need: journal and pen, room to cast a circle, undisturbed time and place
> » Time: up to an hour

Begin by offering an acknowledgment of sacred land and grounding and centering yourself.

Speak an intention such as *My intention is to gather some of my wisdoms.*

Cast a circle. Run the Pearl Pentacle from within the circle you've cast. Conclude by dropping into the point of Wisdom. Allow it to open out like a flower or a scent gradually filling a room so that Wisdom is present and filling the circle.

Moving to or turning to face the south (in the Southern Hemisphere) or the north (in the Northern Hemisphere), let your mind turn to the experience of your own birth. What wisdoms did you bring into the world with you or receive in that process of being born?

Spend a few moments thinking and feeling into this, then jot down some notes in your journal.

Turn next to the east in either hemisphere. Allow yourself to remember your childhood from the perspective of your current age. What wisdoms did you gather as you were growing up? These may have been passed down to you from others, realized on your own, or learned as part of a group of children. Often these wisdoms were very hard won and may have memories of trauma, grief, and pain woven inseparably within them. Remember your grounding and cast circle; if you need or wish, run the pentacle again, asking to be held within Love, Law, Wisdom, Liberty, and Knowledge.

Spend a few moments with the wisdoms of your childhood, and record what you wish to remember.

Turning then to the north (in the Southern Hemisphere) or the south (in the Northern Hemisphere), recall your young adulthood. Perhaps this is the stage of life you are at now or perhaps that was a long time ago. What wisdoms did you gain at this time?

Take a few moments and then record your wisdoms of youth, perhaps using dot points.

Then turn to the west in either hemisphere. Here is the maturity and aging in life—a place you may have spent twenty or forty or more years in, so there may be a lot to record. Or maybe you haven't reached this time yet, in which case you can either leave your journal blank for this piece or write down your observations of the wisdoms others around you are carrying from this part of their lives.

What about the Great Above? What wisdoms have you gained from the stars, the celestial, the aether? Perhaps these are wisdoms passed to you within a spiritual or magical tradition or wisdom that has come to you through dreams, practice, magic, or direct encounters with the divine. Take some notes about the wisdom you feel you have received.

Finally, address the Great Below. Have you been granted wisdoms connected with death, the underworld, and the mysteries? After contemplating this for a little while, record what you can, or wish to, of this.

Find a way to complete your ritual. Maybe you will stand in the center of the circle and read aloud all your wisdoms. Maybe you will thank each direction and attendant part of your life before offering blessings to yourself and all beings who seek and find wisdom. Maybe you want to decide what you might do now with these wisdoms—share them with your children or community, write a poem or create an artwork, or lead a similar ritual for others.

Make sure to release the circle you cast.

WE ARE THE WISDOM OF
OUR LIVING TRADITION

HILARY BUFFUM

It begins with an invocation. A call from a circle of witches and activists. It begins with a shared breath; a longing, fierce love and a spark for what's to come. It begins with us.

Wisdom—as it lives in my body—is intangible. Wisdom is experiential and adaptive. It is mistakes, desire, perspective, and mystery. Wisdom is the instinct curled inside the hollow of your bones, the clear discernment that comes from inside of yourself. Some say that it comes from our ancestors of blood, of craft, of resistance, of existence. Wisdom can be a message that you might not want but need to hear. The taste of fear in your mouth as you face your challenges head-on. The hut at the edge of the clearing in the forest I stumble upon after winding my way down a dark and mysterious path. When I open the door and inside is the Wise One, an ancient witch with a key and a question, or an empty room now containing you and your wisdom of becoming. For wisdom, my dear one, is not linear or bound by time; wisdom simply is.

Where does wisdom come from? Where does trust in the intuitive process live? A mentor and elder of mine, Seed, said to examine the root of the word to understand it. *Wisdom is the quality of clear sight,* she said. It asks, *What do you discern? What do you regard with clarity?* It is not an act performed with the eyes. It is the somatic experience of perception. The textural, experiential, and relational act of taking in our world is a way to grow your wise self. In my experience this is the truth. Each time I have chosen to behold, to witness, to be witnessed, my wisdom has widened. It arrives in pieces each time I step into myself.

While some wisdom is innate, other wisdom is learned. There are many who say that the only way to grow wisdom is over the stretch of time. While there is deep and rich wisdom that comes from time, wisdom itself is nonlinear.

I had the privilege of growing up in Reclaiming. This queer, anarchist, ecofeminist, activist, witchcraft community taught me a great deal about wisdom from a very young age. It was not so much that adults taught me definitions of wisdom according to their experience and ideology but in observing how wisdom was enacted by the ones whom I trusted. There was no road map or procedure, no high authority on the subject. Instead, I watched those around me show what it means to carry wisdom in community. I listened as they placed pieces of wisdom at each other's feet and tucked them into beloveds' pockets for safekeeping. I learned that I too possessed wisdom from the ways community carved out space for me in conversations, asked for my perspective in decisions, and listened to my interpretations of the divine and messages from the land. I have stood in circle with our community as we made mistakes, took accountability and sometimes not, stepped forward to claim pieces of wisdom, and stepped back to make space for the wise ways of others.

What does it mean to grow into wisdom in an emerging, living tradition? Much of my wisdom was found amongst the rocks, sticks, and tall redwood trees on the land of the Northern Pomo people in a state campground colonially known as the Mendocino Woodlands. This is the site of my first ever WitchCamp, Witchlets in the Woods. When I entered camp at eight years old, I was unsure about placing my trust in the community my parents were so excited about. They were eager for me to connect with witches my own age, while I was deeply skeptical. We packed our 1990s Volvo station wagon and drove the four hours from Ramaytush Ohlone land, so-called San Francisco, to this land of old trees and children's laughter, following the call of community wisdom into the forest.

Witchlets in the Woods was a brand-new camp, just a few years old, and was a place where some of the first Reclaiming witches to have children could come together and create magic. Witchlets was committing to a multigenerational community in a way that had barely been dreamed of in the fledgling experience of Reclaiming. Witchlets grew out of the wisdom of parenthood and communal caregiving. It began as a way for caregivers to support one another in the complexities of raising children in a new pagan tradition. It made a circle that encouraged the interruptions of children and called the chaos and joy that ran through their rituals' deep and wise magic.

Community wisdom raised me. I can trace my wisdom lineage to the scraped knees, firelight spells, 2 a.m. cups of hot cocoa, and secrets whispered between the trees on that land. Community wisdom raised me in the songs of joy, in the relationships with myth and deity, in the whispers of the forest. Community wisdom raised me as we celebrated, processed, fought, organized, marched, grieved, and dreamed together. Through this tradition I was connected to mentors and friends of all ages to consult with when I did not have access to the answers on my own.

I learned what wisdom meant, what forms it took, and where to look for it by watching how others valued it. Where it was buried, where they saw it in me, even when I could not. It started with the simple act of making space for me in ritual. *You are your own spiritual authority*, they said. In a culture where adults do not traditionally listen to children, this community taught me that my voice not only mattered, but there were wisdoms of deity and magic that I could perceive better because I was a child. They made space for me to take on priestessing roles and invocations, encouraged me to help plan rituals, to help plan our camp. Elders and mentors asked me and my friends for our perspective on magic, on how to shape the community culture. Every ask was a way of saying, *We see you, Wise One.*

Sometimes it was quiet, more subtle.

I remember being seventeen, standing on the edge of a riverbank preparing to come out of the ritual role we call aspecting. My tender, a dear friend and mentor, asked the godd[7] I had welcomed into my being if they had any messages for the body that was carrying them before they left me. The deity spoke through my mouth and said, *She needs to just jump; stop thinking about what's below, and jump.* My tender did not move, did not explain; she held space and watched. It was a metaphor, but she was ready to catch me in case I tried to launch myself onto the rocky riverbed below. She held space in an affirmation of her

---

7 "Godd" is a gender-encompassing version of god/dess.

trust in my body's wisdom. The witnessing, the tending, saying, *I trust the wisdom of your body. And I am here to catch you, remind you, hold you, when you forget it yourself.* Since that moment she has said that to me in a myriad of ways a thousand times over. She knew I would not jump, that my body held the wisdom of its vastness and limitations. By her trusting my body wisdom, it showed me it was safe for me to trust it too.

Embodied wisdom expanded into the wisdom of clear boundaries and communication. Copper Persephone, one of my first teachers—a beloved friend and mentor—taught me that boundaries are a gift. They show others how to love you well. Boundaries are the rich soil in which your authentic *yes* can flourish. In and outside Reclaiming I have sometimes felt like I could not say *no* to what was being asked of me in community. When I lost my words, mentors stepped in, put their hand on mine, and said, *You don't have to listen to that; you don't have to justify; you can just say* no, *no matter who you are speaking to.* They gave me permission to trust my no and reminded me that community care does not mean crossing your own boundaries for others' comfort. Boundaries are deep body wisdom. This wisdom allows us to show up fully in our own story in community and in relationships.

It was through Witchlets and other camps that I deepened into the wisdom of story. The mythological wisdom of deity can appear in unexpected ways. If we choose a myth that begins with a storm, we should not be surprised when the first day we arrive at camp, our carefully laid plans have a flavor of chaos and the unexpected and we end up digging pit toilets instead of meeting as a teaching team. Or if you choose a story where the forest is fighting for its sovereignty, then the trees falling and blocking half the cabins for the first night should come as no surprise. The year that you work with Baba Yaga, the teenagers find themselves compelled to nap on the stoves to keep warm in the middle of the night. I learned that the wisdom of the myths and the narratives we tell will work us in ways we cannot expect, but if I lean into the mystery, I might be able to catch some of it. As it is said in the story of Vasilisa the Brave and Beautiful and Baba Yaga, the morning is always wiser than the evening.

Witchlets taught me the wisdom of the land through the way we engaged with story. The wisdom of silence and listening to the plant world. To be mindful. To think about who the first peoples of the land are before engaging in ritual in a place. To ask the Indigenous peoples of the land you are on what you can do to honor their wisdom and support the land thriving. To fight the colonial erasure of Indigenous wisdom. To listen to the trees and to ask the plants before you pick them. To practice reciprocity. To listen for the wisdom that comes from the nonhuman entities in a place. How each time we arrive in a place we are part of the story and yet we are a small piece of the larger narrative of the land. The wisdom of place and history of the ground our feet touches extends far beyond us.

Change is a deep wisdom within Reclaiming. One year at Witchlets we decided to modify the story we chose to better fit our camp. Three days into camp, Rose May Dance—a teacher, elder, and trickster—said that she wanted to have a meeting with the story cell. Cautiously, we agreed. She gathered us around and told us that she did not usually believe in changing myths but loved what we had done with the story. Rose wanted us to know that she loved the magic that came out of the story at camp. I was struck by how she had taken the time to share her appreciation. She showed me the wisdom of change, of always learning. Acknowledging change and changing your own biases is wisdom. It was a gift that she made sure we took the time to receive.

In an ecstatic witchcraft tradition, joy is an integral gift of our wisdom. Witchlets has now begun holding an entirely child-planned and priestexed ritual. These rituals are powerful and lots and lots of fun. I am so impressed by the things I have learned about magic from the next generation of witches. This camp continues to show me the value of intergenerational wisdom. The willingness to create a structure and then play within it, knowing the magic will go where it will. Improvisational wisdom invites us to be present with one another in magical space. To say yes to following the energy of a ritual, especially when it takes us somewhere we were not expecting. In my experience, young people, especially teenagers, have incredible access to this wisdom. I had a friend tell me once that every person over thirty should have a mentor in their twenties. Teaching at Witchlets and taking part in these rituals has shown me that every person should have at least one mentor in each decade. That intergenerational relationship is one of the deepest wells of wisdom for all involved.

When I became a Reclaiming student teacher, Rose May Dance offered to be my mentor. I was flattered and a little bit intimidated. So when she texted me and said we should probably have a meeting, I remember feeling as though I was going to meet Baba Yaga in her hut. When I arrived, we had tea. I sat down and she said, *So what are we supposed to talk about?* I laughed. Neither of us knew. Between cups of tea and curling steam, we co-created a mentorship lineage together. When I reflect on that moment, what she was teaching me was the wisdom of co-creation.

We are the Wise One together and apart.

In our journey to wisdom we come back to one another. The collective wisdom of co-created magic and a messy, imperfect community is the path that unfolds when we dare to dream together. When the lineage is being created as we speak, we follow one another into the forest. Knowing when to be still and when to jump. Trusting our feet to know the way.

What is the wisdom of Reclaiming? Where do the roots find hold, where do we adapt, where are we pulling from? What wisdom are we growing of our own? How are we building the soil for future wisdom to grow?

The wisdom of a living tradition is that it is alive, ever changing, ever growing. We make mistakes and dream new ways of being, just as Wisdom in the Pearl Pentacle is suspended in the continuum of the points, connected to and a part of the whole. Wisdom in the context of Reclaiming is held in the lifeline of living tradition, floating in the threads of relationship between the beings who co-create this tradition.

As I sit down to write this, I am flooded with uncertainty. I'm supposed to write from the perspective of having grown up in Reclaiming, and I am feeling the weight of that responsibility. Who am I to take on that? What is this wisdom? Who has it? I feel as though there is an assumption of experience in being asked to write about community wisdom, and I do not feel qualified, yet I know I have experience. My own experience. I know who I am. I know that being raised in Reclaiming is integral to who I am. How do I start? I come back to the Pearl. The irritant rubbing over and over to make something beautiful. Where have the raw challenges I've encountered worried pearls of wisdom into the edges of my being?

In a living tradition, accountability and adaptability are deep wisdoms. Copper modeled this for me. She and I had many conversations about the place that sacred sexuality held in Reclaiming. For her it was deep and powerful magic and an important part of community. She helped found the bower space, a dedicated space for sacred sexual practice at many camps. As I got older I began asking her questions about the way in which sex magic fit into her practice, noticing how it didn't feel as easily accessible to me. She was generous with her listening and insight as I began to explore my own understanding. Once during our conversations, in an attempt to reassure me, she offered that she didn't think I was on the asexual spectrum because of my strengths as a priestess. Instead of assuaging my concerns, it knocked my confidence in one fell swoop, causing me to question my legitimacy and leadership in community and my relationship to magic.

I continued to have these conversations with her as I explored this part of our magical tradition and my relationship to my own sexuality. Eventually I expressed the impact of that conversation. I shared what the moment had felt like to me, how her reassurance had landed in my body like erasure. Copper took the time to hear me, to listen to the impact, and then she changed the way she talked about sex magic. She expanded how she taught, wrote about, and made space for sacred sexuality. When I wrote and shared my own experience, she supported me. Copper showed me the impact of accountability wisdom and the value of my personal embodied wisdom to her. That trust changed our community conversation and wisdom around ecstatic witchcraft.

As our community ages, grows, and changes, our wisdom expands and changes with it. We are creating it together, as did those first members of our community in the 1980s protesting nuclear power in the so-called San Francisco Bay Area. Like the ones who gathered for a family camping trip because they couldn't bring their babies to Witch-Camp. Like the wisdom of community care, wisdom we have gained from those witches who nursed our queer ancestors through the AIDS crisis. Like the continuing care wisdom I have learned as my beloved mentors, teachers, and elders of this tradition have lain dying over the past decade.

We are a community of people who are edge walkers, threshold keepers, living at the margins. If we gather our wisdoms together and collectively care for one another . . . if we are willing to make mistakes . . . to love, live, die, grieve, celebrate, birth, and rebirth alongside one another, we unfurl the pearlescent threads of our collective wisdom. We are the wisdom of the living tradition.

we blaze forth, seeking liberty

liberation liberté freedom release

from all slavery from oppression

and in this work we mantle

ourselves yet again, smoothing

out the edges of how it is to be

embodied, a soul born to a community

of souls and this pearl forming

changing growing

LIBERTY

iberty is the fourth point of the Pearl Pentacle, and its power leaps forward into the world, strident after the subtlety of Wisdom. In Liberty we examine our freedoms and also our limitations: our obligations and commitments, the restrictions placed upon us, and how and in what ways systemic oppressions control and limit us. These oppressions may come in the form of tyrannical governments, poverty, class and gender and income, systems of capitalism, fascism or communism, human laws that are applied unequally across race, class, age, gender and sexuality, body types, education, and many other categories. We also meet internal oppressions where we have integrated these systems into our own lives and self-talk so that we may no longer be free even to make the choices that are available to us. Liberty is heavy lifting.

Placed over the Iron Pentacle point of Power, Liberty needs every bit of that power we can feed it. We can write all the social media or blog posts we want; at a certain point, it's where we place our bodies that counts. Will we seek out comrades and form networks of empowerment, knowing that sometimes we do the personal work each of us is gifted in this life and sometimes we do the work of world changing, and sometimes these two things are not different? Will we stand or march or sit or speak for what we believe, what we value, for the Love-Law-Wisdom of life? Liberty is held in—or released from—the right hand as we gesture, as we plant trees, as we reach out to hold another's hand, as we make our vows.

THE WORK OF LIBERATION

Liberty in the Pearl Pentacle arrives after Wisdom, implying that once we are wise we can find freedom. If only it were that simple! So far in the Pearl Pentacle we have decided that these qualities—of love, law, and wisdom—are coexistent with ourselves, and when we slow down—listen—show up—pay attention, there they are, not having to be worked for so much as made room for. Is Liberty the same? Is it there all along, and our strivings, yearnings, and sufferings toward it are only the long way around? It's true that when we look at the natural world, liberty abounds. The wind is free, the birds and insects follow their own laws, the mountain is free, the pademelons are free. Yet it is also not true; all of these parts of nature are determined in their existence and behavior by other parts of nature, as well as their own logic, and sometimes by human interference.

The mountain is mined, the stream diverted, the wind harnessed for energy. The bees are cultivated, the beetles poisoned, the pademelons and their habitat endangered by dogs, roads, and non-native plantings. As for us humans, many of us, and for much or even all of our lives, live within not just limitations on our liberty but interlocked systems of oppression including race, class, the capitalist economy; even slavery, war, and ecological devastation. Perhaps it is more true that once we have allowed wisdom to be present, we can then show up to the work of liberty. We can analyze these systems we are enmeshed with, learn our own strengths, discover ways to join with others, and pick our fights, as well as seek liberty within our minds, hearts, and bodies both individually and communally.

The words *liberty* and *freedom* may come across to some as self-righteous sloganism or philosophic rhetoric. The freedom to do whatever we like—if we have enough financial leverage or societal clout and lack of considered empathy, perhaps—screams through the airwaves, the street, and social media. And yet this is also the time of so-called social justice warriors and of *wokeness*—originally an American Black term referring to being awake to injustice and oppression and doing something about that. We are living in a time of multiple and diverse liberationist and justice movements that seek to dismantle the destructive structures and systems we live within, such as patriarchy, capitalism, and racism.

If one considers our personal freedoms or liberties in English-speaking colonized countries (Australia, the United States, Canada, etcetera) and contrasts these with the personal and social freedoms of citizens of China, Sudan, Iran, or North Korea, then we come across obvious difference, an immediately unnerving divide. The right to express oneself without being persecuted or killed by the state, the right to protest, to hard-won and fought-for rights of workers, women, and queer people differs extremely between countries. However, all of us still live in the glamourized and commandeered wreckage of imperialism and colonialism: almost every piece of actual earth has by now been deeply affected by this mass and systemic wielding of coercive power. Many, many peoples are dispossessed, while others have lives filled with possessions. And not only humans—countless species have been dispossessed of their homelands, food sources, and shelter, and under these pressures and persecutions have become statistics in the rapid extinction era we are now in.

Some say the road becomes narrower the more we know or the more dedicated we become to justice and liberation. That is, the choices in our lives have narrowed down due to our previous choices of following our ethics. This concept carries connotations of less options, perhaps images of people operating robotically in larger state-structures, even wearing prescribed clothing and undertaking work assigned by the state rather than having any veneer of personal choice. But the narrow path as I (JM) was taught is a particularly joyous experience, where the confrontation and complexity of competing choices—a sort of discordance that many of us experience, not feeling confident with our ability to make the best choices, and possibly even feeling controlled by forces outside ourselves—falls away. Instead, we realize all our previous choices have led us here, and the path ahead simplifies. The choice becomes more one of saying yes and thus continuing to show up to ourselves and for ourselves and less a choice about competing possibilities. The more we know who we are and the more practice we have in making decisions on that basis, the more our way ahead becomes clear. This is a type of liberation, but—as with most types of liberation—it usually leads to more responsibility, not less.

The work of liberation is not done alone. The road may narrow because we become aware that it is the collective, the community, the network who are responsible—and each of us within it. The road narrows because together we may need to resolve our various interests, investments, and agendas into a form that is both singular and specific, holding both complexity and intricacy. It is also salient in the work of dismantling oppressive structures and systems, within ourselves and around the world, to consider that this work is never an either/or circumstance. Liberation demands our attention and requires us all to participate, be responsible, and commit ourselves. The road narrows, bringing clarity and power.

Once we begin the work of liberty, we discover there's a great deal to be done in this point of the pentacle even on a simple or personal level, let alone when we are discussing liberty in its wider contexts. As it happened, we received the contract for this book while we were writing the notes for this essay. How liberating—to be offered to have our work published and even, at some future point, to be paid for it. Then we sit there with twenty-one pages of legalese to read through, trying to decide if this is all correct before we sign on the dotted line and suddenly—no freedom any longer! We have to deliver an 80,000 word manuscript on October 13, including ten pieces by other people whom we have undertaken to curate, invite, and edit. Oh, Liberty—what were we thinking?

I (JM) have an abiding memory of the first time we locked ourselves away for a weekend to do Pearl Pentacle work together, prior to teaching it. This happened to overlap with reading through proofs of our Iron Pentacle book—definitely unplanned timing on our part. Proofs are an excruciating and essential part of the production of a book, and how we do it is to read aloud (taking turns), critiquing and picking up on flaws. The person reading includes all punctuation, saying (for example): *Capital A as we read aloud we include all punctuation comma saying open bracket for example close bracket colon.* We were within the point of Liberty in our Pearl exploration and wrangling this Iron manuscript when Fio turned to me, as exasperated as I have ever seen them, and half shouted, *This is the least free I have ever felt!* All we could do was laugh—then and now, recalling it. Oh, Liberty. Why are you so un-free?

To truly sign up to liberty involves a deep examination of all the places we are not free, not liberated; where we are oppressed and where others are oppressed and work to change that. *Liberté* is a cry for revolution arising from the oppressed masses—in the French Revolution it was the first word of their essential three-word demand: *Liberté. Égalité. Fraternité.* That's still the motto of France, and it is written everywhere, inscribed on schools and public buildings, a foundational value on which to build. Every time there's riots in the street in France, I (JM) recall the willingness of the people of this country to front up to oppression, to take on the battle, to show by human numbers and action what their thoughts and feelings are about whatever's happening on the political stage.

Liberty is inextricably bound to equality. Working for liberation in any realm, we realize *How can I truly be free if others are not?* We may work on a very local level—with young unhoused people in the city or to remove rubbish from a creek or to create better support and outcomes for BIPOC families at the school our children attend—yet when we lift our heads up from that work for a moment, we can see how it ties into liberation movements much more broadly, both thematically and geographically. Realizing these links, we can learn to be more at ease understanding that we can't be everywhere at once; our time, energy, and resources are limited; and everything we do in this work feeds toward making a difference overall. If we are called to environmental work, Amnesty International, programs for girls' education, making soup in a local soup kitchen, protesting on the steps of Parliament House, or being active in Indigenous and First Nations movements, whatever it is, we are part of the overlapping movements for liberation, for human equality and justice, and justice and rights for the natural world. If we can't decide which is the most important or most deserving issue, we learn to start where we are. Our workplace has no recycling program. The street where we live doesn't have trees planted. I want my child or my niece or my grandchild to grow up free of gender stereotypes. It all counts.

It is nearly impossible to create significant social or political change as an individual. When we consider the layering of the Pearl and Iron Pentacles, we remember that Liberty arises from Power—both in response to power and also fueled by power. In Reclaiming we analyze power through a lens of examining power-over, power-from-within, and power-with. Power-over is the type of power we're used to associating with the word *power*—the power of institutions (police, government, dictators, media) but also, more benignly, the power a teacher has in a classroom or a facilitator in a meeting or an organizer at an event. Essentially their use of power dictates, to some extent, others' behavior and experiences. Sometimes this power is granted to them by consensus, such as choosing a facilitator; sometimes it's mandatory, and sometimes it's enforced. Power-over is not automatically or always bad. Humans have always designated roles and responsibilities within group settings, and in organizing for change we continue to do so. In Reclaiming we like to say that when power-over is temporary; assigned to a role, not a person; and with clear and agreed-upon guidelines, it can be a functional way of getting things done.

Power-from-within is the power of being alive, the power that each of us has to almost always choose how to act, react, create, love, and be an active participant with life. It might seem a very small power compared with the enormity and complexity of the multiple powers-over that we live with. However, it is always within us and can be a compass for change, inspiration, and empowerment. It also has the ability— when added together with many other power-withins (usually other humans, although eco-rights movements have expanded this concept to speak with rivers and other parts of the more-than-human world)— to become mighty and shake even the institutions, oppressions, and injustices embedded as the power-over systems. Consider the critical reexamination of the institution of the police in Minneapolis after the murder of George Floyd in 2020 by police and the riots stemming from that terrible event.

This adding together of many individual power-from-withins we name power-with. Consciously choosing to work in power-with, we can create art exhibitions, open universities, mass political protest movements, networks of support and empowerment, reforestation . . . things it would be impossible for any one of us to do on our own. And this conscious use of power can open the doorway to liberty, liberating us from helplessness, from being too small or too isolated or too quiet with just one voice—liberating ourselves and our comrades through solidarity, community, and action.

When discussing liberty we might wish to consider the following: What do we seek freedom from? What do we desire to have freedom to do/be/become? What and whom do we seek freedom with? Freedom from, freedom to, freedom with—just like power-over, power-from-within, and power-with—engender questions and considerations around empowerment and differences of power. Humans are unequally powerful, privileged, and free. This depends on many factors, including and not limited to location, class, skin color, ethnicity, language, age, gender, wealth, sexuality, body type, health, education, income, employment, and the list continues. Our experiences are more about inequalities than equality.

At times in our human histories, liberty seems to erupt and shriek through the status quo, breaking the deceptive peace and order of societies. *Liberté* as a cry for revolution in the French streets, perhaps distilled in a spontaneous moment of protest by women over the price and scarcity of bread, catalyzed a revolution. The intense and furious nature of liberty—when people have been under the heel, systematically oppressed—will always create uprisings. The world has witnessed this in the Haitian revolution for those African and Taíno peoples who were stolen and enslaved, in the Stonewall and Compton Cafeteria riots for queer and trans people in the US, in the 1978 gay and lesbian Mardi Gras protest on the streets for those communities in Australia, in the work of the suffragettes for women in many places. As much as there are uprisings that are violent, often in final response to intense and ongoing violence, there are also organized and peaceful acts of civil disobedience, frontline protest, and direct action, such as with the

Occupy movement, the First Nations Uluru Statement from the Heart, and the worldwide movement of school strikes.

We are discussing liberty sitting in the Blue Mountains Cultural Center—Darug and Gundungurra country—and also discussing my (Fio's) imminent travel to the United States and how much more scary that country seems year by year. I told a story about the time I was caught in gang gunfire in the Mission in San Francisco, which I luckily escaped. Jane Meredith then tells me that the leading cause of the death of children in the United States is guns. This is an issue that horrifies many people the world over, and yet the seemingly society sanctioned gun violence ricochets through the media and our minds. This right to bear arms—especially against a centralized and authoritarian government (or more specifically against an enemy imperialist military)—is enshrined in the US constitution. The specific and original contexts and nuances are usually forgotten in favor of engineered patriotism within a coopted argument around individual liberties.

Liberty, as an American concept today, has become quite different from other forms of this word. The French *liberté*—the Statue of Liberty herself a gift from the French government, inspired by the centenary of the American Declaration of Independence—celebrates not the individual's rights but the rights of the common people to live free of oppression by monied overlords or aristocracy. The form *liberation* is still used worldwide to declare a social movement of a united group or class of individuals against a common oppression, whether that be of law, culture, class, or all three. I (JM) prefer the liberté form of the Liberty point, especially in the US context. Liberté is the very opposite of the freedom to do whatever the hell I want (regardless of how it impacts another); instead, it calls for deep social justice, in which each must be responsible for not only themselves, but for the well-being and equality of all peoples.

There are many political thinkers, religious leaders, and theologians, scholars, and activists who challenge and provoke notions of contemporary nationalism. To be proud of your people, your culture, the land that raised you, and of your ancestors is distinct to an ideological weddedness to patriotic principles of nationhood. In Australia, the

US, and similar countries, ethnic and cultural distinctions—especially if they don't look, sound, or seem like the dominating colonizing culture—are asked or subtly commanded to assimilate or get out. What is put forward as *liberty* or *the fair go* (respectively, the values the US and Australia fetishize the most) are neither liberating nor fair.

The beliefs of many self-styled patriots dovetail with those who worship the inviolate individual, claiming a sovereignty that supersedes the common good. These movements demonstrate against trans rights, abortion, and sex education—the very opposite of the self-determination and individual rights they supposedly promote. That style of sovereignty is in stark contrast to the concepts of sovereignty spoken of by Indigenous communities and many witches and pagans. Sovereignty is certainly a term that I (Fio) have an intimate relationship with and consider to be especially important to witchcraft. In Reclaiming's Principles of Unity, we say that we are our own spiritual authorities. We like to use the terms *autonomy* and *anarchism* in our tradition as well. What might be left out is the underlying field of context we are expressing these concepts within. In *The Spiral Dance*, Starhawk has written that the Goddess tradition (as she articulates Earth-based witchcraft) has three main principles: immanence, interconnection, and community. These three principles form the field—we could say the field of liberation—in which terms such as sovereignty, authority, and autonomy begin to come alive and make sense.

In some British and Irish stories and myths, there is a central character originally seen as a hag who is revealed to be a lovely young woman. A young knight or king meets with her and is tested in the form of kissing or making love with the loathly lady or old woman. As he embraces her dreadful form, perhaps already perceiving her intrinsic power and beauty, he is revealed as the noble one worthy of that love and power. In the loathly lady story in Chaucer's writing and in later ballads there is a challenge issued from women to a knight, or King Arthur himself, to discover what women desire most of all. In meeting a loathly lady, it is discovered—either because she ultimately tells the knight outright or because he acknowledges her fully—that women most desire sovereignty.

In so-called Australia, where we both live, sovereignty is a term evoked by Indigenous peoples as well as their allies and accomplices. The phrase *sovereignty never ceded* is heard in acknowledgments of country, which happen everywhere all the time more and more, as well as being chanted at protest rallies and events. In this case sovereignty is understood to refer to both the belongingness of Indigenous people in and with country and the ancestral embeddedness, responsibility, and authority held with country. Indigenous sovereignty is political. It is assertive, saying no to empire and colonization while affirming the rightful ownership of land.

The histories and continuation of imperialist and colonialist systems of domination and control mean that for large percentages of humanity (and almost all of the nonhuman species and biosystems) there are unequal opportunities, rights, and protections. In so-called Australia, the reality of stolen land and occupied country is the foundational cause of the disproportionate social, health, economic, and ecological ills and horrors that Indigenous people face. In the so-called United States, the legacy of invasion of Native land and the stealing and enslavement of African people and their descendants continues to affect Indigenous and Black people throughout many strata of the socioeconomic reality. Further, the widespread and long rooted misogyny, marginalization, and oppression—such as the use of free labor—of those assigned female at birth and of women at large is central to how most colonial and capitalist systems continue to thrive.

Fannie Lou Hamer (1917–1977) was a Black civil rights and women's rights activist born in Mississippi. In a speech she gave in 1971 at the founding of the National Women's Political Caucus—in which she was deeply instrumental—Hamer spoke these words that have become powerful for many people: "Nobody's free until everybody's free." The work of liberation requires responsibility. It requires diligence, effort, and focus, because only together can we effectively dismantle, transform, and create systems of power that work for all of us, and also because these systems, processes, and structures always require finessing, checks, critique, feedback, and reflection. The work of liberty is the excavation and application of power. Again we are talking about the work of many, perhaps over many generations. Liberation is not an individual work; it is collective.

Currently as a society we are becoming more deeply aware of the marginalization and persecution of non-binary and gender diverse people of all backgrounds, as well as people who experience neuro-divergency and disabling, those whose sexualities or lack thereof dif-fer from the model of man-with-woman and heteronormative mar-riage. Other systemic discriminations impact the ways Traveler and Rom peoples live with the land, those who speak a language other than English, or are disabled, or are at either end of the age spectrum. Essentially many structures and systems are designed to benefit the able bodied, those classed as neurotypical, and generally those assigned male at birth, who continue to present as male in the world.

In 1989 Kimberlé Crenshaw, a Black feminist, utilized the term *inter-sectionality* to bring awareness to the places in which Blackness and womanness collide and experience one another. This term has since drawn focus to the places of intersecting identities and experiences that potentially increase disadvantage, marginalization, and persecu-tion, so that we more specifically advocate for needs and rights. The experience of a white middle-class cis woman with no children living in Australia is quite different from the experience of a regional Aborig-inal woman with two children or an Asian trans woman living in a city doing survival sex work. The intersections of oppression and the experience of marginalization—the material impacts of living in what bell hooks (1952–2021) named *imperialist, white supremacist, capitalist patriarchy*—are important to engage with and learn from.

There are entangled histories of oppression including the witch hunts of the past and the present, the murder of Jewish people hun-dreds of years ago up until now, the genocide of First Nations peoples, the genocide occurring in Palestine as we edit this book in late 2024, the invasions by Rome and many other empires since, the subjugation of women everywhere and anywhere, the persecution of people we now call queer and trans . . . In the face of this, it may seem hopeless-ness and despair would become inevitable, and these are legitimate emotions, but analyzing and knowing about systems of domination and oppression can empower us. When we bring our attention to the realities of unequal power distribution and the histories and value systems that make this so, we reclaim some of our own power. If we work with the power, if we begin to join together with others in solidarity and advocate on behalf of one another, then we can become very powerful.

Entire civil rights movements that have helped to change the face of many modern societies are testament to this. We can draw inspiration from these activist mighty dead of liberation, including from bell hooks, who died only in recent years. We can draw strength and inspiration from Martin Luther King Jr., Maya Angelou, Marsha P. Johnson, Harvey Milk, Yunupingu, Eddie Mabo, Emily Davison, and the many, many liberation activists, storytellers, and frontline extraordinary folks who have helped fight for the rights that we might have today. So we tell one another stories about Robin Hood, Mary Magdalene, Christ, Tara, and Kwan Yin; the bodhisattvas who vow to return again and again until all achieve liberation. And for many modern witches, the legends of Aradia are a source of inspiration and insight into the work of liberation.

A catalytic and foundational text for the modern revivalist witchcraft movement is *Aradia, or The Gospel of the Witches*. This book was published in 1899 and authored and collected by an American folklorist Charles Godfrey Leland (1824–1903). In *Aradia* are several creation stories concerning Diana, who is Darkness, and Lucifer, who is Light, and their daughter Aradia, who is mortal. Diana says to her, *You will be the first of witches known.* Aradia comes to Earth to teach the poor, the peasants, and the oppressed the arts of sorcery and witchery, including how to bind the lords in their towers with power, how to ruin their crops, and all manner of magics that also include healing, charming, beauty, and blessing. These are traditional witch magics, and as the saying goes, *the witch who cannot hex cannot heal.* And I (Fio) can testify that these are the magics that people still come to witches for.

Aradia's name is chanted by thousands upon thousands of witches today. We invoke her to teach us the arts of liberation, to empower our magic and our rituals so that we are allied with justice, to assist those experiencing subjugation. Many women both cis and trans, non-binary people, disabled folks, and queer people find homes in witchcraft because traditionally witches emphasize and work for liberation. Aradia is a spirit who is known to have existed for centuries, but she is certainly a very modern goddess as well—a goddess of witches today working for justice.

Reclaiming as a tradition of witchcraft is distinguished from many other magical communities and practices by the fact that it is overtly liberationist and outspokenly political. Our anarchist, political, feminist roots are in protest on the streets, civil disobedience at nuclear power plants, women's class and consciousness-raising groups, and organizing to protect forests and rivers. More recently Reclaiming has had a presence within the Occupy movement, and Reclaimers are active within the Red Rebels, Black Lives Matter, Extinction Rebellion, and other protest and liberation movements. Reclaiming is dedicated to this work of justice as an expression of our magic and commitment to the immanent life force.

There are ways to participate in solidarity and allyship that fundamentally trust those experiencing the impacts of oppressive systems. We know that largely the global systems of governance and economy endorse violence, oppression, and ecocide; we know this affects all of us. Our friend Urania, a skilled Reclaiming priestess and witch, says that not one person can be left behind. No one, not even the bullies and abusers. Bullying and abuse are not tolerated, but if we are truly working toward collective liberation—liberty for all—we must bring all along with us, with many dynamic threads weaving together. This is not an endorsement to agree with conservative agendas, but it is a deeper holding of the inherent interconnectedness of us all. Perhaps it is also a radical hope that as more people remember and center the sacred immanence and the dance of the life force, they are inspired to transform, behave, and think differently.

What would a world, a society, a nation look like if everyone agreed that Love, Law, Wisdom, Liberty, and Knowledge for example, were the values? That we each could interpret, discuss, debate, and experience them personally, distinctly, but we agreed that these are what we share? Ultimately there will never be dynamic peace and trust in our world until we can see that there might be some common realities for our lives as part of this planet.

In the last twelve months Fio's sister has given birth to two children and Jane Meredith's son and extra-daughter have had a baby. These children have been born in Sydney, Australia. We consider their liberties, both those they inherit simply by being born into this time and place and those they will enjoy as they grow up. We do not know how to compare their privileged situations with that of a child born in the Northern Territory in the same year or in a Syrian refugee camp or an African witch camp (enclaves for those accused of sorcery) or on the streets of Rio de Janeiro or in a thousand other places upon this earth. It is not just poverty our niblings and grandchild have avoided, but that their freedoms—compared to a child born in Hong Kong, in Russia, in Palestine—seem immense. That is even while laws against protesters—more severe than any in living memory—are imposed in this country, by left wing as well as right wing governments. Still we have freedom of speech, the right to rally and protest, the right to stand for election, and the obligation to vote.

We can only hope that these babies grow up understanding the need for solidarity between oppressed and marginalized peoples and the necessity for allies and liberationists within all communities. That they are able to find ways to work as fierce and caring accomplices with others and with each other, not losing their beautiful diversity and difference but appreciating and respecting one another in their fullnesses. Our commitment to them is to continue our work for liberty, for liberté, and for liberation, knowing that always and everywhere no one is free until everyone is free.

We have discovered that the points of the Pearl Pentacle in our journey thus far in this book—Love, Law, Wisdom—are already there, rippling through existence as the deep and core realities. Liberty may be something that we have to reach toward, to action in our lives and with one another. A beloved teacher and Reclaiming elder Rose May Dance (1948–2021) once passed on a teaching from Victor Anderson: that when all the other points of the pentacle are balanced or in harmony, then the Power point lights up. She was speaking then about the Iron Pentacle, but in retrospect—and knowing her—she also meant the same for the Pearl Pentacle counterpart of Liberty. For the Iron Power to become Pearl Liberty, we must love one another so fiercely—as is the law—that we remember the wisdom we already have and delight in the wisdom shared by others . . . maybe then, together, we will be free.

WHAT BINDS YOU

All of us are bound, even if only into the process of living and dying. Most of us have a whole heap of other bindings as well: job contracts, ringing our mother once a week, watering the garden, returning our library books on time, and paying taxes. We may also have more joyful obligations such as to a community, tradition, practice, or beloveds. At this Pearl point of Liberty, we are invited to examine our personal lives closely to find out what binds us and what sets us free.

Boundaries and what binds us appear to be the opposite of liberty. We often perceive boundaries and bindings as placed on us by external forces—the state, our job, family, relationship, or social conventions. But some bindings and boundaries are our own—commitments we've made that ring deeply true to us, boundaries protecting ourselves or our beloveds, bindings to a spiritual tradition, relationship, or way of being. When we examine what these bindings actually are, assessing or reassessing them and recognizing their impact on us, we get an opportunity to free ourselves from outdated, inappropriate, or exploitative bindings, while still showing up to those commitments, agreements, or obligations that have meaning and worth to us.

This process is in two parts: What Binds You, directly below, and a Ritual of Unbinding (page 175). Part 1 is a journaling exercise in preparation for part 2, which is a dynamic ritual. It is recommended to leave a space of time between parts 1 and 2; for example, a week. This way we get a chance, having articulated the bonds, to sit with them and feel into them before choosing what and how we will release.

> » You will need: journal and pen; a quiet,
>   undisturbed space
> » Time: 40 minutes

Listing the Bindings

Begin with the outermost levels of what binds you: the laws of the universe and those of local time and space. Acknowledge the impact these have upon you, how you are entirely held within them, and start your list of bindings with a recognition of this.

Move a step closer to you: the laws of your country that bind you. You can either list specific laws you feel bound by or find a general statement that summarizes how you are bound by these laws.

You might want to consider how you are bound by the demographics you are categorized by, including age, race, class, gender, sexual orientation, ethnicity, able-bodiness, education, and income.

Reflect on how you are bound by your current organizations and activities; for example, your job, community, volunteer work, leisure activities. You may coach a sports team, have signed a contract for your work, be halfway through a degree, be managing a family and household, or be the treasurer for a community organization.

What else binds you within the world? For example, a financial loan, a lease, contracts with clients, customers, or suppliers.

What immediate relationships bind you? These might be joyfully held bonds that are not perceived as restricting in any way—most of us have agreements, spoken or unspoken, with lovers, partners, children, parents, friends, and pets.

You may also have chosen bonds with one or more spiritual traditions, deities, covens, or other groups. You may have practices you are committed to do each day, week, month, or year.

Consider what binds you internally, including:

» family patterns and traits you enact

» limitations you place on yourself

» expectations you place on yourself

» values and ethics

» fears

» habits

» anything else you can think of

This will be a long list. As we often like to pretend we are quite free, it may be daunting, confronting, or even seem absurd to you. Not all bonds are imposed on us; as we can see from our lists, many we have chosen ourselves and even delight in the richness, joy, meaning, and love they bring into our lives.

Over the next few days, lean into your awareness of these bonds and bindings. You might like to discuss them with a friend, partner, or someone else.

When you are ready, begin to prepare for the Ritual of Unbinding, which is part 2 of this process.

RITUAL OF UNBINDING

Once we have understood all the bonds we are held by, we understand that a binding, freely undertaken, can in itself be a liberating thing. You may have made a fierce commitment to follow your creativity, and yes, you're bound by it willingly and understand this commitment frees you up to focus on what matters most to you. Other bonds may not be so welcome, so freely entered into, or even up-to-date. Perhaps we have been bound by family traditions since we were small children, stuck in a situation, group, or friendship that's really not serving us, or be held by an out-of-date relationship agreement.

Where bonds, commitments, and agreements involve other humans, ideally we check in with those people (or at least notify them) before changing the status quo. Sometimes this isn't possible or feasible—the person is dead or I'm not in touch with the person or the person is dangerous to me—in which case I can still acknowledge them either before I begin the ritual or as I release the bond and claim my liberty, offering them the same in return.

Like any ritual, we can have one plan inside our head or on paper and then find the ritual goes its own way. We can end up cutting ties we weren't initially planning to, but it felt so right at the time we had to do it, or retaining other bonds we thought we were ready to let go of. It's always okay to take a few calming breaths and remember or reinstate our groundedness before allowing the flow of the ritual to continue. You might even stop midway and do some journaling if you are discovering deeper layers of bindings and are not sure what to do about them. This might be a ritual we do more than once as different layers of bindings reveal themselves or we become ready to let go.

This is part 2 of a process, the follow-on from the previous process, What Binds You, working with that material we discerned specific to ourselves. If you have not done part 1, it is recommended to do that first.

» You will need: A safe and private space to do the ritual. An altar for Liberty. Journal and pen, including the notes you wrote for the previous process, What Binds You. Cords, ribbons, or threads to symbolize the bindings. Scissors or a sharp ritual knife/athame. An empty bowl. Optional: drum, rattle, dance music, a chant about unbinding or the Pearl Pentacle.

» Time: 60–90 minutes

Set up your altar for Liberty. For example, on the altar might be a pearl necklace, some books that have helped you on your path to liberty, your cords/ribbons/threads and scissors/knife and bowl to use in this ritual, a photograph of yourself showing how freedom or liberty looks and feels to you, and any symbol of liberty you wish to include. You may also include candles, incense, flowers, oils, or any other altar item.

Be clear on your intention before you begin the ritual. This could be as simple as: *To release myself from what binds me against my will* or be more specific: *To release myself from all past relationships and outdated commitments.*

Begin with a land acknowledgment and grounding. You might also wish to cast a circle.

Invoke the Pearl Pentacle and the point of Liberty in particular. You might like to run the Pearl current within yourself and open to the point of Liberty.

Speak your intention aloud. Some people like to do this three times.

Read through everything you wrote during part 1, What Binds You. You might like to circle or underline the pieces you will be directly working with in this ritual.

Take up your cord, ribbon, or thread. For each binding that you are going to be releasing, either tie the thread around yourself somewhere (ankles and wrists are easy, but you might choose waist, breasts, or hips) or else place a circle of the cord around you, on the ground. I have done this ritual both ways. You can either choose to release yourself from one binding at a time or do several at once.

Feel deeply into each binding, exactly how and where it holds you, both metaphorically but also in real life.

Now imagine the Pearl energy of Love building up and leading to Law, gathering together and finding Wisdom, and then, like a river fed from many sources, all coming together into Liberty. You might feel this coursing through your body or moving like winds through your life or see a Pearl Pentacle shining as point by point lights up.

When you are ready, pick up your scissors, knife, or athame and cut the binding. It might be enough to just cut open the thread so it falls away and you are released, or you might wish to cut it into tiny pieces. Bundle up the pieces and place them in the bowl on the altar. Later you can burn, bury, or otherwise dispose of them.

Breathe into your liberty. Dance, drum, sing, or just let yourself expand into the spaciousness of liberty. Take at least ten minutes to really feel this.

You might wish to journal, to record the ritual and also note how you are feeling now about having released yourself from those particular bonds.

To complete the ritual, run the Pearl Pentacle again, feeling especially into Liberty. If you cast a circle, release it, and be sure to extinguish any candles you lit.

Leave the altar up for a few days or weeks if you wish, letting it remind you each time you see it of your new liberties. Find an appropriate way to dispose of the symbols of your bonds; you might even leave them on the altar as a reminder.

AM I FREE?

SUSANNERAE

From the pile of dust on the floor I pull a small rectangle of cardboard deco-rated with purple. I shake the dust from it and turn it over in my hand. The words beautifully handwritten in black pen speak to me: You are free! *This had been plucked from a tray during a Reclaiming Pearl Pentacle Liberty rit-ual years ago. I laugh and sigh all at once and rub the cardboard rectangle along my thigh. I finger the edge of the card.* Am I free? Could I be? What is freedom anyway? *I tap the card against the wall and look around for some-where to put it. A room full of half-sorted boxes yawns up at me. Things to go, things to keep, and things to give away or return. Piles of dust. I have been in this house for fourteen years, and now I am leaving. I never thought I would. A cat winds its way around my legs, looking for a place to sit amongst the upheaval.*

I push the card into the back pocket of my jeans and squat down to collect the dust. Dust that had escaped years of sweeping and vacuuming. The dust that reveals itself when the last piece of furniture is pulled from the wall, the debris of years. You are free, dust! You are free! *I chuckle.*

I take the ill-matched dustpan and brush and sweep up the detritus of a life. We had built this extension on the back of the house, tucked away at the end of the garden, hidden beneath wisteria, through summers of heat and flood. A place to retreat to, a place to work, away from the hurly-burly of a blended household of teenagers and friends. I used it to write my PhD thesis, to plan, to sit in meditation.

Freedom: it breathes in and it breathes out. Across time and space freedom comes and goes. It opens up and then it closes in. The con-straints of my life have taught me that. And all the time I seek it, desire it, to realize the sovereignty of my heart.

As a child I didn't feel free. So many rules and regulations for ways to be and dress and talk. So much to learn about, the ways to interact with this one and that. When to be quiet and when to be loud. At school I felt contained and restrained. At times my mind would gallop away with what we learned. But there were the bells, uniforms, assign-ments, and exams. I was gaining an education. The careers advisor said I could do anything I wanted. Was that freedom?

If I sat on the back veranda and looked into the dark night skies, the spaces between the stars, I felt free. Or when I walked with the chickens or wandered with my dog along the creeks . . . I would be free to expand, to be someone else, to explore. But even then there were limits, amorphous strange beings that challenged and danced on the edge of my mind, luring, teaching, and taunting me all at once.

I pick up the pan and take it to the bin. The dust flies through the air and catches the sunlight as the heavier pieces tinkle into the garbage bin. Go well, *I shout. Bits of my skin, cat hair, spider webs, and shoe dirt catch in the breeze. For a moment I watch the light dance in the dust looking for rainbows.* Be free! *I pull out the card and turn it around in my hands.*

She held the tray out to me. There was movement all around and people laughing, chanting, singing. I was in that state between the worlds, in ritual with beloveds from across the lands gathered for a weekend of Pearl Pentacle magic. My hand extended and chose a purple and patterned card from the silver tray. The tray whirled away to be offered to another. *You are free!* said the card. I laughed out loud and felt relief, elated, light, and then the question: *Was I?* It is that same card that had returned this day, somehow moving from where it was on the altar in the other room to that pile of dust.

I'm moving house. My parents have died. The world is locked down. My relationship of fifteen years has been over for five years. It's time to move on. With the sale of the house I am able to purchase a four-wheel drive car that can take me wherever I want to go. I am able to move 1,000 kilometers away and buy a fully furnished house in the desert mining town of Broken Hill on Wilyakali country. Now it is time for me to be free and I am ready.

I have been able to transition my business fully online. This is something the pandemic gave us—freeing us from the brick and mortar of offices and cities, providing us opportunities to explore the online space. Liberation from the constraints of hours of commutes and drudgery in an office to freely choose the pajama-bottomed life of working from home. A new freedom, they said.

I thought I could be free to be me if I moved to the place that makes my heart sing. The land where my heart had lived since I was ten years old, of huge horizons and wide plains. These are the lands of the Wilyakali and Barkandji peoples and the great Darling-Baaka River in far western so-called New South Wales. I wondered if being free is letting the heart sing its sovereign song?

Strings of memories rolled through my mind, bobbles and jewels clustered together. Glimpses and flickering recollections of my sovereign self. Standing naked on top of a hill in Maputo in eastern Zimbabwe on the day I didn't see zebras. Driving through the lands of England, Wales, and Scotland, walking a labyrinth a day. Sitting in deep meditation on day six of a ten-day retreat, the limits of me dissolved. The futility of trying, gone. Walking the wilds of the west coast of Islay, battered by Atlantic waves and wind. Standing on the edge of the Mundi Mundi plains—my vision stretching out toward the western horizon, searching for the faint smear where the Flinders Ranges lie.

Breathe in and out.

Maybe freedom is being alone, without human interaction? Yet freedom is there because of others.

A cat moves between the packing boxes as if leading a ceremonial procession. It finds itself a position on the windowsill to peruse the progress and begins cleaning itself. I return to packing.

It wasn't the first time in my life I had gone west to express myself and find my freedom. In 1978, having dropped out of tertiary studies twice, I got on a train in Sydney with a new short haircut and a half-opened butterfly tattooed on my left shoulder. The mark of the devil. After all, I was a witch, wasn't I?

I had been living with friends in Double Bay, a suburb of Sydney, where I had a room off the kitchen. Yoga and meditation were my interests. A wild '70s camp scene of drag queens, sex workers, actors, and politicians cavorted through the living room. I was going to Adelaide to be a lesbian. To ignite the part of myself that I felt couldn't be explored in Sydney near my family and old friends who had a particular view of me. Adelaide had liberal laws. I wanted to join the Women's Liberation Movement. Free to be me!

It's a privilege. I am a white, educated, woman-bodied being. My ancestors worked in the mines and the mills of Wales and England and the fields of west coast Scotland. Hard working manual laborers stitching, sewing, digging, building, and forging iron. As laborers they suffered the impact of economic decisions made by the land owners and bosses: the land clearances, wars, and economic depressions. They migrated to Australia in search of a better and freer life. They inadvertently supported the colonization and the mining industry of this country: cutting down trees to make farms, exploiting the ground and opportunity. They sought freedom. I have benefited from that. I doubt they understood the cost of their own freedom in settling here. Does that make me free?

My freedom, my privilege, has come at the cost of others losing their freedom, their land, and their liberty. The First Nations people of so-called Australia, by percentage, are the most incarcerated group of humans on this planet. I was born into this stolen land from settler ancestry. As a descendant of early colonizers, my presence here denies the First People of their land and their liberty, despite my best efforts and whether I like it or not.

Nobody's free until everybody's free. The words of Fannie Lou Hamer and Martin Luther King Jr. filter through to me.

I had moved to Adelaide to become a lesbian, to explore my sexuality, and to get involved in the Women's Liberation Movement. Initially I stayed with friends and then moved into a household of women. I soon become engaged with lesbian separatism. We thought at the time that was where our true liberation lay. It's not that I disliked men; it was more that I found women exciting. I had a voice and felt mostly understood in the company of women. Times were exciting and tumultuous. We were going to change the world. We were loud, brash, and uncompromising. We cared and ideas flourished. Conversation was analytical, at times academic, critical, and unforgiving.

We walked and painted the streets, demanding freedom for women to choose what happened to their bodies. For lesbians to have the right to express their love. We fought for abortion on demand, free childcare, affordable housing, and against uranium mining. I learned a lot about myself: my passions, my strengths, confronted my fears, and learned to stand tall before a world that hated what I stood for.

I pull a pile of exercise books off the shelf. My life, my journey through time, contained within pages and words, photos and cards. Stacking them into a box, I choose a green-covered volume. Sliding down the wall, I land amongst boxes and dust to read.

The light from the afternoon sun streamed through the arched stained glass window, sending its colored shards down the corridor. My home was shared with the regular visits of my daughter and friends. A house filled with nature spirits and the wisdom of the Ice Lady—a beautiful, slender, high-collar-wearing witch from the seventeenth century—my guardian and helper. In that house I was myself totally. I lived with two cats, made art, worked at the hospital, grew flowers and vegetables in the backyard, and ate no meat. The only men in my life were the patients at the hospital where I worked and within my family of origin, my father and brothers.

I moved to this house in King Street to be by myself after years of living in shared households. Since I had left home I had shared accommodation with over one hundred and fifty different people and their assorted friends and lovers. I think I deserved some time on my own. So was I free?

I thought I was free outside of mainstream society, yet my freedom was claimed within the constraints of the patriarchal, capitalist society that marked the boundaries of my existence, both in physical and my internal worlds. Much later in my life, when I chose to live with a white man, I experienced the freedom of heterosexuality. In conversation, in society, in relationship to the world, I had the ability and option to move freely and not have to justify myself. It was easier, yet was it freedom? Whole parts of me had to be cut away, suppressed, hidden, ignored, and silenced. But still I was willing to choose this path, and so I danced with the patriarchy.

It was in an anarcho-feminist group that I found my political will. Always reluctant to follow regulations without question, feeling constrained by communist ideologies, the grassroots nature of anarcho-syndicalism appealed to me: freedom from wage slavery, liberation of all worker and private ownership, social responsibility. There was a cost to freedom, and that was responsibility.

I traveled the world. I saw and felt the impact of apartheid, the legalized system of racialized segregation, in South Africa. I protested for the right of Indigenous Africans to have freedom of expression and association in their own country. Everything that I knew and understood about the world was challenged in that journey. I began to understand my white privilege, and it was not comfortable. Over time I began to understand that it was impossible to liberate only one section of the population without all others, that everyone's liberty and freedom are interconnected. I moved away from a separatist stance and found a deeper inner freedom in understanding how everything is connected. I came to understand Kimberlé Crenshaw's explanations of intersectionality, though I didn't call it that then.

Back in colonized Australia, I was a marshal during the 1988 March on Sydney to protest the invasion of the continent two hundred years prior. We were protesting for the rights of First Nations people to their stolen lands and cultures. I began to learn the Indigenous names of the places in which I lived and worked. I was beginning to acknowledge the relentless war against First Nations people on these lands and work for peace. So how can I be free?

In the corner of the room is a sad pile of cloth, fast fashion they call it now. No longer fitting garments of various descriptions and sizes. Limp expressions of previous joys on their way to the op shop. I grab a plastic bag and start stuffing them in. What should I do with that pile? Will it all end up on the streets of Lusaka, Zambia? My mind swims with images from the bus trip into Lusaka through the markets. The roadside littered with plastic bags embedded in the soil and plastic bottles squashed flat creating a scaled covering for the road. Piles and piles of recycled clothing on either side of the road. My freedom to purchase cheap serviceable garments is connected to enslaved labor somewhere in the world. Someone clothes me with their sweat. And somewhere these western-style rubbish clothes are offered to others.

After twelve months of traveling in Asia and Africa in 1987, I found myself in a supermarket in Edinburgh, Scotland. I was newly arrived from Zimbabwe where there had been one type of peanut butter, one type of sugar, one type of flour. All I wanted was tea, sugar, and bread, but I had lost the power of choice. In the Edinburgh supermarket there was a whole aisle of sugar! Brown, cubed, coffee, white, granulated, castor, all differently packaged by their brands. The freedom to choose! I was overwhelmed and left without any of what I needed. *We are offered such variety as an illusion of freedom,* I thought. *There is actually no choice. It is just sugar after all. Is freedom choice?*

The coffee cup is warm in my hands as I find a place in the sun away from the breeze. Taking a break from packing, I punch the code into my phone. With a mobile phone I am able to move about and be called at any time of the day or night. It's so freeing. I start scrolling, checking notifications and exploring what my people are up to. In my newsfeed there is a plethora of smiling white well-groomed humans that the algorithms have sent me. They are luring me to find my true worth, inner wisdom, and personal freedom. I scroll through them. I know what they are getting at. I once gave someone a lot of money to help me find my authentic self. They still smile back at me from Facebook as they travel the world expressing themselves. Good luck, I smile! *You can be whoever you want, and it's easier if you have an income, if you have access to privilege.*

If I don't have the money for food and rent and travel, can I be free? And then I think of the mystic, the wandering sage, those who choose to live outside of society. Are they free?

Buddhism has taught me much about freedom and provided insights for ways to attain my own liberation. Sitting for a time each day, following the breath in meditation, just being, has definitely brought me an inner sense of freedom. Meditation has brought me a deep inner knowing and freedom from the constraints of others' expectations. This practice has helped me see how to be, how to be with it all and be who I am. And yet it is still hard to be myself. From the kitchen sink to the bedroom, the fingers of patriarchal capitalism creep and pry.

I have been in the desert for nearly three years. I was able to purchase a humble home where I can live and play. I acknowledge my privilege in this and attempt to take responsibility for what this freedom affords me. I'm learning about the weather, the land, and the people. I feel free to be me. On Wilyakali country with its magnificent sunsets I live close to the intensity of colonial impact. Racism, mining, land degradation, water theft; it's in my face and sometimes overwhelming. The land has been denuded of its trees to support the mines. The river has been emptied of its water to feed the cotton and wine farms.

Freedom and liberty are not just about people. Trees and wild spaces, rivers and creatures should be free from interference by humans who would seek to control and manage them. They are sovereign beings in their own right. We cherish and desire the wild. The land is not a commodity to be consumed; without it we would not survive. The wild places, beings, trees, and beasts have a right to be free. Liberty and freedom exist when there is knowledge and wisdom, when there is right relationship to the law, and when there is love of self and planet.

I wish to be free to fly in my own mind and journey. To not be shackled by the rules of others. I know I am free from deep within my sovereignty. Many times in my life I have forgotten myself. Now I have a glimmer of who I am. I like to dance. To breathe into my full self. To show myself to the world. I have discovered new words to describe my non-binary self.

Breathe in. Breathe out.

I look for the card. In my mind's eye it was purple on one side and held the words *You are free!* on the other. Where did I put it when I unpacked my boxes into this desert house? This home on top of a hill, protected by a massive peppercorn tree and the Greenman. I am amused at this search for freedom. At the back of my altar, underneath a crystal of quartz, I find it. Picking it up, I hold it in my hand. It has changed. On the purple side the word *Liberty* is beautifully scribed in silver ink. I don't remember that . . . and then I do. The small card sits snuggly in my hand, lying across my palm, from heel to the base of my fingers. *You are free!*

I clasp the card to my heart.

ALLIES AND WITNESSES

In the work of mutual liberation, we need allies and witnesses. There's honestly no other way. Mutual aid and investment in one another and our webs of relationship—human held by the more-than-human—is not just desired; it is required! How do we come into a vital and collaborative synergy or partnership so that we can challenge and invite one another, but perhaps more importantly create a fabric of love and liberation ethos that can hold all that work?

In Reclaiming we sometimes conduct ally circles. These are emotionally immersive and sometimes intense spaces in which the group holds a circle with our bodies and breath. We often create ritual space together, and then one by one someone moves into the center (or speaks to the center if unable to move there), makes a statement and sometimes a gesture, and those who resonate with what is offered move to the center of the circle. The others hold silent solidarity at the edge. These are amazingly healing and enriching spaces, and the concept can be thrown out wider. In this process we will do just that.

This process is multi-leveled and ongoing. I (Fio) am going to borrow from a Wildwood training three-concentric-circle model in order to illustrate and anchor this magical work.

I want to pause for a moment here and speak to the fact that when my friend Kate and I had the opportunity to sit and listen with a Munanjali elder in October, 2016, in Yuggera, Jagera, and Turrbal country, she revealed to us that she used a three-concentric-circle map to teach about her Indigenous ethos. Kate and I, both Wildwood priestesses, were listening in awe as she used two of the same words and the model/map was exactly the same. We were gobsmacked.

> » You will need: a journal and pen; a quiet space at
> home or in a park
> » Time: 30 minutes for part 1; up to an hour for part
> 2; the rest of your life for part 3. Part 1 and part 2 are
> ideally spaced apart by a week.

Part 1

Begin by situating yourself in a quiet space with a journal and pen. On a clean page draw three concentric circles. Mark the innermost one SELF, the circle wrapped around that COMMUNITY, and mark the outermost circle COSMOS.

Ground and center yourself. Breathe deeply and pay attention especially to the spaces between the inhalation and the exhalation.

Guide your pen and your attention to the circle marked SELF. Consider how you are an ally and witness to yourself. Inside this central circle, draw symbols and icons to intuitively express how you turn up for yourself. This may go for a few minutes.

Repeat this with the circle marked COMMUNITY. Reflect on how you are an ally and witness in your community or communities. Intuitively draw symbols and icons in this circle.

And then repeat this process with the outermost circle marked COSMOS. How are you an ally and witness to your experience of the great unfolding cosmos? This will be the vaster, wider realities, including the bioregion, the lands connected, the seas, the rivers, the clouds, the biosphere, up into the solar system, the gods and spirits, etcetera.

Conclude with reflection and journaling to wrap up.

Part 2

This might be a week later.

Part 2 is invitational and works best with other willing humans involved in the process. If there is a group, each person needs to have completed part 1 on their own. However, if you need or want to do part 2 alone, take the piece of paper you drew the three circles on and place it in the center of your quiet and private space.

Acknowledge country, ground, center, align your souls, do whatever you need or want to do to affirm the sacred, and consciously immerse within.

Imagine that you are within the circle of SELF and that the circle of COMMUNITY wraps around you and the circle of COSMOS wraps around that circle.

If there are other humans with you, do this all together with your eyes open and gazing at one another, feeling silently through the space to begin. You will need to be fairly spread out, and eventually you will all begin to move around the space as each person holds their own awareness of their own three circles.

Notice how these circles overlap and relate to one another. You are invited to pause as you meet each other—in partners—and speak to how you can be an ally and witness in one another's lives. You could ask questions, offer, negotiate, and come to agreements in the name of Liberty.

If alone, you might imagine people in your community—or more-than-humans in your communities—and what you might offer. Try offering this aloud verbally and open to perceive what an energetic or magical response might be from the god souls of these humans or the consciousness of these spirits and life systems.

When you are complete, journal your reflections and findings.

Part 3
Continue to do this work.

It is a good idea to check in on agreements you have made on how you turn up as an ally and witness in your own life and in the lives of others. If you have made specific accountability check-in dates, keep to them as best you can. Practice calling one another in, asking questions of discernment and clarity, and working together truthfully and responsibly. This is the work of a lifetime and lifetimes.

LIBERATION PLEDGE WITH BRIGID

When we wrote *Magic of the Iron Pentacle*—which is a marvelous companion to this book—we included a ritual for the making of a vow to Passion. In this book we are invited into the making of a Liberation pledge!

Since 1982 Reclaiming witches have been gathering in stolen Ramaytush-Ohlone lands—colonially known as San Francisco—and marking the witches' feast of Imbolc or Brigid with a specific pledge-making and sealing ritual. Witches and pagans gather together, and there is often a priestex or maybe three aspecting the Irish goddess Brigid. She is often reported to be a welcoming deity to any and all who desire to do healing and justice work in the world. She is beloved by many in Reclaiming.

Brigid is a goddess who many believe has survived under the guise of the beloved and popular Irish Catholic Saint Brigid. The tenth-century *Cormac's Glossary* speaks of the goddess Brigid as being three sisters who are respectively deities of poetry, smithcraft, and healing. It is in the spirit and inspiration of the goddess Brigid and the early Reclaiming San Francisco Brigid ritual that I (Fio) dedicate this writing. The usual amount of time for these pledges is a year and a day.

» You will need: A small fire in a fireproof cauldron or container, you can make this outside with firewood and kindling, old newspaper, and a little bit of methylated spirits or rubbing alcohol. If you go ahead with this kind of fire, please have a fire extinguisher or a bucket of water in the ritual space as well. If not a fire, then a large candle in a fireproof container. Biodegradable offerings for Brigid. A journal and pen to record your pledge if you desire.

» Time: an hour

Before anything else, make sure you have the fire (or the candle) and all the fire accouterments ready to be lit in the ritual.

Begin the ritual by acknowledging country, grounding and centering, and aligning your three souls. For this ritual casting a circle will be very useful. Honor the elements of life.

When you feel ready, invoke the goddess Brigid (and perhaps others). You may desire to use the following words or you might spontaneously hum, sing, tone, or invoke her with your own words.

Great Goddess Brigid,
I ask you to come join me in this circle!
She of Poetry
She of the Forge
She of the Well of Healing
I call you, Great One—Exalted Mystery!
I call for you to witness me as you have witnessed so many
Throughout all lands and all worlds.
Great Brigid, I ask for you to witness my
liberation pledge between the worlds.

When you can sense or imagine Brigid's presence in your ritual space, you may begin counting your breath to enter a trance state.

A common way of doing this is to inhale to the count of four, hold for four, exhale for four, hold for four. We call this the square breath as it has four parts, or sides. I (Fio) like to imagine and feel into a wheel of starlight moving through me. As I inhale it swoops down through my head, and as I hold the in-breath it moves down through the whole of me. When I exhale it moves out of me, and then as I hold it, it moves up in front of me, ready to come down through my head at my next inhalation. By counting your breath and surrendering into that rhythm, you can guide yourself into a juicy trance state.

Once you are in trance, begin to actively journey in that state, meditating into what pledge you will take for the coming year and a day (the traditional amount of time for this pledge) in the name of Liberation. This pledge will also be made between the worlds and witnessed and held by Brigid. Be very mindful; Brigid remembers these pledges.

At California WitchCamp 2023, Brigid Camp, three priestexes in aspect voiced, *Every year we hear you make your pledges, and we are holding you to them. We remember.*

When you have the wording of your pledge, bring yourself up and out of trance and back into the circle here and now.

At this point you might want to run the Iron and the Pearl Pentacle currents (see page 271).

Move to the container/cauldron and light the fire, asking Brigid to bless the flames. When you are ready, voice or express—perhaps in gesture or dance—your pledge over the fire, witnessed by the goddess Brigid. Imagine that you can hear three hammer strikes (you might hear them anyway) of the anvil sealing the pledge as this is how we generally do this ritual in Reclaiming.

Pour out or lay down your offerings for Brigid and thank her. Honor and praise the elements of life. Farewell any other spirits and mysterious ones you invoked. Release the circle. Ground and go do something relaxing or fun. You might also want to record the pledge in your journal.

ENVISIONING GENDER LIBERATION

ALEX IANTAFFI

In this essay I share some of my own experiences over the past two decades within Reclaiming community and reflections about possible visions for gender liberation. Please note—and yes, this is your content note—**that there are mentions of intimate partner and domestic violence, childhood sexual abuse, sexual assault, cisgenderism and transphobia within this essay.** Take care of yourself as needed while you read this. If taking care of yourself means skipping this essay, that is okay too. However, if you are a cisgender person—that is, someone whose current gender identity aligns with your gender assigned at birth—I would like to offer an invitation to reflect on why you might choose to skip this essay. It can be uncomfortable to read about areas where we felt we didn't have privilege before and realize that maybe there is a degree of privilege in moving through this world within a cisgender bodymind, for example.

As we're talking about privilege, let me also position myself. I am a conditionally white, immigrant, Italian, trans masculine, non-binary, bisexual, queer, polyamorous, kinky, disabled, neurodivergent witch. I am a Reclaiming, Feri, and Queer Spirit initiate, and I have taught both within my home communities and at WitchCamps. I am also a gender scholar who has written extensively for both academic and general audiences about this topic and a systemic psychotherapist who works with people of all gender identities and expressions, both individually and within families and groups. What I share here, I share from my own positionality.

I want to acknowledge that not all of us begin from the same starting point in this conversation. Many Indigenous nations, cultures, communities, and languages, for example, do not view gender as a binary rooted in biology. This biology is, by the way, a science far more complex than what most of us were taught in school. I don't want to assume that everyone reading this essay was brought up within Anglo dominant and/or western cultural and linguistic paradigms, so if you haven't, I hope you can still find something of value or interest in these words. I also want to recognize that those of us who are trans, non-binary, and gender expansive have likely had more demands placed on us to interrogate our own gender identities, histories, expressions, roles, and experiences, especially if we are Black, Brown, and Indigenous.

I have woven and integrated this essay in my own experiences because the personal is indeed political, and it includes gender scholarship as well as a potential vision for collective gender liberation. My vision includes freedom and expansiveness for all gender identities and expressions. I would love to invite you to dream into yours after reading this essay or maybe even before you begin. May this work be supportive of your own magic around the Liberty point.

When I attended my first Reclaiming Winter WitchCamp, one of the things I really appreciated was that there was no gender segregation in the sleeping arrangements in cabins. The bathroom door between the gendered bathrooms at the state park site was permanently open, enabling easy communication and movement between the two spaces. Even though I was not yet out as trans, I had already been out as queer for several years, and I had never been comfortable with binary expectations of gender. I loved this camp for many reasons, but the queer understanding of gender was definitely a major draw for me. A couple of years later, we moved sites for this camp, and one of the first things that some of us did was to liberate the gendered bathrooms by placing All Genders Bathroom signs over the gendered signs.

This was a simple act to make many of us more comfortable with using the bathroom, but it instigated fear, anxiety, and nervousness in others. Over the years we had some cisgender women who would not come to Winter WitchCamp because we refused to segregate the dormitories by gender. I remember the challenging conversations at that time: *We were a feminist tradition; how could we not understand that some women did not feel safe around men? Were we placing the comfort of one group of people over another, and whose comfort or safety mattered?*

As a survivor of domestic and sexual violence both as a child and adult, I could understand the fear and anxiety that some people were experiencing, but I also knew that it was a red herring. Binary understandings of gender and bathroom divisions never kept me or many other people I knew safe. The threat of violence and the actual violence we had experienced might have more often than not come from men—it did in my case—but the systems enabling these violations can be upheld by people of all genders, including cis women. Placing walls and doors between us would not stop the misogynistic patriarchy that keeps perpetuating violence. It's often easier to deal with an externalized monster as a threat than to face how we have internalized the reproduction of systems of power, oppression, and privilege.

One of the hardest things for me to come to terms with as a survivor was not just the violence experienced at the hands of men but rather how the women around these men, including women who were supposed to protect me, enabled this to occur. Initially I told myself that my mom, grandmother, aunts, and great-aunts were also victims of the patriarchy and that they had no power or agency either in those situations. However, as I grew older and reflected further on how systems reproduce oppression—including completing a doctorate in what was at the time Women's Studies—I came to realize that these women around me did not always lack agency, and that they had taught me not only to cower when faced with violence but to take responsibility for it.

Growing up I heard countless times how if I were able to just be quieter, smaller, more careful, I could avoid patriarchal violence, but it was a lie. No matter how small or quiet I made myself, it was never enough. Later, much later, I would also realize that much of the violence, harassment, and discrimination I experienced over the years was not just because of gender. There were so many other aspects and intersections at play too, such as my own undiagnosed neurodivergence that made me vulnerable in a number of ways, especially growing up, while also contributing to my resilience in other ways. In many of my adult relationships within the UK I also experienced being stigmatized, harassed, and abused because of my own ethnicity and culture. In fact, oppression rarely comes packaged in neat, singular shapes.

I'm honestly not sure why the narratives of *all men are dangerous* and *penis = man = danger* common within the feminist movement in the 1980s never stuck with me despite my being heavily influenced by second-wave feminism. Maybe it's because I am trans and something deep inside told me that an easy binary wasn't the answer. Maybe it's because I'm neurodivergent and I saw patterns that did not fit these beliefs. Or maybe because as I experienced women's only spaces, which were supposed to be safe, I wasn't experiencing safety for a number of reasons. I wasn't Anglo in Anglo, white-dominated spaces; I wasn't straight; and I wasn't a lesbian either, given that I was bisexual. Eventually it also turned out that I wasn't a woman, but that came later. Those direct experiences told me that the gender liberation movement of second-wave feminism was no liberation at all for some of us.

This might seem harsh in some ways, and I am grateful to so much feminist scholarship and activism. At the same time, I cannot deny that second-wave feminism really struggled with issues of race, sexuality, and gender, among others, in ways that didn't bring liberation to many people within the movement. Black women, queer women, trans women, trans men, gender expansive people, and disabled women were already part of the movement, but our liberation was not viewed as essential. In fact, many second-wave feminists didn't construe trans women, for example, as belonging to a women's movement at all, even though they were there with us and in some cases had been part of feminist groups and movements for decades.

Rejecting those narratives wasn't easy. As someone who was exploring Anglo-based paganism and started being a gender scholar nearly thirty years ago, the narrative of women-only spaces as safe, healing, magical, spiritual places was pervasive. There was refuge and community in giving into this narrative. I wanted to embrace it, but I just couldn't. I wanted that comfort, but I couldn't ignore the harassment, and at times violence, experienced within those spaces. In my experience this was not healing or liberating; it was segregation and safety that was reserved only for some and not all bodyminds. One problem was that the Reclaiming tradition I embraced twenty years ago and in which I am initiated was heavily founded on feminism of the second-wave kind, even though it was by no means a separatist tradition. That's why when I first attended Winter WitchCamp in 2005, I felt such relief. Here was a camp and a community within my tradition that was queer at heart. However, that did not mean that we were completely exempt from the same colonial, patriarchal, and Christian supremacist notions of gender as binary, which brings us back to the episode of liberating the gendered bathrooms.

This act generated numerous discussions in our community that would continue over the next few years as our tradition also came to terms with updating language in the Principles of Unity. All these discussions had one thing in common: equating penis with men and danger. This is a position that is founded in gender essentialism, the very thing that as feminists we are supposed to abhor since it's at the roots of gendered oppression, as well as being a part of biological determinism, a stance deeply rooted in racism, colonialism, and eugenic beliefs. Yet here we were, having conversations that conflated safety with an absence of penis in the same bathrooms or dorms as people with vulvas. The latter also often just meant cisgender women, which erased the existence of trans masculine people as well as denying the reality of violence that far too many trans feminine people experience, especially Black, Brown, and Indigenous trans feminine people.

During these conversations I heard statements such as *I cannot feel comfortable showering if I am sharing the bathroom with a man who might sexualize me* or *How can I feel safe sleeping in the same room as a man?* I am summarizing some of the major points that were being made by various cisgender women. There were many assumptions that were implicitly being made about both gender and sexuality.

I want to take a moment to make some of these implicit assumptions explicit. While it is true that many cisgender white straight North American men are unable to be around nudity without sexualizing it, this is a very specific cultural experience that presumes who is in the room when we're talking about segregating spaces like bathrooms. The reality is also that, as pagans, we're sometimes naked around each other in ritual, regardless of gender. If someone is sexualizing other people on the basis of nudity alone, this needs to be addressed within our community, no matter what our bathroom arrangements are. Similarly, if we cannot feel safe if a man is in the same dorm, we are likely not to feel safe in other situations with men either. We're also denying the reality that many people, often cisgender straight white men, do not need permission to access a space and be violent. The main message that I am trying to communicate here is that gender essentialism gives us the illusion of safety while perpetuating the very system that is ultimately harming us all, albeit in different ways.

A couple of other arguments that I have heard for the past three decades are that challenging gender binaries is a *young people's thing* or that trans, non-binary, and gender expansive people need to *wait their turn given that we don't even have equality for women yet.* Those arguments are, in my opinion, fairly easy to dismantle. First of all, I am in my 50s. I know non-binary people who are in their 60s, 70s, and 80s. Some are even gender-blessed ancestors. Challenging a binary construct of gender is not just for young people, and anyone who thinks so is either not paying attention or just doesn't know any non-binary and/or gender expansive people. The other argument is a little more insidious as it implies that trans people are newer and have not fought alongside cisgender women for body autonomy and reproductive justice or that our issues are separate and not a priority within the movement for gender liberation.

In reality our struggles are not separate, even though divisive conservative forces would like us to think otherwise. Audre Lorde, among others, beautifully stated how ultimately the battle is the same in her poem *Outlines* and how we're trying to imagine something that is beyond the past and moves us into possibility.

Gender liberation can indeed be a place of potentiality and new possibilities within our communities, but we do need to choose each other.

What does that mean in practice? We need to understand that gender essentialism, on which constructions of gender as binary are founded, is the threat. We also need to stop viewing people with gender identities different from our own as the enemy. We need to acknowledge what we want when we organize spaces for only certain genders, which can be helpful and healing. If we just say the space is for women and non-binary people only, what does that mean? The reality is that many people will see this as a space for people with vulvas only, but is that what is wanted or are you looking for a space that does not include cisgender men? Is the space trans inclusive or not? If not, why not? We can get better at asking questions about intention, needs, and desire when organizing these spaces in community.

We might also want to ask ourselves what our vision for gender liberation is. Personally, I dream of a world where all gender identities, expressions, roles, histories, and experiences are considered valid and legitimate. When I talk about gender liberation, I am not envisioning an androgynous, genderless world but rather a world where people are not pre-assigned a gender lane that they need to adhere to. This world is not going to be possible without racial and disability justice, as Professor Crenshaw clearly illustrated in her theory of intersectionality.[8] These threads are tightly woven together, binding us into collective contraction as we navigate systems of power, privilege, and oppression that are not separate from our everyday actions and interactions. I believe that healing needs to include expansion so we can widen our notions of gender into a much vaster landscape than the current binary offers us.

How can we practice living as if gender was already expansive in our world? What can it mean for our spiritual practices? There are a few things I would like to invite you, reader, to consider as I stroll toward concluding this essay.

The masculine, feminine, and what is beyond conceptions of masculine and feminine do not need to be bound by biological determinism. This means that when we embrace ideas like the divine feminine, we do not need to conceptualize this as cisgender femininity alone. For those of us who work with deities, for example, we could ask ourselves: *What if Freya was what we nowadays call a trans woman?* or *Why do we usually assume that all divine beings are cisgender unless it is clearly stated that they are fluid, such as Avalokiteshvara?*

---

8   K. W. Crenshaw, "Mapping the Margins: Intersectionality, Identity Politics, and Violence Against Women of Color," in *The Public Nature of Private Violence*, ed. Martha Albertson Fineman (Routledge, 2013), 93–118.

During meetings, whether there are trans and/or non-binary people present or not, we can make sure we include pronouns in our introduction check-ins. Not everyone likes this practice as it can single out trans people, especially if cisgender people say things like *you can call me anything* or make light of it in other ways. I find that asking something like *Please share your name and, if you want, your pronouns, if any, for today* also gives people permission to try a new pronoun on if they feel safe to do so or to not include their pronouns if they're not ready.

When we organize rituals, classes, or intensive retreats such as WitchCamps, we can make sure that there are all-gender accessible bathrooms available. If not, is it possible to find a better venue? If overnight stays are involved, is there an expectation that accommodation will be segregated by gender? If so, how will this impact people who don't fit into a gender binary?

When we teach, facilitate ritual, write, or speak, let's consider whether our language is inclusive. I want to do this not because it's politically correct but because I care deeply about not alienating, erasing, or harming whoever might be in the same room as me. I also want to make sure I don't only do this when people who are potentially impacted by my linguistic choices are in the room because I care about building beloved community, and how can we do so if we're erasing, misgendering, or otherwise being harmful in our language? After all, our words are indeed part of our power as witches.

In everything we do, let's not assume that everyone in the room with us at any given point is likely to be cisgender. When we assume that the baseline is being cisgender and that other gender identities deviate from this, we are implying a hierarchy of identities in which being cisgender is somewhat superior to other gender identities.

When someone tells us that we haven't been respectful of their gender identities and/or expressions, we need to listen. I have learned so much from my trans feminine siblings! Let's try to not be defensive or spiral into shame, since that doesn't help us focus on being accountable for any potential harm. Instead, I invite us all to listen, learn, and do better. After all, if someone is letting us know we hurt them, they care enough to share this with us, which is a vulnerable move. They likely want us to do better.

Liberation is not tolerance, acceptance, or inclusion.

Liberation is expansion and freedom from normative expectations so that we can all be our most amazing magical selves.

In order to practice liberation, we need to unlearn so much of what we have been taking for granted, to undo epistemologies (ways of knowing) and ontologies (ways of being) deeply rooted in colonialism and imperialism. If this seems like a tall order, that's because it is. It's not easy to uncouple appearance from gender, for example, because cisgenderism is the air that we breathe, and we have learned to associate certain traits with a binary construction of gender. For example, when we see someone with a beard, we usually think of them as men or masculine, even though anyone can rock a beard: women, men, and intersex people. We might also associate certain pronouns with appearance or mannerism; for example, automatically using *she* if someone wears makeup and moves with fluidity.

Our paths toward gender liberation will vary but hopefully can be connected by our desires to be free from harmful notions of gender as a rigid binary determined by a false understanding of biology as dimorphic. We cannot do this work alone because liberation can only be achieved relationally, in community. There are plenty of moments when I feel the joy of freedom in relation to my own non-binary identity, but those moments are fleeting if others around me negate my joy, my freedom, and my gender, or if I negate theirs. "Our liberation is truly bound to one another," as Lilla Watson, an Aboriginal Gangulu artist and activist, reminds us.[9]

I cannot wait to witness the gender-liberated world we could co-create together if we're willing.

---

9 Joanne Watson, "Lilla Watson," *Queensland Review* 14 , no. 1 (2007): 47, https://doi.org/10.1017/S132181660000595X.

down we twist into the depths

    finding what we know and

        don't know yet but yearning

            driving—igniting—delving to refine

                to let ourselves be revealed

                to let the pearl of us

                shine forth to carry in the heart of us

        we know

    we know we are pearl and you are pearl

we know the end and the beginning

KNOWLEDGE

The fifth and final point of the Pearl Pentacle, the way we are working it here, is Knowledge. Where Wisdom is broad and available to some extent everywhere, Knowledge is specific, narrow, local. Knowledge calls for precision; it requires discipline; it insists, at some point, on specialization and perfection. It is also a gateway. Knowing something we have not previously known changes us, perhaps in very minor ways or perhaps more major. Knowing how to write an essay enables us to pass our degree; knowing how to live on the land empowers us to survive. Knowledge that is transmitted in initiations, in mystery traditions, and in moments of deep personal breakthrough does not just change our understanding of the way of things; it changes us. We can be rewritten by knowledge.

This is an era where a vastness of knowledge exists, and, parallel with that, false, fake, and deep-fake "knowledge" ramps up within social media, conspiracy theories, and even changing the way knowledge is understood in our society. In the Iron Pentacle this fifth point is Passion, and we can consider how passion drives the quest for knowledge and how following a passion leads us to develop specialized knowledge. This point is placed in the left foot, the foot holding steady as the right foot steps forward. This is the foot that can then continue that path or make an adjustment; this is the foot holding our balance. Will you allow your knowledge to wash you back, like the incoming tide, to Love—the origin and return point of the Pearl Pentacle? Love beckons to us through passion and the quest for knowledge and meets us, again, at the end of our journey through Love, Law, Wisdom, Liberty, and Knowledge. All comes back to Love.

KNOWLEDGE REWRITES US

Knowledge, knowing, to know. This is the fifth and final point of the Pearl Pentacle. We could imagine it as the final layer of the nacre that creates the pearl. Following the richness and challenge of Liberty, Knowledge sounds a little dry. Really? After all this buildup through the realms of love and law, wisdom and liberty, that's supposed to lead to knowledge? But it's here the secrets are held and revealed to those willing to partake. We move into the mysteries through the doorway, across the threshold, and into the intimacy of knowledge. The insights we receive rewrite us; it's an alchemical process. We emerge changed. Liberty was so large and expansive whereas Knowledge draws us back in, within, and as it changes us and completes the pentacle, we find the doorway back to the starting point of Love.

The thing about knowledge is that you can't go back. It's irreversible. You can fall out of love. You can slip sideways from the law. Wisdom comes and goes in its presence. Liberty is to be fought for but rarely gained, or gained only incrementally or conditionally. But knowledge is an absolute. It happened. Bite into this apple and be changed forever. Take the red pill. It's like downloading the latest update—everything gets rewritten and we're moving on from here. You wanted to continue as you were prior to receiving that knowledge? Bad luck. Knowledge really doesn't work like that. Knowledge might not sound sexy, but it's got gravitas, and when we look again, that is sexy. The serpent whispers *Thou shalt be as gods*. And we've got shivers down our spines—we are tempted, we've bitten into the apple, we've eaten it.

This biblical apple grows on the Tree of Knowledge of Good and Evil. There is a story of a first man, Adam, and a first woman, Eve. It was a story in the air of the society we grew up in. We knew that a serpent—who was said to be Satan, who is cast as evil—tempted Eve into eating an apple from the Tree of Knowledge. She ate the apple, and she convinced Adam to eat as well. Then they knew they were naked; they knew that they had erred and gone against God's wishes. And so they hid from the god who had apparently made and brought them to life. Later we discovered different ways of interpreting this story, passed inside witch and feminist traditions that taught us about knowledge as an awakening to our own divinity and power. Eating the apple, we remember who and what we are, where we have come from, and the capacity within us *to know*. This is one facet of Knowledge in the Pearl Pentacle.

There is another tree in that paradise: the Tree of Life. The Tree of Life, as worked with in Jewish Kabbalistic tradition, contains a dark, mysterious space called *Da'ath*—Hebrew for *Knowledge*—beckoning and foreboding from within the Tree. Here we recall the types of knowledge passed down in initiations, as well as knowledge belonging to certain lineages, cultures, or specific to time and place. Knowledge of land, of ways of being in harmony with the earth; knowledge within magical traditions: of ceremonies and mysteries and the divine. Knowledge that is coded in layers, like rock, like myth, like doors that open one to the next within a temple, leading us to the deeper revelations held within. Even knowledge about the other points in this pentacle: knowledge of love and law, wisdom and liberty.

To arrive at Knowledge after the transition from Wisdom through Liberty opens these realms up in a particular and deep way. We might imagine knowledge as held in dusty tomes on high shelves in the library, of scientific papers (filled with knowledge, no doubt; all great stuff!) but inaccessible to the general reader. We recall the rigor of academia and the requirements of passing exams. Perhaps we think of specific knowledge, such as that of a car mechanic or an electrician or a doctor. Useful, essential, but do we want to know about it or do we just want the car fixed, our house wired, and someone to understand this medical condition?

Knowledge has never just been about the halls of academia, hidden occult traditions, or what is transmitted in schools and universities. The knowledge pooled and shared within universities arrives courtesy of the work of liberty. Science and knowledge are close kin—the word *science* comes from the Latin root *to know*—and science is the practical application of working with what we know and don't know as we test what is possible. Scientific discoveries have sometimes catalyzed spontaneously; an effect is noticed, a pattern discerned, and a series of data is drawn out and tested over and over to observe potential outcomes.

We are liberated from our previous constraints, and knowledge grants us access into the unimagined new.

Knowledge comes in different forms and differing levels of accessibility, but it always changes us. Before we didn't know it. Now we do. And things are different. I go through childbirth. You witness a death. We cross through the portal of initiation. Many people fall in love and experience betrayal. Some people move through the world perceived as a gender they were not assigned at birth. We learn another language or travel to a different country or attend a workshop on something we're fascinated by. Now we know something that we didn't before, and knowing this has created change in the way we see the world, maybe in our values and understandings, or who we are as people. Knowledge has rewritten us.

And it doesn't just happen once. We live in a sea of knowledge, an ocean of it. Like love and law and all the others, it's washing all around us and through us, and we're in constant change, constant unfurling, constant nacring of this pearl that is us. This pearl that has been born in love, has learned law, allowed space for wisdom and opened up to liberty and now is dropping deep and hard into knowledge. Some knowledges bite deeper than others. Some even come with a warning—like the snake/garden/apple—and some are inevitable, unavoidable. Birth. Death. Change.

In spite of being so all-and-everywhere, knowledge is very specific. When I pursue my (JM's) degree in education, I do it at the expense of accepting an apprenticeship in stained glass. I choose which sets of knowledge I'll take on and put the time into learning and becoming an expert. And these are not only choices about where I'll put in the 10,000 hours, but they also direct my life. Because I've gone down one avenue, I quite specifically have not gone down another. Imagine a Paradise where Eve didn't eat the apple but instead wrote a poem or painted a picture about it . . . well, we might not even be here!

There's often a confusion differentiating between knowledge and wisdom, although working within the Pearl Pentacle it becomes quite clear what we mean by each term and how they differ. Where wisdom references the numinous and an experience of being with or within the

All, knowledge is particularities, specifics, the 10,000 hours it suppos-edly takes to become expert in something. Wisdom—in itself and also possibly how much we can access of it—is unlimited, except by the usual human constraints of mortality, distractibility, quirks of person-ality, competing demands of the environment, etcetera etcetera. With knowledge one has to select pieces, and when we do this, the other paths from that crossroads of life will disappear.

We can only go down one track at that time, and so although imme-diately we start to gain intimate and complex knowledge about this particular journey, we have no idea at all about what lies down a dif-ferent track. This is the realm of knowledge that's specific to time and place, and the further in we go, the more we know about this and the less we know about anything else. Think of looking through a micro-scope or a telescope and how what's in view is close up, all the detail there to be read, but to do that we have to ignore everything else that isn't in focus. Knowledge is the focused and practical learning of a time, place, subject, practice. It's intimate.

We say that wisdom is accessible to all, there when we show up to it, but knowledge isn't the same. It has to be worked for, won, courted. Sometimes it comes to us—secret knowledge in dreams, a divination that rings true, a teacher or beloved or even a stranger passing us just what we need to know at just the right time, placing our hand on a book in a library or bookshop and lo, it holds what we are seeking. But mostly we work for it. Whereas the process of accessing wisdom could be seen as making room for it—clearing out, showing up, paying atten-tion—the process of knowledge is adding layers, depth, responding to the grit of provocation, which could be longing or need or ambition, with layer after layer of hard work. There's some knowledge that just comes—an intuition that someone will call us, a feeling to go some-where or do something—but we'd argue that this is based on years of listening to and trusting our gut, and of knowing in the wider sense, knowing patterns, threads in the weaving, and being able to see, just below the level of the conscious, what's actually happening.

There's a very instructional, apprentice-type aspect to knowledge. Recently I (JM) learned about skirting boards, though I would have said there wasn't much to know about them apart from that they cover the gap between the bottom of the wall and the floor. Apparently they come in different heights and something called profiles. Once we had them, it was suggested I paint them before they were attached to the walls. *Ah, but do put a primer on first.* In the paint shop another customer tells me to make sure I paint the wall color over the primer before two coats of the semigloss, because otherwise the semigloss will sort of blur. Then the builders point out that there'll be a whole lot of nail holes when they're put onto the walls, so it's best to fill the holes before the final coat—after you've sanded them, obviously. Also, here's some gap filler for between the top of the skirting board and the wall.

I watch one of the builders spending hours crafting a crocodile-toothed skirting board to fit the stairs. Each tooth is measured and replicated perfectly—hours of measuring, drawing lines on walls, matching different bits up so they meet smoothly at the joins. How does this type of knowledge have anything to do with love, let alone the Love of the Pearl Pentacle? Is it initiatory knowledge? The secrets of building houses (a tiny part)? Do I love my house more because of all this skirting board labor? Oddly, yes. Or perhaps not oddly at all, as it has hours of my labor and dedication now woven into it. Do I love the builders more because I got a tiny insight into the constant complexity of rendering raw materials into functional and beautiful housing? Yes. Am I meditating on the vast depths of knowledge that exist in the world that I will never even know about? Yes. Do I imagine that this complexity somehow has something to do with God, the divine, and the start of the universe all the way through to this tiny moment of me lying on the stairs trying to gap-fill these nail holes? Perhaps not peculiarly at all, yes.

And it's important to note that I'd (JM) really have none of this knowledge, nor the link back to love, without doing it myself. If I just watched the builders do it or hired someone to paint, I'd know very little more than I did at the beginning, and it seems unlikely I'd be drawn into love over it. We might associate knowledge with books, libraries, and educational institutions, but it's really more of an apprenticeship; you have to do it. When we are genuinely pursuing knowledge, whether of skirting boards or the structure of the universe, it is leading us from the thing that has our interest, our necessity, and even our passion into the depth, the complexity, the initiation of knowledge.

There's an abiding fear of knowledge, of the powers it has of transformation, clearly encoded in the paradise story of the serpent, tree, and fruit; with the contradictory warning not to eat alongside the temptation to eat. Knowledge changes us and changes everything. There are stories about the stealing of fire from the gods, an intense desire for knowledge often coupled with punishment. This has tragically played out in history where the seekers and finders of knowledge have been punished, including with death, as they posited that the earth moved around the sun, for example, or studied topics not condoned by the powers that be, whether that was alchemy, comparative religion, science, or simply girls trying to get an education in 2025 in various locations in our dangerous world.

According to Australian journalist Waleed Aly and academic Scott Stephens in an episode of their podcast The Minefield,[10] there's a whole moral field related to knowledge, following the Islamic concept of knowledge as something that leaves an indelible mark upon you. Perhaps the root of this is that such knowledge is considered to be knowledge of God—'Ilm—so that we can imagine ourselves being rewritten, or inscribed, over and over again as we learn more and more deeply. Bringing us once again back to love, if we heretically cross the Pearl Pentacle over this Islamic teaching, some might say (Fio says), *Just the sort of thing Victor Anderson would have done himself, and likely did.*

Aly and Stephens also explore the differentiation between information and knowledge—knowledge being the thing that changes us, forms us, whereas information simply *in*forms us; and a further distinction within knowledge of knowledge that does not benefit, or as they put it, "knowledge not directed toward the good."[11] This strays into the arena of false knowledge, manufactured knowledge, and the post-truth era we are supposedly entering (reluctantly, desperately,

---

10   Aly and Stephens, "'Knowledge that does not benefit.'"

11   Ibid.

terrifyingly) and highlights Aly and Stephens' focus on discerning moralities of knowledge. Knowledge that does not benefit, in their definition, is knowledge wielded as a tool of manipulation, such as when statistics or studies might be used not as general education but to humiliate another or aggrandize the person or organization sharing it. Obviously the media and politicians are in the front lines for this, but Aly and Stephens also suggest academics and broader movements with political agendas are liable here.

The information overload we are currently subjected to, with digital media on 24/7 and constant grabs for our attention in all directions, means it can be difficult to determine what is knowledge and what is merely information, or disinformation. It may lead to a general disinterest and dismissal of even very important information/knowledge, such as that of our warming planet, species extinction crisis, and the general world shift further away from democracy. Knowledge, and the entire concept of knowledge, can also be wielded as a weapon by the unscrupulous. Remember Donald Rumsfeld's—former US Secretary of Defense—*known knowns, known unknowns,* and *unknown unknowns* underlying the War on Terror and the invasion by the United States of both Afghanistan and Iraq in the 2000s, partly based on the theoretical weapons of mass destruction, a wholly fabricated premise.

This raises the concept of secret knowledge—knowledge that may be encoded in a lost language such as that inscribed on the Rosetta stone or lying forgotten in archives of a university library or knowledge that exists with only one living person, such as is happening today with more than one Aboriginal language. Do we still count this as knowledge or has it become something more like potential knowledge? If no one knows it or no one shares it, even though it has existed previously or may be shared in the future, is that still knowledge? Was the apple (persimmon, fig, pomegranate) knowledge in itself or did it only become that when we ate of it, ingested it, and it changed us? Certainly in the Pearl Pentacle the point of Knowledge is not academic, remote, theoretical; it's potent—the type you eat and that changes you. Otherwise we could not turn through the point to complete the pentacle back at Love.

Knowledge may also be strategically and systemically hoarded or kept away from certain groups of people in order to restrain and subjugate them in society. Access to education—the kind of education that might grant you the privilege of moving further into the landscape of social power—has been and still is kept from groups of people. It can also be seen that often one member of an oppressed or marginalized group gaining access to this knowledge effectively removes them (and therefore the knowledge as well) from belonging within that group. Resources and privileges allocated by governments to private and religious schools and those given to state schools are often bizarrely disproportionate. Going to certain schools funnels easy passage into certain universities and careers.

But what is this exclusive knowledge that is reserved or kept away? One portion of it is the entire realm of finance: financial independence and financial strategy. Many people from working class and lower middle-class backgrounds are not taught about money. Often this is because folks raised in lower socioeconomic situations never imagine having enough money to act with power and agency in the economy. Cycles of poverty are also known to increase depression and anxiety, and disempower and entrap people into settling for limited life options. The field of financial knowledge can be wielded over and through entire groups of socially disadvantaged people.

Those who are taught Latin, usually only in exclusive private schools, have an advantage for entering certain academic streams such as law and medicine. The cultivation of a certain aesthetic and concept of civilization and culture has been used throughout the contemporary world, as well as throughout history, to divide classes and reify social stratification and subjugation. However, there is something to be said for the intimate knowledge grown in working class families. This is the knowledge of the street, of the marketplace, of navigation of life's stresses and hurdles in immediate and potent ways. This knowledge can form rivers and bodies of extremely practical, visceral, and emotional ways that help generations survive, laugh, eat, and relate kindly and intimately to one another through turbulent times of inevitable stress and conflict.

Related to this is an inquiry around the production and consumption of knowledge. Here we can move into a critical examination of who is producing, discovering, or disseminating knowledge, and how and what their motives are. The corporate world, which funds much of medical research? The media, largely owned by a wealthy elite few? Entrenched systems of government, historical morality, and the war machine economy? There are also many benign systems of production and consumption of knowledge—family recipes are developed and handed on, books are written and placed in libraries, TED Talks are recorded and uploaded to the internet. These examples are much closer to what we might understand as the ideal in relation to knowledge: a mutual sharing, a co-discovery and co-creation of knowledge. We may also recall peculiar stories of scientists or spirit workers in different locations in the world, unconnected with each other, making comparable discoveries at the same time—knowledge that seemingly wants to come into the world or that the world is ready for.

Another way that knowledge can enter our world is through the realm of dreams and divination. We spend a third of our lives sleeping, and within that time we dream—this is core to the human experience—and we can become lucid and skilled in this art of dreaming. Most traditional cultures are rich in dream magic and divination. These magics belong to the people. It is the magic that rises up from what Carl Jung called the collective unconscious and joins people and cultures through the older than old, the archetypal.

Jeremy Taylor (1943–2018)—a dream worker, teacher, and Unitarian Universalist minister—offered six basic hints for those exploring their dreams. Hint number four can be paraphrased as *a dream tells you something you didn't know before*. Jeremy Taylor–style dream work as described in *The Wisdom of Your Dreams* has had some influence on Reclaiming magic and community. Another form of dream work practiced in Reclaiming, which Rose May Dance taught, is trancing into a dream either solo with a group supporting you or as the whole group trancing into the same dream together. In many cultures, including my (Fio's) father's culture, dream interpretation and dream knowledge is a specialized skill, although of course everyone can learn to interpret their own dreams.

My (still Fio's) *dadong*—the Balinese term for grandmother—was a wise woman, or as my parents and their community name her, a holy woman. Every story about her is told with deep respect and admiration for her skill, magical power, and knowledge. My mother, Ros, who was living in Bali at the time, has often told me a story of my dadong helping her by tracking her dreams. Ros had returned home one day and my grandmother noticed immediately something was wrong. After Ros replied that she did indeed feel dizzy and "off," my dadong gave her special oil and told her to observe her dreams. The first night she dreamed of five caged ducks; this continued for about four nights until one night she dreamed of the ducks free and a little boy in white robes who took her hand. At this point my dadong was happy with the result and said, *All is okay now.*

I (Fio) have dreamed many times of spirits and gods visiting me, revealing hidden names and words, only to discover later that those exact names and words were incredibly rich and meaningful in their context. I have also dreamed true and known things before I could possibly know them. This is exactly the kind of foreknowledge that dreams and visions sometimes bestow on witches, artists, mystics, scientists, healers, and really anyone and all the time, perhaps without us paying heed. And I (JM) have dreamed of magical rituals, spells, and experiences so intense and resonant that I knew their happening was as real and impactful as if I had done them awake, though awake I had not necessarily had the knowledge needed to perform them; but asleep and dreaming, I knew.

There are beautiful affirming dreams in the world, and there are also nightmares. Knowledge too is both beneficial and potentially destructive. Some knowledge terrifies us, though it also may teach us: knowledge of the atomic bomb, genetic manipulation, and the whole minefield of Artificial Intelligence. Here we return to our consideration of evil that we began in the point of Love. When we countenance evil as descriptive of particular human actions and intentions, we can ask ourselves, *Can knowledge itself be evil?* Or is it only its application, the human actions utilizing the knowledge, that can truly be classed this way? And does the possibility of evil—for example, the way human actions result very directly in climate crisis and species extinction—create also the possibility for love in action? Knowledge, even of evil, can create a pathway back to love.

Humans have often fallen into the fallacy of externalizing evil, either to the realms of gods/demons or onto other humans. Certain groups of humans are described as evil or the origin of evil, particular spirits or deities are considered to wreak evil or perhaps there is a Satan figure. This has often meant that individuals and entire societies fall foul to the notion that we are being misled deliberately or that evil is being enacted upon us by seen or unseen players. As a human concept, evil is more correctly a way of reflecting upon our own behavior and conduct in the world. It is not outside of us. The seduction of external evil has produced many convenient tropes and narratives.

Conspiracy theories represent a worldview that a person might cling to because revealed in it—they sense or hope—is the comprehensive answer for the chaos of the time or the world or the difficulties of their lives. Conspiracy theories may contain grains of truth, but many draw from intensively racist, anti-Semitic, and scientifically inaccurate notions of the history of civilization and culture, and may themselves contribute to human evil. For instance, the term *cabal* is directly anti-Semitic. It refers to sinister and secret groups of elites performing evil deeds to control and confuse us. The word has its roots in the medieval Christian term *cabbala,* which comes from the Hebrew *kabbalah,* meaning *to recieve* and the name of the Jewish mystical tradition. It is true that there is a small percentage of wealthy elite, the oligarchs, that control many of the major decisions in the world. Do they sacrifice children to evil spirits, as QAnon declares? Is Donald Trump trying to expose the deep state and liberate people from ignorance? Highly unlikely. The world is full of misinformation, and the avenues of gaining knowledge are so instantaneous that supposedly we can watch a few YouTube videos or listen to a podcast and access special knowledge that allows us to understand the secret levels of geopolitics.

How are we meant to trust any knowledge? Perhaps this is why Knowledge comes last in the Pearl Pentacle, as a culmination. If we journey around the perimeter of the pentacle: Love—Wisdom—Knowledge—Law—Liberty, we must at least have been initiated by Love and held in Wisdom in order to kiss Knowledge. In the journey of the Pearl Pentacle current through the star, we begin in Love, move down to Law, spiral up to Wisdom, leap across to Liberty, and then cascade into Knowledge. As the Pearl evolves from the Iron Pentacle, so then it makes sense to consider the underlying Iron point of Passion in our quest to trust knowledge.

Knowledge is the pearlescence that now shimmers forth, wrapped around the grit of Iron Pentacle Passion. Ravyn Stanfield, a Reclaiming teacher and priestess whose essay on initiatory tradition is on page 239, offers the affirmation *I care* for the Iron Pentacle point of Passion. What do you care so much about that you would live your life for it? When we care this much about something, be that returning to animistic spirit working or dancing in the Tree of Life or learning to love one another deeply and sustainably, we apprentice to those knowledges. Our trust is gained breath by breath with our learning, with our descent down the narrow path of hard-won knowledge.

We might even become obsessed. Two variations on the Iron Pentacle are the Rust and Gilded pentacles, which came out of the work of Gabriel Carillo, Steven Hewell, T. Thorn Coyle, and Reclaiming. The Gilded Pentacle takes each Iron point to its extreme and the Rust into its deficit. Both are unbalanced and sometimes used as diagnostic tools to discover where and how our Iron points may be out of alignment and right relationship. *Obsession* is the Gilded point related back to the Iron point of Passion. The Rusted point is *Apathy*. So what might this tell us about moving toward Knowledge? Dawn Isidora, in her Bridges Pentacle (see page 248), came to the idea that *Temperance* may help guide us from Passion into Knowledge. I (Fio) am immediately brought magically into the forge by this word, and in Reclaiming and many witchcraft communities we like to refer to the forge when we speak of initiation.

As we journey through realms of initiation—and if we are lucky, we are held and witnessed by living human initiates—we go through the forge. We experience being taken apart, dismembered; it might get very hot or intense in our lives. We may even feel that life is hitting us hard; just as the hammer hits the metal on the anvil to shape it, and we might swing through extremes, the intensity of fire and the quenching of water or cold air. We must be cooled and heated over and again until we are strong, substantial, so that we are not brittle. This is tempering in the forge, and this describes passion as well as knowledge. If knowledge requires us to passionately pursue something—apprentice, deepen, refine, focus, hone, discover, renew—we must do this over the years and not just in sudden and hot bursts.

Formal initiation into a tradition—the type offered by mentors, teachers, and sometimes peers—draws from the knowledge we have of initiatory experiences in ancient and contemporary magical and Indigenous traditions, what we know of the psychology of change and development, and the rich cauldron of our own desires, needs, and fears. Both times I (JM) have asked for initiation and passed through its gates and tests, I have been changed forever. That was the point. These were changes I needed, yearned for, but could not bring about entirely by myself. I needed a larger frame, a community and a mystery, to hold them. The initiations stripped me bare of doubt, artifice, and hesitation and left me revealed to myself in strength and beauty.

I (Fio) have experienced initiation many times over, into four traditions of witchcraft, into the specific mysteries and magics of great ones and gods. I consider all of these initiations whole and complete unto themselves and also part of the labyrinth of initiation that is my life and will be my death. When I reflect on the seventeen-year-old who was initiated by Coven of the Wildwood, I remember that it radically catalyzed me to finish my first manuscript and send it to Llewellyn. That initiation challenged me to step into increasingly visible leadership in my local and then broader magical community. I have gone through the rites of witchcraft initiation on three continents, and each time I have been fiercely and powerfully held and witnessed by remarkable humans, living and now dead, who continue to hold and witness me to this day. Initiation is for everyone, and there are many mysteries that we humans dance with. Initiation gifts us a knowing that is intrinsically and simultaneously personal and cosmic.

Both Passion and Knowledge in their respective pentacles play the role of strengthening and culminating the currents. Through the quenching and the tempering in the forge, we may come back to life renewed and refined; we may remember what we really care about. This is knowledge we can trust: we have been changed by it; it has rewritten us. And the framework of Knowledge creates a container to hold all the other points, the Love and Law, the Wisdom and Liberty that bring light, shining like moonlight on the sea, into the gritty depths of our Iron Sex, Pride, Self, Power, and Passion. Pearl and Iron combine, dance, and reveal that they were always one.

Knowledge is still the apple on the tree. Knowledge is the secrets in the heart whispering to us in our quiet moments. Knowledge can set us free. Knowledge is in the beauty and wonder shared between lovers and friends. Knowledge is transmitted in Indigenous cultures the world over and within spiritual and scientific enclaves and schools. Knowledge is always on offer. Knowledge awaits us to commit, dedicate, and care. Knowledge can be what happens, what unfolds, when we say yes to the path not yet trodden and move down the road that rises to meet us. We will be changed.

GATES OF KNOWLEDGE

Knowledge to me (JM) is something like Eve eating the apple: once it's done, it can't be undone. Eating knowledge, imbibing knowledge, rewrites us; we are irretrievably changed, and this knowledge that we've learned isn't just academic or maybe isn't academic at all—we've learned more about who we are and what we're capable of and there's no going back.

I like to think of these moments as gates that we pass through. Although wisdom is something we can be aware of but still ignore, knowledge is who we have become; there's no avoiding it once it's occurred. All of us have passed through these gates of knowledge—times where what happened to us or what we did literally rewrote who we are. Being born is a gate of knowledge we have all passed through, through the gateway of our mother's flesh. Other gateways we may pass through include menstruation, sexual maturity, falling in love for the first time, pregnancy and birth, experiencing serious pain, witnessing a death, the loss of a loved one.

Then there are other gates of knowledge we may seek to enter: for example, initiation, parenthood, commitment to a partner, tradition, or community. Some of these things may involve years of study or preparation, yet however much we've learned, we can never acquire this sort of knowledge beforehand; it's to do with what happens to us in those crucial moments, when we are within the gate, so to speak. Death, or at least mortality, brushes nearby and shares the gate with us as we hover between one state and the next.

This activity provides an opportunity to reflect on the gates of knowledge you have passed through in your life as well as explore one of those gates in more depth. You can split it into two parts done at different times, firstly the reflection on gates you've passed through and at a later time the exploration into a single gate.

» You will need: journal and pen, art materials if you choose to create a visual representation of your chosen gate

» Time: 60–90 minutes or more depending on the format and depth of your exploration piece

Reflection

Divide a page of your journal into three columns—perhaps turn the page sideways or use a double page.

Think into what constitutes a gate of knowledge for you. We learn things all the time, but some events are pivotal and change forever who we are or how we understand the world. This is a gate of knowledge. Some are universal—basically everyone experiences them, such as the death of a loved one—and some are individual to us, such as initiation into a particular magical tradition.

In the first column, write down gates of knowledge you have passed through, and in the second column, your age and (if relevant) circumstances at the time. So my own list would begin with the *gate of birth*, and the second gate I'd write down would be *the death of a loved one*—my best friend Kerin when we were seven. Fill in the first and second columns. It doesn't matter if you forget some or they're not in strict chronological order.

In the third column, write down some of the knowledge that you earned in passing through this gate. I might write *embodiment* for my first gate and *inexplicable mortality* for my second.

Possibly you have passed through many gates of knowledge or perhaps there are only a few you can isolate or locate. This activity is not about the number of them but about the quality, the sense of what happens within and after passing through a gate of knowledge. Our awareness and understanding of this may feed our own wisdom and the wisdom we can pass to others, as well as our ability to be present for others when they transition into and through such gates.

Exploring a Gate of Knowledge

We can go even deeper into understanding gates of knowledge by focusing on a single one of these and not only thinking about the effect it had on us and our lives but finding a way to represent that. This may be something we keep private, share with just a few people, or we may choose to put it out in the world in some way, *#gateofknowledge*.

Choose one of the gates of knowledge that you have passed through listed in your reflection above.

Then choose how to explore this gate. Options include:

» writing a poem, story, or memoir
» drawing or painting
» creating an interactive or 3D artwork
» composing a song or other piece of music

Focus on the transformation aspect, or you may choose to see this as the Knowledge aspect of passing through this gate. Perhaps it is a gate many others may identify with or have similar or related experiences of, or it may be something few people have experienced. Either way, you will have a unique experience, understanding, and expression of this piece of knowledge.

APPLES AND POMEGRANATES

In the story of the Garden of Eden that appears in the book of Genesis from the Torah, the first five books of the Hebrew Bible, there is a tree of knowledge and a fruit. There is a serpent and there is a woman named Eve. *Eve* comes from the Hebrew meaning *living one*; some also say *source of life*. Eve eats a fruit because, as many Christians believe, Satan, in the form of a serpent, tempted her to eat.

Genesis does not indicate that the fruit on the tree is an apple, but much of European history and culture declares it to be so. Apples appear as significant to the otherworld and the gods throughout pre-Christian and non-Jewish cultures in Europe and Asia. Apples are often thought of as the fruit of immortality; consider the golden apples that the Norse gods eat and the red fruits that the dead feast upon in the Isle of Apples, also called Avalon.

Pomegranates are another mysterious fruit sacred in both Jewish and non-Jewish cultures. The pomegranate is intimately connected to the mystery that unfolds between the ancient Greek gods Hades and Persephone. The eating of pomegranate seeds offered by Hades to Persephone seal fate; Persephone then spends half or some say three or four months of the year in the underworld.

In Starhawk's *Spiral Dance* Samhain ritual, the priestexes of the ritual declare that the apple is the fruit of death that holds the five-point star of life within. The pomegranate is the fruit of life that holds the seeds of death.

This is a spell for opening to forbidden knowledge, occult knowledge, the knowledge of witches and mystics. Only do this spell if you dare. Daring is required in the pursuit of magical knowledge.

> » You will need: an apple and a pomegranate, a sharp cutting knife (which could be your witch knife), and a working altar or quiet and private space to do the spell (could be your sacred kitchen)
> » Time: 30 minutes

With a fresh apple and pomegranate before you, perhaps on your altar or on the dining table, acknowledge country, ground, center, and align your souls.

Pick up the apple in whichever hand is called to hold it. Pick up the pomegranate in the other hand. Or you can start by picking up the pomegranate and then the apple.

Through your breath drop your attention into the fruits of life and death, into the fruits of immortality and the otherworld/underworld. Imagine into all the stories, folktales, legends, and myths you have heard about apples and pomegranates. Let them run through your mind. Maybe some in particular stand out to you, maybe something begins to unfold in your awareness that you have never consciously come across or barely remember.

Allow your senses to become aroused or ignited by all this apple-ness and pomegranate-ness. Begin to dance in your own way with the fruits and raise the power. Dance and sing of apples and trees and knowledge, of hidden and magical knowledge.

As you raise the power to receive this knowledge—and it could be specific knowledge you've decided upon ahead of time—remember the daring, the holy risk, in this work. Things will change; you will be rewritten in the receiving of this knowledge. As you dance and raise the power, remember that people have been hunted and killed for this kind of knowledge and let whatever grief or rage that you feel about that help bolster the power. You might even feel the mighty dead, the powerful witches who have died with a strong sense of who they are, gather around you.

Release the power you have raised into the apple and the pomegranate. Ground yourself.

Then cut the apple open crossways with the sharp knife and behold the five-point star made by the seeds in the heart of the apple. Collect the seeds and later place them on your altar or bury or plant them if you desire. Take a bite of the apple; relish it if you can. Honor the apple and all the histories of the apple.

Then cut open the pomegranate with the knife or your hands. Marvel at the glittering deep red and purple jewels; they are like garnets! Eat a few of the seeds and honor the pomegranate, remembering the stories of this fruit.

When you feel complete, you can throw the fruits into the compost reverently or bury them or place them on your altar.

It is done.

DISTILLING THE KNOWLEDGE
OF A TRADITION
IRISANYA MOON

I knew nothing when I got in the car with a woman who'd offered a ride to me, an unknown passenger. I'd met her in person only minutes before shoving my suitcase into her small hatchback. All I knew was that Reclaiming's California WitchCamp was my next stop, my next adventure. I packed what was suggested, but I didn't know a thing about what I was going to experience. Thankfully, my new friend patiently explained all of the pieces of a WitchCamp to me (well, most of them), from the outline of rituals to the way the week would flow, as we drove north. I can still remember the turn of road where I learned about aspecting, Reclaiming's approach to possessory work, and how it would look in ritual. What she didn't tell me was how I would learn to possess myself, how I would learn to heal and grow, and how my inherent and gained knowledge would impact the group. I would learn that along the way through classes, teaching, and planning rituals. And I wouldn't do it alone. Ever.

With so many people, life circumstances, and beliefs, how could we bring the best of ourselves to ourselves as well as each other at a one hundred–plus person WitchCamp? I wondered what would or could bring this group of witches together and keep us together. Could we recognize ourselves in our shared values? And what were those values anyway? Thankfully, I found an answer in Reclaiming's Principles of Unity (see page 13). Each piece of the Principles distills the tradition's knowledge and has helped me feel progressively less lost the further this journey has taken me.

We are an evolving, dynamic tradition and proudly call ourselves
Witches. Our diverse practices and experiences of the divine weave
a tapestry of many different threads.

The Principles of Unity were born out of necessity and circumstance. During the late 1970s, a group called the Reclaiming Collective was forming in the San Francisco Bay Area. What was once a small group of witches and activists started to build momentum but became unwieldy in size. The collective was too small and too big at the same time. A change needed to happen to consolidate what was true about this group and its shared knowledge and values.

The front door is purple. The steps are narrow enough that you have to hold onto the wall or the banister to make sure you don't fall backward. You walk two stories up and past the bathroom with the clawfoot tub to the room where it happened. It's sometimes musty and often not quite the right temperature. The walls are lined with altars, and there is a view of a wild garden. There is a back porch where you can see Sutro Tower in the distance, assuming it's not too foggy. In this room the Reclaiming Collective came together between meetings that took place over two years: several larger community meetings, retreats, and smaller meetings between collective members and community members to discuss concerns. In this room the collective brought wisdom and knowledge gathered from more voices than their own, distilling and reordering the pieces until the Principles were born.

The Principles of Unity is a document that contains the beliefs and shared knowledge of individuals committed to social change, magick, and each other. Each piece of this document is a reference point for members of the Reclaiming community. Reclaiming Witchcraft became a tradition, and the Principles of Unity became the document we could agree to, anywhere in the world, and identify as Reclaiming. You are empowered to step into this dynamic tradition, one that evolves and encourages ongoing evolution, to weave a value-based tapestry.

Our practice arises from a deep, spiritual commitment to the earth, to healing and to the linking of magic with political action.

Some of the Reclaiming witches that came together were activists leading, organizing, and participating in political actions to fight for environmental causes. They brought their knowledge to enhance protective magick, to enable ongoing grounding in high stress situations, and to help keep bodies safe from harm during actions. Not only did the knowledge of magick help support the humans in activism, but the magick helped empower the spell of justice and change. Singing, spiral dances, and chanting were able to bring the collective attention and intention together, raising energy within the group and adding power to the action.

From Elements of Magic as a core class that builds relationships with earth, air, fire, water, and spirit to rituals that send energy across timelines of activists to give the support they/we need, there is a promise to be committed to the earth. Before nearly every ritual there is a land acknowledgment, a clearly defined time to bring attention to the impacts of colonization on the lands and the people of the stolen lands. Rituals celebrate the turning of the wheel of the year and how the earth changes. Classes and camps trance through the water cycle, and groups plan or attend actions to continue to bring attention to the climate crisis as it arrives more loudly each year.

Each of us embodies the divine. Our ultimate spiritual authority is within, and we need no other person to interpret the sacred to us.

There is a knowing we are born with, maybe from past lives, maybe from where we are born into, and maybe from our cells and bones. Within each of us is the ability to discern what is best and right, to align our actions with our beliefs. We are inherently divine and can trust our knowing to guide us. This can be described as having your own spiritual authority rooted in community, as it is taught in Reclaiming. In this way, each person can make decisions based on their inherent knowledge, need, and ability.

My choices, while valid and wise, are also choices that can impact those around me. While I might want to dance for the goddess and wave my arms around wildly in my ecstasy, this might harm someone near me whose spiritual authority asks for closed eyes and a still presence. We do not need someone else to tell us what to do, and we can also consider those around us during our decision-making. Witches and magick makers can follow their hearts to access the divine.

We include those who honor Mysterious Ones, Goddesses, and Gods of myriad expressions, genders, and states of being, remembering that mystery goes beyond form.

Over many years there was a fervent call to expand the language of the Principles of Unity from the binary of god and goddess and add language to affirm trans and non-binary people. Prior to the 2012 update of the Principles of Unity, feedback was requested from the global Reclaiming community via email lists and smaller community gatherings. After all, if a group wants to be inclusive and welcoming, it is helpful to have the deities and other divine beings represent the practitioners and their practices. We can make room for animists, monotheists, polytheists, and other flavors of divine connection. At a Dandelion gathering outside of Portland, Oregon, in 2012, Reclaiming witches came together to discuss what changes might be possible and supportive to trans and non-binary people within the tradition. Some people brought the idea of mysterious ones, and this was discussed, reflected on, and eventually consensed into a Principles of Unity update.

This new wording helped bring the knowledge of some people into the collective knowledge and experience of the group. Today in Reclaiming gatherings, classes, and WitchCamps, you will see rituals that include deities and divine beings of many forms, faces, and figures. Some rituals don't include deities at all, calling on energies or fairy-tale characters instead, while others include entire pantheons (perhaps that's an exaggeration). Classes bring this knowledge of many divine possibilities by offering stories of a wide range of divine beings.

We make decisions by consensus, and balance individual autonomy with social responsibility.

Many activists and some other groups use a form of consensus-based decision-making. This process invites all voices to be heard, resulting in more balanced, creative, and inclusive decisions. Consensus requires that everyone has a voice, not just those in positions of leadership or those with the most experience. Consensus is the thoughtful discussion of all ideas, all pieces of knowing, and all voices to create a proposal that reflects the needs and desires of community. In the end, the decision is one that everyone can agree to, making it community-informed and led.

We work in diverse ways, including nonviolent direct action, for all forms of justice: environmental, social, political, racial, gender and economic. We are an anti-racist tradition that strives to uplift and center BIPOC voices (Black, Indigenous, People of Color).

The benefit of being an evolving tradition is that things can be examined and challenged, and things SHOULD be examined and challenged to support the ongoing and emerging needs of the community. In 2019, another global Dandelion gathering of Reclaiming witches took place in Petaluma, California, over several days, starting with a meeting about how to communicate and hold space for the discussions to come. I was sitting at a table eating a snack when a paper was passed to me: a letter penned by the DARC (Decolonizing Actions in Reclaiming Communities) cell, which had previously been shared with the wider Reclaiming community.

The letter describes itself as being

> a broad statement and invitation for dialogue, inquiry and growth to the broader Reclaiming community as we approach the 2019 International Dandelion Gathering. It has been developed in active dialogue with Black, Indigenous, People of Color (BIPOC) and Mixed Race witches—priestesses, activists, teachers and organizers—who are actively involved in this tradition of witchcraft.

This letter is an invitation for white-identified people in the tradition to more thoughtfully and carefully engage with people of color in the tradition. It outlines nine clear principles and practices to follow, including the recognition of Reclaiming as an ethnically diverse tradition and therefore, the use of *we* to encompass all Reclaiming witches is not necessarily accurate.

Highlighting the knowledge of BIPOC experience enables greater understanding and stronger boundaries for community care. By calling attention to harmful practices and thinking, this DARC letter inspired conversation long after that meeting, spreading that knowledge out to other groups and communities. There was a growing awareness of the need for shifts in language, thinking, and practice, and how that might look in different places. It called into question older language in the Principles of Unity that spoke of nonviolence, which is not always a realistic possibility for those living in Black and Brown bodies. Actions or strategies deemed violent by white or privileged classes may very well be what is needed to protect and defend one's life.

In addition, the Principles of Unity, and therefore the tradition as a whole, was not clear on anti-racism. Realizing this was not only requested by people of color within Reclaiming, but also essential in a culture steeped in white supremacy, there was a call to update the Principles of Unity again. Through meetings and community conversations, a consensus-based decision was made to include a stronger statement about Reclaiming being an anti-racist tradition in 2021. Not only does this make a strong statement and start to attend to the requests in the DARC letter, it also invites us to step into this shared aspiration.

We welcome all genders, all gender histories, all races, all ages and sexual orientations and all those differences of life situation, background, and ability that increase our diversity.

When a group makes it clear who is welcome, it is easier for someone new to step into that community. Knowing you are considered and called into the group creates a sense of belonging. However, statements are only a part of the practice, as action needs to follow.

During an Elements of Magic class in San Francisco, we spent some time in a park for our magickal work. It was warm and sunny, and a nice break from sitting in a loft apartment. On the way back from the park, a bystander started to yell at a person of color in the class. The yeller started with insults and then profanities. The person who was facing all of the verbal assault started to yell back. I was scared of violence; my brain frozen, I hesitated and could not think of what to do. I wanted to support the person in what they felt was the right response, but I was also sure I could do something else. Later I asked the student what could have happened to help them feel safer. They admitted to not knowing as it was a common, everyday occurrence. They said they weren't feeling unsafe, or maybe not more unsafe than they typically would, but they offered that the class of many white bodies could have surrounded them to act as a physical obstacle in case the yeller decided to get closer.

Being welcoming is not just what we say. Welcoming is also a practice of knowing when to step in to support others facing harm. Even though this student was not physically harmed, it is wise to remember that ongoing harm and verbal assaults are trauma given out in small, potent doses. Welcoming can also include getting to know everyone in a class, asking them what they need, and taking the time to learn what might have gone better. Collecting knowledge inspires creative actions and more ways to support those who may be exhausted from having to deal with everyday injustices.

We strive to make our public rituals and events accessible and safe.

Creating access in groups requires a careful examination of what makes an event accessible and safe. To learn more, we need to reach out to those who are often left voiceless because they can't get to events or they have limits to what they can do and when they can do it. This is a lesson in making the invisible visible and finding what has been lost.

Asking questions about accessibility is a great start, but listening to feedback is also essential. By listening to what is being offered, we learn about the lived experience and the impact of that. Today, Reclaiming groups committed to ongoing and expanded accessibility have self-selected, created their own rituals, and offer feedback to ritual planners and organizers. Access is a conversation that expands into how people move through spaces and what other barriers there are; for example, financial barriers.

We work to create and sustain communities and cultures that embody our values, that can help to heal the wounds of the earth and her peoples, and that can sustain us and nurture future generations.

Communities grow where they are nurtured. I think of how communities come together in the very first core class in Reclaiming: Elements of Magic. This class teaches about Reclaiming culture, ritual practices, and magick, and also how to work together in a group. At the end of this class is a co-created, collaborative ritual, planned and facilitated by the students, which brings together their knowledge and skills. This final ritual acts as a template for ongoing local community work where each participant adds their knowledge to practice magick together.

One of the practices I teach is embodiment exercises in which we tap into the knowledge of our bodies to inform the lessons. I've invited students to move as I read the Principles of Unity and then freeze when I stop reading. I encourage them to look around to see how the movements or positions are similar and how they are different. Often the positions will share some similarities, and students will smile at the shared experience.

Knowledge is shaped from different experiences, and everyone has something to contribute. Not only does this allow for the possibility of stepping into the wider community less encumbered by shadow and more energized by passion, but it also encourages sharing. When I get to use what I know, I am engaged, and I feel alive. I know that I am adding value to the greater whole.

A group of humans who feel passionate and who are honored for their knowing are hard to stop and even harder to control. It is often said that Reclaiming is an anarchist tradition. The Principles of Unity is a document that distills shared values, but it also offers a collective spell that evolves and responds. Twice amended by consensus, the Principles changed in response to a call to expand beyond the binary and clearly define Reclaiming's anti-racism stance.

In an overculture that seeks to separate humans on the basis of unearned privileges, prejudices, class, and ranking systems and encourage rugged individualism, the knowledge we share and celebrate is the pathway to sustainable collaboration, community, and co-creation. It is the ongoing commitment to ourselves, to others, and to the world. It is the renewal of hope that asks us to pack up what we have traveled with, get in the car, and drive into the woods to gather with witches and activists once more.

BRINGING YOUR
KNOWLEDGE INTO THE WORLD

Bringing our knowledge into the world is a lifelong process. We share knowledge through conversation, art, community work, raising children, planting gardens, social media, and how we show up in the world and in the way we interact with others. Many of us are engaged with some sort of knowledge sharing as part of our job. Some knowledge is secret or only to be shared under certain circumstances, whereas other knowledge is better the wider it is spread; for example, knowledge about consent, diversity, and justice. Knowledge is often specialist: how to graft a fruit tree, structural engineering specifications for building a house, all sorts of technical, scientific, and historical areas, just to mention a few fields.

Often we may hold a depth of knowledge on a particular topic that is not much use to the general public, but part of it may be, or to a certain level. That is, while not everyone will want to know the ins and outs of how batteries that store solar energy work, many or even most people may want to know how viable they are, what circumstances they are appropriate for, or how to obtain and use them. Being a specialist in something that sounds ordinary—how to use your local library, creating healthy meals that kids love, how to stay sane on a dating app—can, for others, be a piece of knowledge they would love for you to share!

Sometimes it just randomly happens that our knowledge gets paired into a circumstance where it's recognized, valued, and received; other times we have to search for or even create those circumstances. Leaving secret knowledge to one side for now, knowledge—like Eve's apple—is meant to be offered, shared, and partaken of. Even secret knowledge, under the right circumstances, is the same. Perhaps you already are someone who shares your knowledge in many directions and forums, or maybe not. This process offers a starting point to sharing some of the knowledge you hold, partly with the aim of getting it out there into the world but mostly to have the experience of what it means to deliberately share your knowledge.

» You will need: journal and pen

» Time: For the process, 30–40 minutes. For the knowledge sharing itself, it depends on format and delivery method.

Brainstorming

» What knowledge do you hold that is rare or specialist? This might include professional or academic knowledge. Use dot points in your journal to list some of these things.

» What knowledge have you gathered about everyday things that other people often seem not to know? Again, jot some of these things down in dot points.

» What knowledge have you worked really hard for? Continue with your dot points.

» What knowledge do you have that is quirky, unusual, or particular to you? Everyone has some things. Try for at least two or three dot points.

Choosing a Knowledge-Sharing Forum

Read back through your dot points with an eye to which pieces of knowledge you might wish to or be willing to share with others. Circle these or underline them.

Now consider what forums you have for sharing. Perhaps you write a blog, participate in neighborhood gatherings or a community garden, are a member of a coven, or have big family gatherings. Perhaps you have a leadership or management role at work, coach a sports club, or organize a book club, kids' play group, or something else. Maybe you post on Instagram or TikTok, run workshops or public rituals, or love to hold events in your home.

List the forums you already use or have access to, as well as any others that you've been wanting to explore but haven't quite got to yet (finally getting to a WitchCamp, summer music school, or joining Toastmasters).

Once you have this list, look for obvious or potential matches between the knowledge and the forum. Your expertise in how to make exciting and nutritious kids' lunches matches perfectly with your parents-and-kids Saturday hangouts at the park, and pretty well with Instagram, and also fits in with the large family holidays over summer. Your wealth of knowledge about how to mentor and support other staff goes brilliantly with the in-house training day at work and could also potentially be a blog or online article. Your specialist knowledge about contemporary young adult fiction could be a talk at your local library, a series of videos on YouTube, or a special session at your book club.

Sharing the Knowledge

To start with, pick one from all these options; also choose a backup choice just in case the first doesn't work out.

Form a plan of how you will go about sharing the knowledge of your first choice.

It's possible that we will immediately go into some form of self-doubt or disinterest or spiral into negative thinking about ourselves, our capabilities, and even our knowledge. If this happens, try running the Pearl Pentacle, observing how Love flows into Law, Wisdom, Liberty, and then Knowledge. Think of yourself as completing this point so the Pearl energy can transition back to Love, and even of the sharing of Knowledge as being one of the paths back to Love.

If this doesn't work or fully convince you, I recommend running the Iron Pentacle as a diagnostic. What point or points of Sex, Pride, Self, Power, and Passion are causing stumbling blocks for you here? Perhaps you will need to do some work with one or more of those points before you can bring yourself back to completing this sharing the knowledge exercise.

Once you find a way to share your knowledge, go ahead and do it! Hurray!

Reflection

After you have shared your knowledge in the forum you chose, reflect on this exercise. How easy or difficult was this for you? What has the process brought up? What gifts did it offer you? Would you repeat it or continue it? Are you inspired to encourage and support others to do the same, whether they are your colleagues, your children, or your coven mates?

ACTIVITY

DIVINING KNOWLEDGE

One of my (Fio's) most regular practices is divination. I am almost always divining in order to know something. I might ask, *If I take this action or make this choice, how would my life look and feel? If I go on this trip at this time of year, what might happen, and what is best for me to know?* The words *to know* come up a lot in readings I do for other people. The word *should* comes up a lot too. I'd like to strike that word from the record; I always ask the person to rephrase from *Should I* to *What if* or *How would it be?*

In this practice, it is not necessary to have had a deep apprenticeship to a divination system, but if you are a complete beginner you are invited to work with an oracle deck or a tarot deck whose imagery speaks to you. If you are blind or limited in vision, you might want to assemble a whole host of items that you can touch in a big bowl or bag and feel your way through the divination by touch. And if you are an old hat at the arts of divination, try to anchor into beginner's mind and approach the work with open willingness and curiosity.

In the Reclaiming tradition we often throw cards together in groups and build the reading with many perspectives. We do this with Nordic and Old English runes as well, and with clouds and astrological charts and dreams. The knowledge of the group, greater than the sum of its parts, is one of the reasons we love Reclaiming magic and witchcraft.

> » You will need: a system of divination that works for
> you, a journal and pen, and a quiet, private space
> » Time: 40–60 minutes

Acknowledge country. Ground and center, and align your souls.

Run the Pearl Pentacle (see page 271) through the points several times over, starting gradually and checking in with each point, and then going a little faster as you pick up energy. Each time you get to the Knowledge point (anchored in your left foot), pause and go a little deeper. Enquire into the Knowledge point: *What is best for me to know right now in my life?*

When you feel you have accessed a response—and this might be in words, images, feelings, or knowings—touch your divination system. If this involves a computer and astrology programs, then go to your computer and touch the keys, ready to make those keystrokes! Touch the cards, the rune or ogham staves, the yarrow sticks, or candle that you are about to scry with . . . bring what you need to the system of divination. Cast the reading.

Now it is time to slowly meditate on the original order of the Pearl Pentacle points as they go around the circle. Meditate on each point fully without anchoring them into parts of the body. Let yourself meditate on Love and then Wisdom, then Knowledge (pause here for longer), then Law, culminating with Liberty. When I (Fio) returned to this original order that the Andersons taught to their students, I felt myself receiving rich understandings about both the Iron and the Pearl Pentacles. I invite you to sink into the knowledge encoded in this progression of the points.

Now return your attention to the divination casting and begin to journal your insights, reflections, thoughts, feelings, and knowings.

You may have heard of clairvoyants (those who clearly see) or clairaudients (those who clearly hear) or clairsentients (those who clearly sense). There's also the category of claircognizance, which means clear knowing. This is more common than you would think; this is available to all of us. Our deep, wild, wise bodies know things. We are bodies of knowledge, after all. The knowing will come through you, and this is intrinsically mysterious. Be open and curious about this mystery of knowledge.

When you feel you have written or drawn enough in your journal, you can clear up the space. How you choose to integrate your findings to make decisions in your life is up to you. You may also want to repeat this with different forms of divination about the same question. This can be done at the same time or within days of the previous reading. There is a special layered effect built up between a tarot, Lenormand, rune, and ogham reading.

Divination is all about desiring *to know*. We are desiring to know something of the divine unfolding of things, especially for our nexus of the web, our part of the puzzle. Divination is natural and normal, and we can all learn to do it. I invite you to acknowledge that you are a divine being relating to other divine beings, and that you are your own spiritual authority and need no other person to interpret the sacred to you, as it says in the Reclaiming Principles of Unity. And when you get stuck or feel confused and lost, remember to ask for help. You can always seek divination from a reputable reader and trusted beloved. You still get to decide what you do with that information you receive.

KNOWLEDGE IS INITIATION

RAVYN STANFIELD

I want you to imagine you are in the forest when they come to take you. You have studied. You have memorized. You have prepared. You know something will happen next, but the only instructions they gave you were to come to the edge of the forest and wait. You lift your chin and stare into the darkness, defiant, in case anyone is watching. Inside, you shiver. What will this initiation be like? How will it change me?

Humans collaborate with land and spirits to create initiation processes. These initiations mark rites of transformation and pass knowledge from the more experienced to the less experienced members of a community. A traditional initiation in many First Nations cultures might begin with a symbolic death and climax in a rebirth ritual. Some rituals involve ordeals that test people to their limits; even symbolic death can leave an extreme impact. When we pass through the gates of life and death, whether real or simulated, we learn what is on the other side. What we know after that experience fundamentally changes us. Initiations often culminate in the sharing of knowledge, known only to those who have been through the process already, perhaps learning secrets or receiving a new name.

I was born blue faced and choking, my neck constricted by my mother's cord. Would I live or would I die? Everyone held their breaths as the doctors unwrapped my throat. I sucked in air. I turned pink, knowing breath and sound for the first time. That is when they gave me the name of my grandmother.

When I was a child, I wanted to know the secret names of things, to understand the deeper and wilder workings of the world. I could sense the way everything sings to everything, and I wanted to be a part of that song. I grew up in a conservative Catholic family where many things that were pleasurable were forbidden. I grew up being taught a myth that everyone suffered because the first woman wanted to Know things, and that was a sin. But I knew there was something missing from what I learned in Sunday School. No one was teaching us how to connect to the divine beauty imbued in the way bees danced from flower to flower or the dramatic flash of a lightning storm. Maybe they didn't know?

It made sense to treat your neighbor with respect and not to steal or lie. It didn't make sense that loving who you wanted and refusing to sacrifice your child when God asked were wrong. Still, I thought I could feel the divine sometimes when we sang. When our voices carried us through the rafters and into the expanding clouds, I knew it was holy. I wanted to know more things like that.

What knowledge have you sought in the first half of your life? The second half? What knowledge will you dream of seeking in the future? The pursuit of knowledge requires passion and motivation. Some of us lust after knowledge to make sense of the world. We exchange healing protocols, gardening secrets, breaking science, and life hacks.

In a capitalist society, education is often reserved for the elite. It is no accident that herbal and midwifery apprenticeships were replaced by expensive institutions charging a lot of money for people to study medicine. The quest for knowledge can be radical; to share information reserved for a chosen few can set it free. What has pushed you to learn what you now know? Many of us are susceptible to clicking through the interwebs searching for answers, traveling the strands of the worldwide web of knowledge. What passion keeps us from going to bed until we have what we seek?

I can't seem to stay away from initiatory experiences. Each time my life dropped me at the gates to something new, I took the holy risk to cross over the threshold. There have been births and deaths, marriage and divorce, graduations, all the first and last times, debilitating losses, absolute triumphs, all the changes of an aging body, standing up to powerful forces, and finding and using my voice. Even though it is often life-changing, I recommend taking the holy risk and crossing the threshold. On the other side of every initiation—even the ones I would never have chosen—has been beautiful knowledge. And I have not done it alone.

I want you to imagine that you trust yourself and your initiators. They did come to take you from that dark forest. You chose them because they knew something that you wanted to know. The ones who were wiser or more experienced than you scooped you up and swore to travel beside you as you faced all the challenges before you. They sensed things beyond your comprehension and connected your everyday being to a larger ethereal pattern. They pushed you toward the best version of yourself. Even though the ways they pushed you may have been frightening, I want you to imagine you can trust these challenges will help your transformation.

Knowledge, like air, is all around us and welcomes our inspiration and conspiracy with it to share it with others. Knowledge helps us move forward and answer human questions of *Who? What? Where? When? Why? How?* Knowledge includes my intellect but is not limited to this. Our embodied senses are the gateways to knowledge. It is no accident that we live in a world that asks us to push beyond our senses and ignore the information from them. *I think, therefore I am* is one of the most damaging phrases ever written. Descartes led us down the path of separation from our sight, sound, taste, smell, and touch. We have constructed a world where human comfort is prioritized over relationship to the planet. We participate in these elaborate and destructive systems, even though our eyes dislike the plastic garbage littering the streets and our ears shrink from sounds of constant traffic or gunshots. If we want to enter meaningful relationships with the world around us, we must learn to trust our own knowing again.

The more I know the natural world around me, the deeper I love it. I walk through the forest and see vine maple thrive in the shade of Douglas fir trees. A thrill runs up my spine when I see the first trillium flowers of the spring. Their blossoms mean the forest soil is healthy. In my herbal studies I learn the names, the behaviors, and the seasonal shifts of my more-than-human family. I learn which parts of the plant help different parts of human bodies and how to prepare them for safe ingestion. I wonder about the longtime agreements humans have with them. They create oxygen for us; we eat them. We feed them carbon dioxide; they heal our bodies when we ingest them with intention. We are buried to nourish the ground for new growth. I want to relate with them, my kin. Perhaps we do talk with each other, though not in the English language. It's something deeper that we both understand. I don't know if we have enough time to learn to communicate before the climate collapses and the forests are gone.

Even as the ongoing damage of colonization separates many of us from true intimacy with place, humans are asked to know this stolen land in a way that will help heal climate damage. The love affair between people and places is a devotional relationship built over time. Many First Nations people are cultural experts in making this relationship work when they manage land. Many Indigenous groups are making clear requests about the ways that they would prefer to be supported and how theft of land can be repaired. This is knowledge worth pursuing with passion. There are petitions to be signed, donations to be made, meetings to attend, and causes to support. The movement to return stewardship of land to those from whom it was stolen is growing exponentially. How can non-Indigenous people partner with folks who know ways to approach the land on which we live with respect?

When we know, we make informed decisions. We move closer to action and change.

I imagine you at the point where the challenges of your initiation grow tiresome. You wonder when it will be over. Your body may have already been pushed to the limit. Your heart may have been not just broken but burned to a crisp. Maybe now you fall to your knees and allow sobs to shake you. Maybe you curl up on the ground and wait to be swallowed by the earth. You doubt it will ever end . . . What are you supposed to be learning from this, anyway?

The blood of the coven is thicker than the water of the womb. This saying has been convoluted to mean the opposite of its original intention. Chosen ties, in which we hold sacred knowledge together, may be the strongest bonds. Witches held knowledge and were burned for it. Knowing how to safely deliver a baby, treat a wet cough, or protect yourself from a jealous lover could get you killed. If you wrote the secret down and witch finders found it, you would die. If you named your coven when they tortured you, the coven would die.

Perhaps these days it isn't necessary to suffer in order to learn, but initiatory challenges can test our commitment to carry powerful knowledge. What is our obligation to knowing? Much of the time, it is vital that knowledge doesn't end with us. We pass it from one to another. Knowledge claims our collaboration, a place to unearth new inspiration. We get out of our own heads and share space in the creative void, using the chemistry of two or more to shape something that we would not have formed by ourselves. Creative partnerships or group work can open us to worlds of possibilities that we would never have considered alone.

When people who know themselves come together and work on a project, it is refreshing. The agitations that come up in the community have a much better chance of providing fodder for evolution. Knowledge spreads from the individual to the group: *What did we learn together? Here is where we were successful. This is where we got stuck.* We must remember or record what we have discovered, what we know now. We realize all this together. Take a dream and make it real so the knowledge will stay.

When I pursued the path of becoming a healer, I had to meet the resistance of those around me. In one conversation with my mother, she rattled off reasons why I shouldn't study to be an acupuncturist, why I shouldn't call myself a healer, why the word *witch* was the worst possible word to describe a woman or femme. Something bloomed inside my throat. I felt a warm, tingling force coat the inside of my lungs and expand upward through my vocal cords. *I know what's good for me,* I said.

At the entrance of the Temple of Apollo at Delphi, the words *know thyself* are inscribed. The work of diving deeply into the self and repeatedly asking the questions of who we are can offer us these answers. When I ask who I am and listen without judgment, I get to build a relationship with what's inside me. Carl Jung used the term *shadow* to name the unconscious qualities that each of us carry, both negative and positive. When I bristle at what I perceive as arrogance in a coworker, I have to look at myself and the ways I struggle to allow people to help me. When I admire someone's art, I can also look at myself and the wild creative impulse shining within me. When we have this kind of knowledge rooted in the self, we catch ourselves when we act from shadow. We set ourselves free from our own sabotage by building trust in our bodies, our intuitions, our lessons. With self-knowledge, we start to forgive ourselves for all the errors that we have made. We know that we can recover from hurt and even thrive.

What do we avoid knowing? If we fear knowing what is wrong, we will not face ourselves, recognize harm, and make repair, yet we can take breaks from the barrage of information that comes in through our senses and our screens. That is reasonable and healthy. Knowing ourselves unlocks the gates of the heart in a healthy way. We relinquish the thoroughfare that opens so wide that anything can overwhelm our being and the fortress that protects us from every harmful potential. Instead, our hearts have uncomplicated gates that open and close as we know whether to use our boundaries more and less. When I know myself, I know what I like and what hurts me.

I imagine you standing before that gate, the one from which no one returns. In the stories the gate is guarded by a monstrous being who threatens and interrogates. You may tremble, not knowing how you can possibly conquer this looming behemoth. You are vulnerable, broken in a million places. All you can do is stand there, naked and messy. Whatever this guardian asks, you can only respond from what you Know. That is the only way through.

Sometimes we make the mistake of thinking knowledge gives us control or will ensure that we know how to respond to any situation. Every time someone in my life gets a cancer diagnosis, everything I think that I know is challenged. With the news that *it's cancer*, the bottom can drop out of your world. Over the years, I have sat with some of my most beloveds biting my nails as we wait for test results. The pathology reports from the doctors can hold terrible data or joyful relief. Either way, it is knowledge that we must seek in order to know what to do next.

One of my best friends battled breast cancer twice. She followed the treatment plan that experienced professionals recommended for her. With every choice, there was a side effect to be soothed or a painful protest in a different part of her body. One pain medication caused extreme itching. The other resulted in excess stomach acid that burned hotter than the surgery incision. We both experienced great frustration when she would tell medical staff what she was experiencing and they would tell her it wasn't possible. She soon learned that if she was really going to destroy the tumors and heal from the cancer, then she needed to both listen to the doctors and trust her own intuition. Both kinds of knowledge were necessary if she was going to survive.

When humans don't know what to do, we often panic. We always want to know what the prognosis is, which step to take next, and how to fight obstacles. We want to make a plan. We seek information and ways to organize our lives so that we can find as much ease as possible. We attempt to fill in all the blanks, sometimes seeking to control the future by doing so. The place of not knowing can also be a holy place. This is sometimes the threshold from which we call outside ourselves for knowledge or search for answers within. Our research into the unknown is sacred.

We desperately want to know what's going to happen, but the future is not fixed. The only thing we know for certain is that we will die someday. This knowledge allows us to hold what we love close and search for the magic in everything.

I want you to imagine that you walked, stumbled, crawled, fell, or rolled through that magical gate. You used all your senses to know what is there for you on the other side. Maybe they gave you a new name. Maybe you fell in love with yourself. You are both the same and not at all the same. It may feel impossible to express the difference in what you knew before and what you know now. Or it may feel crystalline and shining, emanating from your skin or your core. It is helpful not to hold this alone. Others who have followed this path can help you integrate and become whole.

In the Pearl Pentacle, we begin and end with Love. This Love comes from red-hot Iron and so it is fierce. Love occurs when we are strong enough to return to life force, even through the initiations of life that feel painful. Love is about the self knowing another, whether this is an animal or plant or the relationship with our planet or another human. Knowledge connects with Love. This version of Knowledge cracks the heart open; it's the way my being moves toward something and makes room to understand it. We form energetic connections between ourselves and other beings as we begin to accept our interdependence.

I sat with my beloved grandmother as she was dying. She was ready to pass through the gates at ninety-two years old. She whispered to the hospice nurses that I was her first-born grandchild and we shared a name. The story goes that she was so excited about my birth, she sped to the airport and jumped onto the first flight she could board. Once seated on the plane, she looked down and realized that she was still wearing her bedroom slippers.

Her last words to me were *I love you more than you know*. They hit me right in the soft part of my belly because she was leaving. She was the person who loved me the best in the world. If she loved me even more than I knew, how much love was there beneath the surface that I didn't consciously perceive? How much love is there for all of us?

More than we know.

we have been rewritten in knowledge

changed

and we remember—

remember we are made for love

through love

in love

falling in love endlessly

deeper and deeper into mystery

deeper into the pearl currents

the ocean of our lives

love is the law after all

law reveals wisdom

and through the wild and fierce heart

we encounter the truth of liberation

our freedom all bound together

this we know . . .

love—law—wisdom—liberty—knowledge—

the pearl current—renews us

A PENTACLE OF BRIDGES

DAWN ISIDORA

Many years ago now, early in my Reclaiming teaching days, my local community was asking for a Pearl Pentacle class. I had taken and taught Iron Pentacle many times, but I had only taken Pearl Pentacle a few times and had never taught it. Confronted with teaching, I attempted a deep dive into running and working with the points of Love, Law, Wisdom, Liberty, and Knowledge in preparation. At that time, as I looked around at the world and my various communities, I felt there was a real dearth of Love, Law, Wisdom, Liberty, and Knowledge. I concluded that while the Iron Pentacle points of Sex, Pride, Self, Power, and Passion were vital and present, the Pearl Pentacle, as yet, was aspirational. We wanted and even needed it to exist, but as yet I could not experience it.

I needed a tool that would help me find my way to the Pearl Pentacle points of Love, Law, Wisdom, Liberty, and Knowledge. I'd studied Pearl Pentacle with my friend Thorn Coyle, who describes the Pearl Pentacle points as emanations—a higher vibration of the Iron Pentacle points. I had also learned from Thorn to associate the pentacle points with the elements of spirit, fire, air, earth, and water, and had been working these associations with the Iron Pentacle. Starting at the Iron Pentacle point and guided by the appropriate elemental point, I pondered, mulled, tranced, and generally ruminated upon how I could move from the experience of the Iron Pentacle point to the Pearl Pentacle point. I felt I needed a path, a road, a bridge that could take me from my vital Iron energies out toward the more etheric Pearl energies.

It would be lovely to report that these points came to me in a sudden blush of inspiration, but they did not. It took me years to complete what I began referring to as my Bridge Pentacle. Several points came nearly instantaneously, a couple of others folded in over time, and the fifth hung awkwardly silent for years. Even once I'd found that fifth bridge, it didn't feel balanced and solid until I finally switched the Pearl Pentacle points of Knowledge and Wisdom, moving Wisdom up to the left hand and Knowledge to the left foot. The name of the bridges that have presented themselves to me are Connection, Integrity, Awareness, Responsibility, and Temperance.

IRON	BRIDGE	PEARL
SEX	CONNECTION	LOVE
PRIDE	INTEGRITY	LAW
SELF	AWARENESS	WISDOM
POWER	RESPONSIBILITY	LIBERTY
PASSION	TEMPERANCE	KNOWLEDGE

Here was a Pentacle of Bridges, my road map of how to move from the Iron Pentacle toward the Pearl Pentacle. Perhaps these bridges will resonate with you or perhaps you will find yourself devising your own pentacle of bridges.

Connection is the journey of Sex to Love, consciously choosing healthy connections to my selves, my intimates, my communities, and the wild and domesticated spaces around me. As long as I worked those healthy connections, my bridge from Sex to Love was strong, clear, and well lit. The sensation of connection is the essence of the sacred element spirit, as I described in my essay on spirit in *Elements of Magic*. For many years I taught workshops on sacred sexuality with Ravyn Stanfield and had explored the relationship between sex and spirit. The pulsing contraction and expansion of the heart at the center ever radiating outward to the circumference of all, her loving arms embracing everything.

Integrity is the journey from Pride to Law. Guided strongly by fire's qualities of action and creativity, right action, or integrity, as I came to call this point, was more complex to sort out. Fire taught me that pride was about what we do and how we move through the worlds. Right-sized pride is not *I have nice hair* or *people like my chicken soup*. Right-sized pride is *I put in a good afternoon's work in the garden* and *I navigated that difficult conversation with some grace*. Fire teaches me that Pride is about what I do and how I act.

So how does this move toward Law? When I teach Pearl Pentacle, I talk about Law's duality. We have natural law and societal law. With natural law there is no arguing, no debate; gravity pulls the falling apple to the earth, the cyclical nature of the seasons is immutable.

These things occur outside of any debate of right and wrong. Societal laws, on the other hand, are all about debate; debate is intrinsic in the earliest notations of laws. Talmudic scholars still debate the meaning of ancient texts—those ten commandments became the basis of so many of our laws and modern concepts of right and wrong. Moving from Pride to Law had to be based in action, not words or thoughts. Taking the right action at the right time, in the right place, and so Integrity moved me into alignment with Law.

Awareness. Emanating from Self toward Wisdom, air drew my attention to the practice of awareness, an opening of all the senses. Wendy Palmer's work on aikido, described in her book *The Intuitive Body* (North Atlantic Books, 2000), helped me learn to be equally present with what is before and behind me, to my left and my right, above and below, noticing the relationships between things, time, and space. For me, Wisdom feels like remembering and re-membering. In times when I have lost my sense of self through inattention or trauma, I have been able to call those lost pieces of myself back to me through gentle yet resolute awareness. Awareness guides me back to a wholeness that has the capacity to remember wisdom. Self—Awareness—Wisdom—yes, that was it! I had been looking for something more complex, airy, and intellectual rather than the profound simplicity and humility of is-ness.

Responsibility. To move from Power toward Liberty takes personal responsibility; ability plus the action of responding. My work here is to find and hold my own power and use it toward the liberty of all beings. Astrologically I am quite Saturnian. I have discovered that responsibility is second nature for me. An impulse to shoulder the load is not something I chafe against. That sense of personal responsibility, of what is mine to do, the next thing needed, is a relief for me. Carrying my share of responsibility brings me a glimpse of the liberty I hope one day we all experience.

Temperance. What is the path that Passion takes to flow into Knowledge? First I had to reclaim passion from its fire associations. Passion aligns with water in the elemental pentacle that Thorn taught me. Passion is about caring deeply. When considering knowledge, I realized I had to haul it back from the musty corridors of academia; I had to reclaim knowledge from the hierarchical, elitist, and colonialist definitions. Knowledge informed by water points to gut knowing, or the kind of knowledge that comes from experience and intuition; a knowledge that is felt in the whole body; every watery cell is infused with it. When finally Temperance arrived, it arrived as Pamela Colman Smith's illustration in the Smith-Waite Tarot. Not the temperance of the early twentieth-century US that outlawed alcohol but the temperance of alchemy and the temperance that asks us to transform, balance, and integrate. Tempering is also a process to toughen ferrous metals—often iron (!) and iron alloys—in blacksmithing. We temper our passions to transform them into knowledge that is strong, balanced, and integrated.

Here is a process to explore this Bridge Pentacle further. Begin by running the Iron Pentacle current (see page 271). When this feels alive within you, move your attention to your center. Feel the ancient energy of iron, of your ferrous blood, pulse in your beating heart. Notice the molten energy of the earth's core—the great below—rise up into your being. Welcome the star energy of the heavens—the great above—and let it flow down into your being. Feel those energies mix and swirl at your center. Take several slow breaths deep down into your belly.

When you feel your energy distilled, from that center, turn your attention toward your head and open to the sacred element of spirit and the Iron point of Sex. Sense into what is here for you. Open to perceive sights, sounds, smells, sensations. Consider that you are surveying the landscapes of Sex and spirit. Now turn your attention to the far horizon. There glows the realm of Love. Imagine, remember, find the bridge that leads from your Sex/spirit toward Love. Perhaps this bridge is called Connection or perhaps your bridge from Sex to Love has another name. Notice the bridge that will carry you toward the Pearl Pentacle point of Love. When you feel ready, return your attention to your center and take a few clearing, cleansing breaths.

Repeat this process respectively with fire and Pride into Law . . . air and Self into Wisdom . . . earth and Power into Liberty . . . water and Passion into Knowledge. Each time open to imagine into and remember the associated bridge or a bridge of your own discovery. Breathe in

IRON PENTACLE

**BRIDGES BETWEEN
IRON AND PEARL**

PEARL PENTACLE

the gifts of these bridges: Connection, Integrity, Awareness, Responsibility, and Temperance. Breathe in curiosity, breathe out gratitude. Blessed be.

This road map of how to get from an Iron to a Pearl experience has made all the difference for me. I have worked with these bridges for many years, and I now feel I can easily access the Pearl Pentacle, experiencing Love, Law, Wisdom, Liberty, and Knowledge. While I still at times experience the Pearl points as aspirational, I also have embodied them as very real and present. Perhaps because I have worked hard to find them, I am now more compassionate and understanding when they appear less than perfectly. Or perhaps years and years of working with and teaching my Bridge Pentacle has pointed me toward what's been there all along. And now I know how to find my way back to them.

RITUAL BASICS

ACKNOWLEDGMENT OF COUNTRY

An acknowledgment of country is a spoken acknowledgment of the Indigenous peoples and lands whose country we are on. The acknowledgment includes the names of those peoples and lands as best we know them. Ideally, it names that we are currently here through a process of invasion, theft, and colonization.

This happens at the very start: that is, before people are introduced (even the speaker), before the grounding, before anything.

An acknowledgment of country recognizes that we are on stolen and occupied land. It acknowledges the violence and horror of that occupation, sometimes including specific information about local atrocities.

It is drawn from ancient protocols of Indigenous peoples, where lands, boundaries, and belonging are recognized and one waits to be welcomed before crossing these boundaries.

At the very least, an acknowledgment is the equivalent of knocking on someone's door before entering their house. We are here for a ritual or activity, but firstly we acknowledge those whose land it rightfully is.

The University of Minnesota Libraries Guide notes that such an acknowledgment also

> respects tribal sovereignty, highlights local Native peoples and groups, and offers suggestions for actions people can take to support Indigenous communities and initiatives.

> A land acknowledgment is a way to educate, inform, and spark action. It is only a first step toward reconciling and addressing past harms and ensuring no further harm is done. **Actions will always speak louder than words.** It is hoped that the knowledge gained in the writing of an acknowledgment will underpin the actions you or your organization will take in the future.[12]

---

12   University of Minnesota Libraries, "Writing Land Acknowledgments."

Such actions, according to the Native Governance Center (United States), might include:

» donations of time and/or money to Indigenous organizations

» actively supporting Indigenous-led movements for change and justice

» commit to returning land to Indigenous groups through local, state, federal, or personal avenues

Anyone can make the acknowledgment of country at the start of a ritual, gathering, meeting, class, or other event. If this has not been planned or allowed for, we can always ask to have it included.

An Acknowledgment of Country Is Not

» a welcome to country, which can only be made by an Indigenous person whose country we are on at the time

» a piece that occurs anywhere within the ritual; it happens at the very beginning

» a trance; we have our eyes open and are fully engaged with each other and the acknowledgment

» a grounding or part of the grounding

» to be replaced by talking about the faeries, land spirits, other deities, or land energies, although sometimes it may include this

» centered on the speaker, who usually does not mention their own name (unless they are Indigenous and making the acknowledgment from that perspective)

» assuming that we have done this many times so we don't need to think about it again

An Acknowledgment of Country May

» name the names of the peoples and lands, insofar as they are known

» ask if there is any Indigenous person present who wishes to speak the acknowledgment

» acknowledge any Indigenous people who are present (usually not by name unless this has been checked with the individuals beforehand or their presence at the gathering is the reason for the gathering)

» make mistakes; we learn by taking risks (perhaps a name will be mispronounced or missed or . . . best practice is that we thank those who point out the imperfections, and keep learning)

» include a heartfelt sentence or two about local historic atrocities, current struggles, or expressions of solidarity

» be brief, especially if the person speaking it is unfamiliar with that land or is new to making acknowledgments

» invite those present to reflect for a moment (silently) on the land and its Indigenous peoples

» invite those present to reflect on the land where they live and its Indigenous peoples

» name specific actions those present can take to align with these intentions of recognizing Native title and land

How to Make an Acknowledgment of Country

Find out the names of the country and its First Peoples. There can be more than one name, there can be disputes about the names and the boundaries of lands, there may be a complex history impacted by colonization. Ask for advice, include this information in the acknowledgment, and be prepared to make mistakes.

Find out if there is an accepted format for an acknowledgment where you are. In Australia one recommended format is:

> Our meeting/conference/workshop is being held on the lands of the [traditional owner's name] people, and I wish to acknowledge them as traditional owners.

> I would also like to pay my respects to their elders, past and present, and Aboriginal elders of other communities who may be here today.[13]

This basic format can be expanded to include a more personal note, as listed above.

If there is no format where you are, ask a few people and then make one up. It can always be different next time. If it conveys respect and acknowledgment, it will be better than not having one at all.

Usually if speakers are going to be on a stage, the acknowledgment would be spoken from the stage. If you are in a circle, the acknowledgment can be spoken either from the middle of the circle or on the edge.

The acknowledgment is in service and on behalf of all the people present, to bring their attention and awareness to Indigenous land and peoples. It is not about the speaker or their personal journey with this material unless that speaker is an Indigenous person.

---

13 State Government of Victoria, "Acknowledgment of Traditional Owners."

GROUNDING

We ground ourselves before magic, at the beginning of ritual, before we start to work with or run the Pearl Pentacle, and at any other moment during our day when we want a reminder of being in our solid body completely here on planet Earth. Along the way, on our journey with magic and ritual, we learn some techniques that work well for us and incorporate them into our daily practice, how we show up to a ritual or magical event, as well as a resource we can call upon in stressful life situations. Ideally each breath would ground us, reminding us we are in a body—this body—and returning our attention to the present moment.

Grounding is a simple practice, although sometimes in larger or group rituals we choose to do it more elaborately. I (JM) like to remind myself and others that this isn't a trance, and to help with that we usually ground ourselves with our eyes open. We don't want to imagine we're somewhere else as the aim is to bring ourselves fully here. Sometimes we might choose to close our eyes for a breath or two, running an internal body check, before opening our eyes again and orienting ourselves to the situation. During the grounding we notice how we are feeling both physically and emotionally and can make small adjustments to bring greater comfort and ease; for example, relaxing our stomach muscles, adjusting our shoulders, repositioning ourselves. We can't force a grounding on ourselves or anyone else; rather, the best practice is a reminder to return to a relaxed but alert state of being, connected to ourselves and the present moment, ready for other things to start happening.

Three Simple Grounding Techniques

1 Take a deep breath, and as it releases shake your hands, arms, and whole body, imagining you are shaking off whatever happened before this moment. Do this for three breaths. Then take a few slow, relaxed breaths with your eyes open. Feel into your center or core, either conceptually or by placing one or both hands on your body, then notice what is around you. You are grounded.

2 Think of a tree. You might imagine you are standing next to a tree or that you are a tree, or just think of calling up treelike qualities. Sink down into the roots of this tree, imagining what it is like below the surface of the earth wherever you are, and think of those roots drawing up nourishment from the soil. Bring this feeling and thought up into your body about as far as your midsection. Then stretch up above—in thought or with your hands or arms—to the starscape, imagining branches and leaves. Allow yourself to draw in nourishment from the sunlight, starlight, and air. Bring this feeling and thought down into your body about as far as your midsection. Allow the two energies of earth and stars to mingle and spread throughout your body. Open your eyes if they've been closed. You are grounded.

3 Become aware of the soles of your feet. Train all your senses there. What can you feel with your feet? You might want to curl your toes, shift your weight, take your shoes off, imagine your feet are kissing the ground, or rub or skim each foot across the floor or earth. Still focusing on the soles of your feet, consider the information they might feed you about the ground, what's below, and how it is to be connected with that ground. Open your eyes if they've been closed. Allow the solidity of the earth to enter into your feet and from there travel up through your whole body. Take some deep breaths of this earthiness. You are grounded.

CREATING MAGICAL SPACE

Before a ritual or a magical working, after acknowledging land and grounding ourselves, usually we dedicate the space and time to our ritual, spell, or whatever it is. Many people might cast a circle, others acknowledge the directions and/or the elements, and some create or revive a temple space or charge an altar.

Creating magical space—however you do it—is great as a demarcation between life as usual and a time and space dedicated to making magic and ritual. By these actions we indicate the nature of our container to ourselves, others there, and also to the gods, other beings, and energetic forms such as the Pearl Pentacle. We move consciously into the work and the magic, and when we're done, we move consciously out of it.

We don't really think that any space is less magical before we begin or after we finish our work; rather, we consider that we are choosing to consciously inhabit the magical realm, deliberately turning our focus and attention there. In inhabiting magical space, what we are really doing is more fully inhabiting our own magical selves, and if we are working with others, we're doing this together.

Creating magical space and casting a circle can be done many, many ways. Some people use magical tools, for example an athame or wand, while others use voices, song, and drumming. Some people like to orient to the elements in different directions; others call to the elements all in the center; still others might not call to the elements at all. Some like to move around the perimeter of the circle (usually clockwise in the Northern Hemisphere and counterclockwise in the Southern Hemisphere, or sunwise in both cases), whereas some prefer to stay in the center. If you have a group of people, you may pass the casting person to person around the edge of the circle. Some start in the north or the south or the east; some might not notice or care which direction they begin in. Some include above and below as directions, others also (or instead) include center.

We have experimented with casting a pentacle rather than a circle when doing pentacle work. Sometimes this might be laid out along the ground with ribbon or chalk; other times it is walked through. Maybe there are small altars at each point—for the Pearl Pentacle there would be altars for Love, Law, Wisdom, Liberty, and Knowledge and we might have a central altar with some pearls, maybe a mirror, and some seawater.

On the whole, dedicating some time and attention right at the beginning of the ritual to the magical space seems to work well. Remembering at the end to unfold, release, or reverse this is definitely best practice. When we do this, we are not so much dismissing the magical space or whatever we have called into it (dismissing the elements, for example, always seems a dangerous practice) as calling ourselves back out of that working, ritual, or magic, putting a full stop to it for now, and directing our attention to return to the daily world.

HONORING THE ELEMENTS

The elements of earth, air, fire, water, and spirit are central to Reclaiming magic and witchcraft. Our ritual form—and the cosmology and mystery these forms express—are incomplete without the recognition and honoring of the elements of life. The articulation of the four classical elements originates from an ancient Greek philosopher called Empedocles. Aristotle later added a fifth essence or quintessence called *aether*, which many modern witches and pagans name *spirit* or *mystery*.

In Reclaiming rituals we start with a ritual intention. We then gather together, acknowledge country, speak the intention aloud three times to make it a spell, and then we ground and cast the circle. Now we reach the part many of us call invocations.

We both have often challenged the language and conceptualization of elements as something we call into the circle, let alone assigning the elements specific directions. Instead, we experience ourselves as praising and honoring the elements of life. In our Reclaiming practice, we often step into the center of the circle and begin to sing or tone or name aloud the qualities or connections we feel are embodied as that element in our lives and the life of the place and time. We consciously bring our attention to the elements, who have neither left nor arrived. We are remembering their presence.

An example of this could be:

> Earth. Holy Earth. Womb and tomb. I invite us all to remember we are earth. Our hair and bones, our skin and muscle, marrow, fat, flesh, and tendon . . . we come from earth; to earth we go. Feel the ground under your feet right now; if you are wearing shoes, they too are formed of earth. We are all earth. No matter how far away these minerals and plastics are engineered from their original forms, they are still earth. Earth is sacred.

Some prefer to say the neopagan *hail and welcome*, which feels right for some people; it often doesn't for us. So before the language of *Earth is sacred, Air is sacred*, etcetera, came into being from the Falling Stars circle—Darug and Gundungurra country, Blue Mountains, Australia—we would say *I honor Earth*, or *Hail Earth*. Starhawk names this recognition of the sacredness of the elements in her Declaration of the Four Sacred Things at the beginning of her novel *The Fifth Sacred Thing*. This relationship to elements is in the spirit of Reclaiming as a witchcraft tradition in the modern world.

Early on in Reclaiming's development, it was more common (and still is in many Reclaiming camps and communities) to face the directions to invoke the Guardians of the Watchtowers aligned with specific elemental powers, with or without invoking pentagrams. This was a decidedly Wiccan and Feri influence, and these practices have great power and meaning within their contexts. At some point this began to be challenged, as mentioned by Starhawk in *Truth or Dare*. Sometimes we turn to a direction and open to perceive what is there—for example, the full moon or a mountain—honoring and invoking that reality into the circle to strengthen and inspire our work.

Reclaiming witchcraft expresses distinctly in different places and times. We offer here the wisdom that has emerged out of our Australian communities. At the end of our rituals and workings, when we are ready to devoke (a term invented to mean the exact opposite of invoke), we might say something like the following:

> We honor you, earth, for all that you hold, sustain,
> nourish, and ground. You are this very ground, these
> very trees, the bones of our ancestors, and my own
> bones formed of them. Thank you. Earth is sacred.

So effectively we begin and end our rituals by reminding ourselves that the elements of life are sacred, and this to us is especially Reclaiming magic.

When you honor the elements, it might look like:

» placing an object for each element onto your altar

» singing a song or chant that honors the elements

» conjuring up a felt sense of each element through your own experiences of them

» dancing to soundtracks you've created for each element

» noticing how the elements show up in this time and place where you are right now

» or whatever feels right in the moment

Earth is sacred.
Air is sacred.
Fire is sacred.
Water is sacred.
Spirit is sacred.

TRIPLE SOUL ALIGNMENT

In 1979 *The Spiral Dance: A Rebirth of the Ancient Religion of the Great Goddess* was published and a poetic description of the triple soul/three selves was included. Starhawk learned about the triple soul from her teachers in the Feri tradition, Cora and Victor Anderson. The discussion on the three selves takes up just three pages. She named these selves younger self, talking self, and high self, which in later editions she renamed deep self.

Originally Starhawk linked these three selves, or souls, with Jungian and Freudian concepts. She then made it explicit in the second edition (1989) that these correlations are not accurate and don't skillfully express the nature of the three souls. This was in the spirit of her teachers, who always taught that the triple soul was real and not metaphoric. We are comprised of these souls; we are a triune being, three in one.

The three selves were often referred to and taught in early Elements of Magic and Iron Pentacle classes, which were first offered in 1980. The three selves were offered as a way of understanding how magic works—specifically that the younger self and deep self are intimately connected and speak to one another through dreams, trance, imagination, story, color, texture, emotion, and instinct. A witch aspires to make this conversation between younger and deep self conscious and useful in this world, which brings in what is sometimes called the talker or talking self, which is often connected to the aura around the body. This is how our magic works here and now.

In the '90s, Reclaiming witches working together in the coven Triskets studied specifically Feri material intensively to prepare for their Feri initiations. There has always been a Feri initiatory lineage running through Reclaiming, though it is neither mandatory nor necessary and only some engage it. Through this group work the Ha Prayer technique of aligning the souls, the Black Heart of Innocence, and the Peacock Angel and Twins began to be transmitted in Reclaiming classes and camps more overtly. This influence waxes and wanes and is either very central to some Reclaiming communities or barely at all to others.

The Feri triple soul and the ways in which they are conceptualized or taught about are distinctly influenced by the system named Huna propounded by Max Freedom Long (1890–1971). This system was first published in 1936, and though Long proclaimed that it was a secret tradition encoded in Hawaiian lore, this has been consistently debunked and rejected by native Hawaiian people. Huna is a clear example of a culturally appropriated esoteric system fetishizing the exoticism of a non-white culture. At the same time, there are techniques in Huna that many people find effective. Certainly Victor Anderson was known to both promote and criticize the work of Long, but it is clear by reading descriptions of how the three selves relate to one another in the literature of the Andersons that they were influenced by Huna.

For this reason, the technique I (Fio) will offer here is one that emerged within the Wildwood tradition and has grounding in a more folkloric and witchcraft sensibility. I have taught this technique publicly for years now, and it has been published in other books as well. It has several layers to it—the three souls that are called fetch (younger self), breath soul (talking self), and holy daimon (deep self); the three cauldrons of hips/pelvis, heart/ribcage, and head/skull; the three realms of underworld, middleworld, and upperworld; and the three great rivers of ancestry: blood, land, and magic.

SOUL	CAULDRON	ANCESTORS	REALM
FETCH	HIPS/PELVIS	BLOOD	UNDERWORLD SEA
BREATH SOUL	HEART/ RIBCAGE	LAND	MIDDLEWORLD LAND
HOLY DAIMON	HEAD/SKULL	INSPIRATION MAGIC ART	UPPERWORLD SKY

The Technique

1. Breathe and be breathed wordlessly by the land. Acknowledge country and the depth of this place, time, and being. As you bring mindfulness to your breathing, you may notice that your breathing deepens, relaxes, and lengthens.

2. If you feel the need for more grounding and centering, you may work with your vision, sensation, emotion, and imagination to send, grow, and anchor roots and tendrils within the land. Not just down but also outward, spiraling and spiraling. In Wildwood practice we often send waves of blessing through the land rather than dump our shit into the earth, hoping it will be transformed.

3. You might wish to sweep your attention up through your skull, where you may be perceiving and feeling branches or connections of some kind spiral up and out into the ether, into the atmosphere, through the biosphere of holy lover–teacher earth. Perhaps you open to the white hot fire of the stars to cascade down as a great river of light, cleansing and invigorating your being. Become a channel that mediates this light into the earth, to the spirits of the land and the dead.

4. In this grounded and centered state—which after a while of practice may take one breath in and out—bring your attention to the cauldron of your hips. Know that it is holding the sea, the underworld. Feel into the red river of blood. Acknowledge all your ancestors: not just one, two, or three of them, but the entire greater-than-the-sum-of-its-parts ancestral web you are woven from. Perhaps you remember, imagine, or sense your genesis within the darkness of the womb, when sperm and ovum met. Animal, fetch, primal soul. Breathe into the fetch, knowing that the fetch instinctively will draw in vitality. As you exhale, send blessings and attention to the ancestors of blood. Do this several times.

5. Move your attention to the cauldron of your ribcage. Know that it is holding the land, the middleworld. The land is in your lungs and in your heart. Feel into the shining aura that is anchored

within the breath emanating from this cauldron, and notice the tone, quality, color, or sound of your breath soul right now, without needing to judge or assess any of it. Perhaps you remember, imagine, or sense your very first breath upon birth into this middleworld, when the fullness of this soul was drawn in and cast a boundary around your heart. Breathe into this soul, trusting that the intuitive expansion, contraction, and rippling of the aura's edge is what it needs to be. As you exhale, send blessings and attention to the ancestors of land. Do this several times.

6. Move your attention to the cauldron of your head. Know that this cauldron is holding the sky, the upperworld. In your brain and its labyrinthine mysteries are reverberating the powers of the stars. Feel into and yearn for communion with your holy daimon, your deep self. Perhaps you remember, imagine, or sense the timelessness of many lifetimes and the deep guidance of your divinity. Breathe into the intrinsic connections with your god soul, the infinite, and mystery. As you exhale, send blessings and attention to the ancestors of the magic or the Craft, the mighty dead, who have helped to braid these roads and ways. Do this several times.

7. After tending to each cauldron, opening to each realm, feeling into each soul, and honoring each great family of ancestors, we often seal this by drawing a deep breath up through each cauldron and blowing that breath up to your holy daimon, who knows what to do with it. Surrender into active trust with your divinity. You may feel your parts sliding-clicking-spiraling into place, and you might meditate silently or wordlessly in this space. Ultimately this process is meant to vividly ground, center, and orient us through and with ourselves and through our relationships with great powers, lineages, and realities.

PEARL PENTACLE TOOLS

THE IRON AND PEARL PENTACLES—
RUNNING THE CURRENTS

The Pearl Pentacle arises from the Iron Pentacle. We wrote an entire book on the magic of the Iron Pentacle together. It was published in 2016, and we highly encourage you to read and regard these books—*Magic of the Iron Pentacle* and *Magic of the Pearl Pentacle*—as companions.

Here is a distillation of the Iron evolving into Pearl:

> » Sex opens to Love
>
> » Pride emblazons as Law
>
> » Self remembers Wisdom
>
> » Power extends into Liberty
>
> » Passion tempers Knowledge

How this happens is for you to discover, but you may find perspective and insight in Dawn Isidora's Pentacle of Bridges on page 248.

In the Reclaiming tradition, when core classes are taught, they often have prerequisites. The prerequisite for all other core classes is Elements of Magic. And much of the time, an additional prerequisite for Pearl Pentacle (depending on the teachers) is Iron Pentacle. I (Fio) was taught about the pentacles alongside one another in both Feri and Reclaiming contexts, though firstly I was taught to engage and run the Iron Pentacle current in Feri.

I was first introduced to the running of the current by Storm Faerywolf, a well-known Feri initiate who was brought into the tradition by teachers saturated in BloodRose conceptualizations and workings. Gabriel Carillo, the main architect and teacher of what came to be called BloodRose Feri and an initiate of Victor and Cora Anderson, developed the practice of running the Iron and Pearl Pentacles through the body. This has become common in Reclaiming as well, although it was not always the main practice in the early days.

Before we run the Pearl Pentacle current through our bodies, let us greet the Iron. For deeper Iron Pentacle work, we direct you to our *Magic of the Iron Pentacle* as well as to *Evolutionary Witchcraft* by T. Thorn Coyle and *Circling the Star* by Anthony Rella.

Running the Iron Pentacle Current

You can do this practice lying down, standing up, sitting, or dancing around the space. This is not a trance journey; it is a checking in and sensing and observing practice, though it rounds up with a powerful moving of life force. This whole process could take between fifteen and thirty minutes at first. Ideally you will spend three to five minutes in each point. Over time this may become faster as you get more intimate with your sense of the points within you.

If you have not already consciously acknowledged country today, do that first. Then ground, center, and align your souls.

Focus on your breath. You may want to give it structure. One of the most effective ways of doing this is the famous square or counting breath. Inhale to the count of four, hold to the count of four, exhale for four counts, and hold for four counts. Continue. While doing this, you can begin to feel or imagine into concentrating and distilling the life force that is everywhere, all the time. When working with the Iron current, we will usually drop our awareness into the iron in the earth, in our blood, and in and rushing out from the stars that have collapsed and exploded forth. We collect this iron energy and concentrate it. When you have a sense of this, move your awareness to your head.

Here in the head we anchor the point of Sex. Say this word aloud several times in whichever language is your primary one. As you whisper or speak or even shout the word—*Sex*—begin to sense into how this makes you feel. Observe your feelings and responses to the word and the idea. You may perceive colors, fragrances, a dance of light and darkness; you might have memories from your waking or dreaming life emerge once more. Remember you are grounded, centered, and aligned, so if you find yourself activated or triggered, come back to your roots in the earth and to the counting breath. If you find yourself overwhelmed or anxious, breathe in through your nose and exhale through the mouth for a longer duration than the in-breath. The running of the Iron Pentacle current can bring up all sorts of unresolved issues, but it is also a filtering and strengthening current and is aiming to heal and affirm us.

When you feel ready, guide your attention down the right side of your body into your right foot or the etheric space there. Here we anchor the point of *Pride*. We undergo a similar process here as with Sex and each point, so speak the word aloud in your language(s) and observe and pay attention to what arises for you. You don't need to go into any stories or trance, just notice and let go.

Then you will continue this same process up in the left-hand region for *Self*, across and through the heart— something we practice is pausing here for several breath cycles and acknowledging your heart—then move across into your right-hand region for *Power*. Eventually transition down into your left-foot region for *Passion*. Sometimes or often this is done standing, with arms outstretched, for some or all of the process, while other times we are seated or even lying down, holding it in our minds or maybe tracing a pentagram across our bodies.

Once you complete this sensing, observing, feeling-into process with each Iron Pentacle point, return your attention to your head. We are now going to run the current, and this goes a little faster—or gathers speed and intensity—and generally our practice is to say aloud the name of each point as we pass into and through it. While we are doing this, you might want to hold the intention that you are cleansing and centering the point within yourself, calling back lost, scattered, or submitted life force and coming into harmony and synergy between all your Iron points. I (Fio) like to run the current between three to nine-times. We go from Sex to Pride to Self to Power to Passion.

When we have finished running the current through the pentagram/star, we then complete the working with the circle. Generally we draw the circle in the original order of the points: Sex, Self, Passion, Pride, Power. Inspired by the Southern Hemisphere, some people may choose to run the circle in the opposite direction: Sex, Power, Pride, Passion, Self. Sometimes we will do both. We encircle the pentagram to make it into a pentacle and also to seal and bless the work.

If this was one of the first times you ever did this you may be reeling or feeling very emotional or raw. Please shower if possible, or eat a meal and drink water, go for a walk later on, and make sure you journal in some way, writing or drawing. For some of us this running of the Pentacle current is a daily or regular practice. We might do it in the shower or bath, laying in bed when we wake up or just before we fall asleep. We might do it in the gym or walking down the road. The options are myriad.

Moving Magically into the Pearl Pentacle

I (Fio) first took Pearl Pentacle as a Reclaiming core class at an Earth-Song WitchCamp in stolen, unceded Dja Dja Wurrung country with Dawn Isidora and SusanneRae. During this class, the following chant came to me magically, I believe from Luanne Blaich (1960–2012), who had already passed. Luanne was a beloved Reclaiming priestess and witch from the California Bay Area.

> By the moon-led sea
> By the waves crashing up on me
> I call thee up!
> O I call thee up!
> (sung twice)
> O Love, Law, Wisdom
> Opening the door
> To Liberty
> And Knowing opens to infinity.

As you sing or whisper these words, or read them again and again, notice your breath; know you are being breathed by the place and the presence of all the spirits here. Follow that breath, ground and center, align your souls, and be here now. Surrender into the process.

Okay, let's run the Pearl Pentacle.

Running the Pearl Pentacle Current

Running the Pearl Pentacle current is very similar to running the Iron Pentacle. This is not meant as a trance journey, but once you are in practice and rhythm with these techniques, you could trance into the landscapes of each point, one at a time, over several moons.

The Pearl Pentacle is said to flower forth or emanate from the Iron points when they are in harmony and synergy with one another. To invoke the Pearl current, let us consider the moon—the pearl in the heavens—and pearls within the rivers and seas. You may want to chant or whisper the Pearl Pentacle song above as you gather this shining pearlescence to you. See Suzanne Sterling's songs in the resources section for a recording of this chant.

Bring your attention to your head. *Love.* Say this word in your language aloud. Sing it, tone it, and open to what love means for you right now in your life. How does love inspire you? How does it frighten you? Where are your blocks to allowing love to dance incandescently through your life? How do you love? How do you receive love? Contemplate all of this for three to five minutes. When you have a sense of the Love point or you can imagine into it, flow down to the right-foot region.

Law. Follow the same instructions here. What does law mean to you right now in your life? When you hear the word, what sensations or memories emerge? What gets you stuck, what frees you up? How does the Law point shine forth more potently? When you are ready, flow up to the left-hand region.

Wisdom. Where are you wise in your life? Where do you want to open to more wisdom? How does wisdom come to you, and how does it feel when it offers itself forth in your being? How do you make room for wisdom, for acting from wisdom, in your life? When you feel the presence of this point, move your awareness into your heart—be here within the heart, honoring yourself as divine—and then extend into the right-hand region.

Liberty. When you say this word aloud, how does it affect you? What comes alive in you? What turns away? Where might you need personal liberation? Where do you commit to the works of liberation in the world around you? How are you dedicated to—or avoiding—this point of Liberty? Spiral your awareness down into the left-foot region.

Knowledge. If there was a landscape, a feeling, a projected image, a memory that distills this point for you, what might that be? Knowing and knowledge; how do you relate to these concepts? Whisper the word, say the word progressively more loudly until you feel a little uncomfortable with the noise, and then return to whispering. Then let the word go. Where are you now with knowledge? How does it feel?

As with the running of the Iron Pentacle current, you will return back to the head, back to the starting point of Love. You are invited now—for three to nine times—to run the current from point to point in the star within you. Open to perceive and feel the Pearl Pentacle current as a palpable force whirling through you. When you are complete, encircle the points either in the original order as given by the Andersons—Love, Wisdom, Knowledge, Law, Liberty—or in whichever direction feels intuitively best.

Ground. Eat. Reflect. Journal. Relax.

PEARL IN 3D AND OUT IN THE WORLD

The invitation inherent in the Pearl Pentacle is to let this work of magic and transformation flow from ourselves out into the world. Pearl is the work of lifetimes, of communities, of relationships and connections. I (JM) am an experimenter, so I'd encourage you to experiment with these ideas presented here but also with whatever occurs to you. Sometimes experiments don't work. The experiments can often be of the moment and we have no inclination to repeat them. The impact of our experiments can change how we do something forever. And sometimes it's an experiment worth repeating or adapting or adding to our box of tricks.

Pearl Pentacle in 3D

Lay your pentacle out on the floor or beach or garden or grove using a marker of some type. Ribbon or tape works well indoors, while marks in the sand, sticks, or stones can work in outside environments. Be mindful of those who live there! Create altars at each of the points: for Love, Law, Wisdom, Liberty, and Knowledge.

Acknowledge the land. Ground yourself. Call to the Pearl Pentacle and begin running it. Move through the pentacle you've drawn, running the energy through that form as well as through yourself.

Walk the lines. Visit the altars. Walk the edges. Sit or stand in the center. Lie down with your head in Love and your arms and legs spreading starfish-like into the other points.

Light candles. Write poetry. Dance. Make magic. Journal. Sing and drum.

Visit the points that are strongest in you and honor and thank them. Visit the points you find challenging or are asking for insight into and make offerings, ask questions, or ask for help.

Build your Pearl Pentacle further out, to encompass a conceptual Iron Pentacle surrounding it, or inward, to hold a miniature Iron Pentacle within it. Add more altars, songs, offerings, magic. Reflect on how the Iron and Pearl points sing to each other, how they show up in you, and what challenges and gifts they offer.

Pearl Out in the World—Place

Take your Pearl Pentacle magic to five locations that reflect the points of the pentacle for you. Perhaps you will choose to visit a wild place in nature for Love, a library for Knowledge, a court for the complexities of Law.

You can create a five-stage spell that you take through all the points or just show up to each place and discover what work needs to be done between you and that point. Perhaps you will create an artwork or a guided walk or trance or a song.

You can do this alone or with others also working the Pearl magic.

Pearl Out in the World—People

Create a discussion group or a series of rituals that explore the points, one each time. If you have a total of six meetings, the final one can address the whole of the Pearl Pentacle.

Create a dinner party or a bush walk or a craft afternoon or a parents' drop-in support session with the theme of Love, Law, Wisdom, Liberty, or Knowledge. See what happens.

Work the Pearl Pentacle with your coven or those you do magic and ritual with.

Deeper Pearl

Invite the Pearl Pentacle and its points into your dreams, art, poetry, rituals. Take a monthlong journey into each point—or a year. Ask the Pearl Pentacle how you can carry its work into your life and out into the world.

The Pearl Pentacle is a living prayer, a profound offering of hope and dedication.

It says: *Love is the ground of all being.*

It sings: *Law is the web of that ground.*

It dances: *Wisdom is the blessing of that web.*

It reminds us: *Liberation is the power of that blessing.*

It whispers: *Knowledge is the being of that power.*

The Pearl is a promise. An invitation. Perhaps it is even a chance for humankind to get something right. Perhaps it is a dare from the Star Goddess to live lives that leave a more beautiful world for those who are to come.

Love. Law. Wisdom. Liberty. Knowledge.

REFERENCES

Abram, David. *Becoming Animal: An Earthly Cosmology.* Vintage, 2011.

Aly, Waleed, and Scott Stephens, presenters. The Minefield. "'Knowledge that does not benefit'—on the uses and abuses of information." ABC Listen, April 23, 2023. Podcast, 53 minutes. https://www.abc.net.au/listen/programs/theminefield/ramadan-on-the-uses-and-abuses-of-knowledge/102170664.

Coyle, T. Thorn. *Evolutionary Witchcraft.* Penguin, 2005.

Hedwig and the Angry Inch (film). Directed by John Cameron Mitchell. New Line Cinema, 2001.

Hoffman, Enid. *Huna: A Beginner's Guide.* Para Research, 1976.

Krauss, Lawrence. *A Universe from Nothing: Why There Is Something Rather Than Nothing.* Atria Books, 2013.

Leland, Charles G. *Aradia or the Gospel of the Witches.* A new translation by Mario Pazzaglini and Dina Pazzaglini. Phoenix Publishing, 1998.

Lorde, Audre. "Outlines." Unpublished poem.

Michaelson, Jay. *Everything Is God: The Radical Path of Nondual Judaism.* Shambhala Publications, 2009.

Native Governance Center. "A Guide to Indigenous Land Acknowledgment." Oct. 22, 2019. https://nativegov.org/news/a-guide-to-indigenous-land-acknowledgment/

Oliver, Mary. *Wild Geese: Selected Poems.* Tarset: Bloodaxe, 2004.

Palmer, Wendy. *The Intuitive Body: Discovering the Wisdom of Conscious Embodiment and Aikido.* Third edition. Blue Snake Books, 2008.

Rella, Anthony. *Circling the Star.* Gods&Radicals Press, 2018.

Schwaner, Jeff. "The Art of Dying: Hospice professionals provide a bridge for the terminally ill and their families." *USA Today Weekend Edition,* October 4–6, 2019.

Scot, Reginald. *The Discoverie of Witchcraft.* Dover, 1972. Originally published in 1584.

Stanghini, Jeremiah. "Jeremy Taylor's Six Basic Hints for Dream Work." May 29, 2011. https://jeremiahstanghini.com/2011/05/29/jeremy-taylors-six-basic-hints-for-dream-work/.

Starhawk. *The Fifth Sacred Thing.* Bantam Press, 1994.

———. *The Spiral Dance: A Rebirth of the Ancient Religion of the Great Goddess.* HarperCollins, 1979, 1989, 1999.

———. *Truth or Dare.* HarperOne, 1989.

State Government of Victoria. "Acknowledgement of Traditional Owners." Updated October 25, 2023. https://www.firstpeoplesrelations.vic.gov.au/acknowledgement-traditional-owners.

Taylor, Jeremy. *The Wisdom of Your Dreams: Using Dreams to Tap into Your Unconscious and Transform Your Life.* TarcherPerigree, 2009.

University of Minnesota Libraries. "Writing Land Acknowledgements." Updated October 5, 2023. https://libguides.umn.edu/LandAcknowledgements.

Ward, Jane. *The Tragedy of Heterosexuality.* NYU Press, 2020.

Yunkaporta, Tyson. *Sand Talk: How Indigenous Thinking Can Save the World.* Text Publishing, 2019.

RECOMMENDED RESOURCES

Books on Reclaiming and Feri

Circle Round by Starhawk, Diane Baker, and Anne Hill

Dreaming the Dark by Starhawk

The Earth Path by Starhawk

Elements of Magic edited by Jane Meredith and Fio Gede Parma

The Empowerment Manual by Starhawk

Enchanted Feminism by Jone Salomonsen

Evolutionary Witchcraft by T. Thorn Coyle

Fifty Years in the Feri Tradition by Cora Anderson

Magic of the Iron Pentacle by Jane Meredith and Fio Gede Parma

The Spiral Dance by Starhawk

Teen Earth Magic by Luke Hauser

Truth or Dare by Starhawk

Twelve Wild Swans by Starhawk and Hilary Valentine

For a list of Pearl Pentacle-related songs and chants,
please visit Suzanne Sterling's website here:

www.suzannesterling.com/pearlpentaclesongs

These are specially recorded for this book.

LOVE

Books

All About Love: New Visions by bell hooks

No One Belongs Here More Than You; stories by Miranda July

Our Missing Hearts by Celeste Ng

Rumi: The Book of Love: Poems of Ecstasy and Longing with translations and commentary by Coleman Barks

The Tragedy of Heterosexuality by Jane Ward

Films

All of Us Strangers

Everything Everywhere All At Once

Howl's Moving Castle

A Monster Calls

Past Lives

LAW

Books

Becoming Kin: An Indigenous Call to Unforgetting the Past and Reimagining Our Future by Patty Krawec

The Fifth Season (The Broken Earth series) by N. K. Jemison

How Far the Light Reaches: A Life in Ten Sea Creatures by Sabrina Imbler

Law: The Way of the Ancestors (First Knowledges series edited by Margo Neale) by Marcia Langton and Aaron Corn

Sand Talk: How Indigenous Thinking Can Save the World by Tyson Yunkaporta

Films

Cloud Atlas

Disclosure (documentary)

Nausicaä of the Valley of the Wind

Our Planet (with David Attenborough) BBC series

Spear (Bangarra Film)

WISDOM

Books

Being Mortal: Medicine and What Matters in the End by Atul Gawande

God Is a Verb: Kabbalah and the Practice of Mystical Judaism by David A Cooper

Life After Life by Kate Atkinson

Songlines: The Power and Promise (First Knowledges Series edited by Margo Neale) by Margo Neale and Lynne Kelly

Soulcraft: Crossing into the Mysteries of Nature and Psyche by Bill Plotkin

Films

Before I Fall

Captain Fantastic

Eternal Sunshine of the Spotless Mind

Spirited Away

Whale Rider

LIBERTY

Books

The Bacchae of Euripides: A Communion Rite by Wole Soyinka

The Dispossessed by Ursula K. Le Guin

Honoring the Wild: Reclaiming Witchcraft and Environmental Activism by Irisanya Moon

Pleasure Activism by adrienne maree brown

Saving St. Brigid's by Regina Lane

Films

Booksmart

Good Luck to You, Leo Grande

Pride

Princess Mononoke

Three Thousand Years of Longing

KNOWLEDGE

Books

Falling Through the Tree of Life: Embodied Kabbalah by Jane Meredith

Notes from the Burning Age by Claire North

Right Story, Wrong Story: Adventures in Indigenous Thinking by Tyson Yunkaporta

The Witch Belongs to the World: A Spell of Becoming by Fio Gede Parma

Witchcraft and the Shamanic Journey by Kenneth Johnson

Films

The Matrix series

Sweet As

Universe (with Brian Cox) BBC series

Wings of Desire (Der Himmel über Berlin)

The Witch

CONTRIBUTORS

ALEX IANTAFFI, PhD, MS, SEP, CST, LMFT (they/he/lui) is a disabled, trans, bi, queer, and polyamorous Italian author, therapist, international speaker, clinical supervisor, teacher, initiate, parent, and witch currently living on Dakota and Anishinaabe territories known as Minnesota in the so-called United States. They have been involved with Reclaiming since 2004 as a co-creator, teacher, weaver, organizer, ritual artist, initiate, and initiator. Alex is also a Feri and Queer Spirit initiate and practices some of the Mediterranean ancestral practices they were brought up with, such as the tarantella. Alex is the author of the award-winning book *Gender Trauma: Healing Cultural, Social, and Historical Gendered Trauma* and co-author of *How to Understand Your Gender, How to Understand Your Sexuality, How to Understand Your Relationships, Life Isn't Binary,* and *Hell Yeah Self-Care: A Trauma-Informed Workbook.* They host the podcast *Gender Stories.* More at www.alexiantaffi.com.

DAWN ISIDORA is a grounded mystic, magical mentor, and longtime priestess in the Reclaiming and Feri traditions. With a Capricorn Sun and Virgo Moon, she jokes she is likely too grounded to be a proper mystic, but with a Sagittarius Rising she feels propelled to always quest for an experience of truth and reality. Dawn has been involved in Reclaiming witchcraft since the early '80s and has taught magic and ritual throughout the Southern and Northern Hemispheres for decades. Through relationships with self, family, friends, communities, the elements, the gods, the land, and Mystery Herself, Dawn finds the sensation of connection to be her reliable pathway to spirit and meaning.

G. RAVYN STANFIELD (she/her) is the author of *Revolution of the Spirit: Awaken the Healer*, an exploratory guide to the crucial need for holistic healing today. Ravyn practices acupuncture and relationship therapy in Portland, Oregon, with a focus on trauma recovery. Her fiction and essays have been published in *The Rumpus, Guernica, Typehouse Literary*, anthologies, and elsewhere. Ravyn designs trainings for emerging leaders and healers internationally and has taught witchcraft in the Reclaiming tradition since 2000. She uses her background in acupuncture, theatre, psychology, writing, and neurobiology to coax more of the extraordinary into the world through the cracks in western civilization. www.gerriravynstanfield.com.

HILARY BUFFUM is a lifelong Reclaiming witch. She is an artist, teacher, and story gatherer. She has taught and organized for both Teen Earth Magic and Witchlets in the Woods. Hilary believes in the depths and power of intergenerational magic. She is a coconspirator with little witches making rituals in streambeds and magic mud pies. She works to weave the deep, complex magic of relationship with ourselves, community, the wider world, and mystery.

IRISANYA MOON (she/they) is an author, witch, teacher, and Reclaiming initiate who has practiced magick for over twenty years. She has taught Reclaiming magick at classes and WitchCamps in the US, Canada, the UK, and Australia, bringing a blend of grounded, graceful, and compassionate facilitation to inspire transformation and liberation at the personal and collective levels. She has written several books: the Pagan Portals series (*Reclaiming Witchcraft*, 2020; *Aphrodite*, 2020; *Iris*, 2021; *Norns*, 2023; *Artemis*, 2024); Earth Spirit series (*Honoring the Wild*, 2023, *Gaia*, 2023); and *Practically Pagan: An Alternative Guide to Health & Well-Being*, 2020. She has written for *Witches & Pagans, Pagan Dawn, Coreopsis Journal*, Moon Books, Revelore Press, Llewellyn, and Epona Muse Publishing. In 2023, they self-published a book of poetry, *wrecked: the insistence of grief*. Irisanya cultivates spaces of self-care/devotion, divine relationship (whatever that means to you), and community service as part of her heart magick and activism. www.irisanyamoon.com.

PANDORA O'MALLORY/ANNE BRANNEN (she/they) has been a witch in the Reclaiming Feri tradition since 1981, teaching in classes, workshops, and various WitchCamps. She is still a witch and has also been a poet, an actress, a crafter in various textiles, a doll maker, a humorist, a rescuer of parrots, and a professor of medieval literature and drama. Currently she is working with mixed media and watercolor, learning Ukrainian, and learning about ADHD, which explains a lot, really. She is still a medievalist, since, like witchcraft, it's a way of understanding the world. She mostly hangs out at TrueCrimeMedieval.com.

RAVEN EDGEWALKER (they/them) is a British witch, teacher, artist, and writer who lives in the magical landscape of Somerset, UK. They are a Reclaiming and Anderson Feri initiate and have worked within the Reclaiming tradition for more than twenty years. They have an ongoing, passionate love affair with the natural world. They see their work in the world as that of building connections with self, with each other, within community, and with deity and the elements. Raven has been lucky enough to teach Reclaiming WitchCamps and workshops across the world, both face to face and as a founder and member of the teaching faculty of World Tree Lyceum, an online pagan Mystery School. Raven owns the popular pagan business Greenwomancrafts and makes their living crafting beautiful pagan tools and jewelry and taking landscape photographs. www.info@worldtreelyceum.org and https://www.etsy.com/shop/greenwomancrafts/.

STARHAWK is an author, activist, permaculture designer and teacher, and prominent voice in modern earth-based spirituality and ecofeminism. She is the author or co-author of thirteen books, including *The Spiral Dance: A Rebirth of the Ancient Religion of the Great Goddess* and the ecotopian novel *The Fifth Sacred Thing* and its sequel *City of Refuge*. Starhawk founded Earth Activist Training, teaching permaculture design grounded in spirituality and with a focus on activism. She travels internationally, lecturing and teaching on earth-based spirituality, the tools of ritual, and the skills of activism. Visit https://starhawk.org/ for more information.

SUSANNERAE (they, them, and sometimes she) has been teaching and organizing in Reclaiming for ten years, including CloudCatcher and WildKin WitchCamps. They are passionate about the earth and ritual. SusanneRae is an Australian born of Anglo, Scots, and Welsh heritage; they have a lifetime's experience working with earth-centered energies. They regularly conduct Reclaiming, labyrinth, meditation, and art classes and workshops in their local community and internationally. SusanneRae has contributed pieces to *Elements of Magic* edited by Jane Meredith and Fio Gede Parma and *Honoring the Wild: Reclaiming Witchcraft and Environmental Activism* by Irisanya Moon. The Meditation Space is an online platform for their teaching and mentoring: themeditationspace.com.au.

WILLOW KELLY—activist, witch, queer, shadow-stalker, lover of the fae and the wyrd. I am a music-making, mischief-conspiring priestess of transformation and have been teaching magic in the Reclaiming tradition of witchcraft internationally since the mid-90s. I am a skeptic and a mystic, seeking a glimmer of understanding into this ocean of ineffable wonder that I inadequately call Spirit. I experience and priestess transformation through the exploration and integration of shadows, sprinkling my work generously with the ecstatic vibrations of music, energy, play, movement, theatre, devotion, and sound. I thrive on collaborative community building, art, and ecstatic magic. I teach and facilitate a variety of events that hold the common threads of authenticity, responsibility, and transformation. I am a certified Professional End-of-Life Doula through the Larner College of Medicine at the University of Vermont as well as a death and dying educator and advocate. My training in the Reclaiming tradition of witchcraft, the Dances of Universal Peace, the Mevlevi Order of America, and other mystical traditions informs my practices and teaching styles. Website: https://willowkelly.com/.

TO WRITE TO THE AUTHORS

If you wish to contact the authors or would like more information about this book, please write to the authors in care of Llewellyn Worldwide and we will forward your request. Both the authors and the publisher appreciate hearing from you and learning of your enjoyment of this book and how it has helped you. Llewellyn Worldwide cannot guarantee that every letter written to the authors can be answered, but all will be forwarded. Please write to:

Jane Meredith and Fio Gede Parma
$c/_o$ Llewellyn Worldwide
2143 Wooddale Drive
Woodbury, MN 55125-2989

Please enclose a self-addressed stamped envelope for reply or $1.00 to cover costs. If outside the USA, enclose an international postal reply coupon.

Many of Llewellyn's authors have websites with additional information and resources. For more information, please visit our website:

WWW.LLEWELLYN.COM